The Ocean Is Alive

About the author

Glenn Edney is an Ocean ecologist, underwater naturalist, sailor and professional diver. He has been exploring the Ocean and interacting with Ocean life for more than 30 years. He has an MSc in Holistic Science from Schumacher College and Plymouth University UK. His research is focused on understanding the Ocean as a living system and the role she plays as the primary life support system for our planet. He has a strong interest in bringing together traditional indigenous Ocean knowledge and modern scientific ecological understanding. Together with his wife Janey they have founded Ocean Spirit, with the aim of fostering a deeper and more harmonious relationship with the living Ocean. They live with their daughter Sam and Skupors the sailor dog on the north east coast of New Zealand, overlooking the Pacific.

Also Available by Glenn Edney

Poor Knights Wonderland: A field guide to the Islands and Marine Reserve

Humpback Whales of the South West Pacific

The Ocean Is Alive

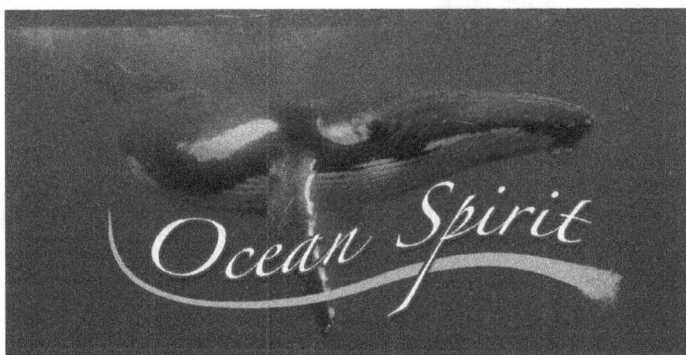

Re-visioning Our Relationship
with the Living Ocean

Glenn Edney

Ocean Spirit

For all my Teachers
In the Ocean and on Land

Contents

Part One

The Living Ocean

Part Two

Re-visioning our Relationship with the Living Ocean

Acknowledgments

The writing of this book has been a two year project, but the journey of discovery that initiated it started more than 40 years ago when I donned mask and snorkel and looked beneath the Ocean's surface for the first time. During that time I have been inspired by the lives and work of many Ocean explorers, scientists and naturalists.

The great Jacques-Yves Cousteau, pioneering Ocean explorer and co-inventor of the aqualung, was my childhood hero and the inspiration for a generation of Ocean explorers that followed. Among that generation, Dr. Sylvia Earle epitomises the bringing together of science with the spirit of adventure that has seen her emerge as one of the most important voices for the protection of the Ocean. Early in my diving career I was fortunate to meet and work with Wade and Jan Doak. Their work as underwater naturalists is unparalleled and their freethinking (unencumbered by overly rigid scientific dogma) has led to many unique insights into the lives of Ocean dwellers.

Wade and Jan introduced me to the design brilliance of Ocean sailor James Wharram. His Polynesian inspired double voyaging canoes prove the skill and wisdom of Oceania's first human explorers, and have enabled many modern sailors (including myself) to explore the Ocean realm. I am grateful to James and his partner Hanneke for our Ocean conversations and their support for my work.

My journey of exploration took a landward turn when I went to Devon in England to study with Gaian scientist and Deep Ecology practitioner, Dr. Stephan Harding, head of Holistic Science at Schumacher College, and long-time collaborator with the father of Gaia Theory, scientist and inventor, James Lovelock. Stephan not only guided me through my research into the Ocean as a living system but has become mentor and friend. I am extremely grateful to Stephan for his critical review and corrections of the Gaian science presented in this book. I also thank Phillip Franses, chaos and complexity theory tutor at the college, for his feedback and uniquely 'left field' insights.

I wish to thank Professor Gerald Pollack for his comments on my presentation of his groundbreaking research into the mysterious qualities of EZ water, and for his kind permission to use some of the illustrations from his excellent book *The Fourth Phase of Water*. Thanks also to Ethan Pollack for his assistance in formatting the images I have used. I am also very grateful to Janet Fernandez Skaalvik and Yannick Beaudoin from Grid-Arendal, and Paul Bown from the Micropalaeontology Unit, University College London, for their help with permissions for the use of images and diagrams throughout the book. I would also like to acknowledge NOAA, NASA's Earth Observatory, Encyclopaedia Britannica online, wikimedia creative commons and PLOS One online journal for making images and diagrams freely available. Special thanks go to Ricky Harris from Eye On Design **www.eyeondesign.co.nz** for his fantastic cover design. Likewise I wish to extend my gratitude to Deirdre Hyde, **www.deirdrehyde.com** an amazing artist and environmental activist, for her design of the Ocean Spirit logo.

It is one thing to sit down and write a manuscript, but turning that manuscript into a book is always a collaborative process. In this I have been blessed with the support of some very special people. Firstly, I want to thank my dear friend Ben Sablerolle, who read the initial draft of the first six chapters and offered enthusiastic but critical support. Likewise my friend and fellow writer, Gill Coombs **www.gillcoombs.co.uk** provided timely advice as I entered into the second half of the writing process.

I was extremely fortunate to have two highly skilled writers to edit and proof read the final manuscript: Gill Coombs and Janey Pares Edney, my wife and fellow Ocean explorer. Between them they have taken my raw words and crafted them into a coherent and readable story. I am extremely fortunate to have such a supportive, enthusiastic and open-minded partner to share this journey of discovery with. It would not be possible without you.

Last, but certainly not least, I want to acknowledge and honour all the Ocean beings who have taught me more about the Ocean than any lecture or textbook could ever achieve. They are the true Ocean elders, and holders of an Ocean wisdom that is as old as life itself. I hope I have done justice to your teachings.

Prologue

*There is, one knows not what sweet mystery about the sea, whose gently
awful stirrings seem to speak of some hidden soul beneath.*
– Herman Melville

Fins on, mask and snorkel in place, I ease myself gently from the bow of
our Polynesian inspired catamaran and slip silently into a blue world. A
world so familiar after all these years that it almost seems more natural to
be in its weightless, physical embrace than the thin, ethereal atmosphere
above.

Floating only thirty metres away is a female humpback whale and her
month old calf. I've done this hundreds of times before but this time feels
different, as if I'm being drawn into the water by a force beyond my control, overriding my methodical preparations. Her immense presence is calling me forth; I could feel it even before I entered the water.

Twenty minutes earlier we had cleared the reef pass in front of our
base on the island of Foa, in the South Pacific Kingdom of Tonga. These
waters are the breeding grounds for a relic population of southern hemisphere humpback whales, long hunted by European and American whalers and brought almost to the point of extinction in the early 1960's by ille-
gal Russian whaling in the humpback's Antarctic feeding grounds. We've
been living here for six years, running a scuba diving and whale watching
business, whose real purpose is to fund my own passion for interacting
with these Ocean giants.

With barely full sails in the morning breeze our catamaran was gliding
serenely through the calm clear waters under a cloudless, azure sky. To
port, the fringing reef and coconut palm-lined beaches offered a picture
perfect backdrop, but all eyes on board were focused seaward, scanning
the horizon for the telltale plume of misty breath that whalers of old would
greet with an excited 'thar she blows'. Instead, the calm was shattered as

---

the female humpback exploded through the surface in a cascade of spray, thrusting her entire 40 ton bulk clear of the water, before succumbing to the alien pull of gravity and crashing thunderously back into the water barely a hundred metres in front of us.

Instinctively I spun the wheel to bring the boat up into the wind while my partner, Janey, and our crew frantically lowered the sails. We were so close to the whale that a collision seemed almost unavoidable and yet she calmly moved herself and her calf out of harm's way and repositioned herself directly in front of our now stationary hulls, as if, having got our attention, she was making sure we couldn't go anywhere. It was at this point that I started feeling her presence urging me into the water.

Ignoring my own rules I leave Janey to brief our passengers on the safety procedures and strict protocols for swimming with these gentle giants. As soon as I enter the water I feel enveloped in her presence. I'm like an iron filing caught in a magnetic field, drawn towards the source and powerless to resist. A few gentle fin strokes bring me within visual range of her massive bulk, but instead of stopping as I usually do, I find myself gliding forwards until I'm floating just three metres away from her enormous head. She is floating completely motionless with just the rise of her broad back above the surface. Her four-metre calf is tucked in close on her left side.

As I float on the surface, fully immersed in her energetic field, I feel the strangest sensation, as if I'm being entered through every pore of my skin. I feel her presence within me, filling my senses with her being. There's a moment when I contemplate resisting; a momentary fear of the unknown perhaps, but there's no sense of danger. I close my eyes, open my arms, my whole being to her internal gaze. Everything outside this connection fades; I hardly feel the chill of the water against my bare skin. I'm aware of myself but can no longer distinguish a clear separation between us. I recognise my own thoughts, feelings and emotions but also experience her emotional being as my own.

The feeling is overwhelming and strange, I feel panic rising within me. Suddenly I'm aware of the calf, he's responding to my unease and is frightened by it. 'My God, he's here as well', a part of this 'mind-meld'. Almost immediately I feel a calm spreading through us. The mother is reassuring us, not with words or thoughts, just a calm presence. I begin to relax, unlike the calf, who still seems unsure and I sense him moving closer to his mother. I shift my focus back to her and try to concentrate on opening myself completely to her gaze. I'm a novice at this and have no idea what I'm doing. I have to trust her completely and just go with it.

I start to feel a sense of expansiveness, as if I'm stretching out through the water like a wave, but with the same feeling of extended consciousness and connection that comes when the mind reaches a deep level of stillness during meditation. There's another quality to this sensation, some deeper meaning, but I can't grasp what it is. I feel her probing me, looking for understanding and somehow I sense that I do understand what it is she's trying to show me. I can't touch it yet, it's lying just out of reach, but I know it's there. Maybe she feels this too because the intensity of her probing diminishes and takes on a lighter feel.

Slowly I feel myself entering into her physical consciousness, although not intentionally and not with the same intensity that I feel her within me. It feels like she's giving me a guided tour of her inner being but I'm aware that I'm only skimming the surface. There's so much more to see, if only I knew how. It doesn't feel as if she's hiding anything from me, just that I'm not capable of seeing it. But I also get the sense that she's more than capable of blocking my access to her if she chooses. She has chosen to communicate with me in this way and it is very much on her terms.

It's as if I'm experiencing her essence rather than specific details. Like hazy memories I'm vaguely aware of other calves, other whales in her life, long migrations, but it's the emotions and feelings being evoked that are clear. There is love, joy, pain and loss, but most of all I'm experiencing again that deep sense of expansive connection.

Quite unexpectedly I feel her withdrawing, and with this an incredible sense of loss as if she's saying 'goodbye'. Then I realise that she *is* saying goodbye, but it's not her that's leaving, it's me and she knows it. It's why she stopped us in the first place, why she initiated this 'mind-meld'. Now I understand: she's trying to show me that the Ocean is so much more than I have ever imagined it to be.

It is Alive!

Introduction

My communion with the humpback whale and her calf was five years ago. It's taken me all this time, and many more Ocean adventures, to feel I really understand the implications of what she showed me in those few moments of connection in the calm waters off Foa Island that day: The Ocean Really is Alive!

This book is an attempt to articulate the living Ocean in a way that does justice to the gift of life she bestows upon us all, especially those beings dwelling full time within her liquid body. My aim is to present a compelling case for the recognition of the Ocean as a living being with intrinsic value far beyond the benefits she provides humanity. A being that deserves our respect and gratitude, but also asserts the right to live unencumbered by the excesses of modern human behaviour. I hope it can also serve as an invitation to embrace our own inescapable reliance on her continued wellbeing. By reliance I'm not just referring to her physiological processes, that in our market economy vocabulary we call 'ecosystem services'. Our reliance is much deeper than this. It reaches to the very depths of our being: even to our 'coming into being' both as a species and as individuals.

The Ocean is the cradle of life in the physical sense but it also serves as a portal into the essence of what it is to be alive; the mystery of meaning that lies beyond physics and chemistry, genes and phenotypes. Words can only hint at this hidden meaning because it is only through our physical, sensed experience that knowledge can be embodied with meaning. The intellect, for all its sophisticated machinations, can only ever give us a representation of our lived experience. We first have to be present to the world; we have to find our personal, bodily connection, from which we can employ our intellect in the service of interpreting meaning into appropriate behaviour. We are alive to the world through our senses and it is through our senses that the living world enters us. Rachel Carson, the 'mother' of modern environmentalism, beautifully illustrates the primacy of the sensed experience:

> To stand at the edge of the sea, to sense the ebb and flow of the tides, to feel the breath of a mist moving over a great salt marsh, to watch the flight of shore birds that have swept up and down the surf lines of the continents for untold thousands of year, to see the running of the old eels and the young shad to the sea, is to have knowledge of things that are as nearly eternal as any earthly life can be.
> – Rachel Carson

* * *

For us terrestrials the Ocean can sometimes seem like a barrier to our senses. After all, none of our five physical senses work very well underwater. Without a diving mask the Ocean is a shadowy world of blurred outlines and unformed movement; our ears are confused by the speed of sound waves pulsing through the water so that we can't tell from which direction sounds are reaching us; we are reluctant to open our taste buds to her saltiness for fear of filling our mouths and lungs with water, while our sense of smell becomes completely redundant. The only sense that continues to function in a similar way is touch, and yet so much of what we encounter in the Ocean seems so alien to us that we are reticent about reaching out; a reticence so often reinforced by well meaning, but over generalised, concerns about damaging delicate marine life. But it's worth remembering that, like most of life's innovations, our senses had their beginnings in the Ocean.

The Ocean reaches out to us, drawing us into her mystery, thrilling our bodies with her sensual caress, feeding our soulful search for life's meaning. For the longest time we have held the mysterious depths of the Ocean as a living testament to the unknowable, allowing us the freedom to imagine, to speculate without limit, life's possibilities. From her depths we conjured monsters to feed our fear and test our courage. We looked upon her limitless horizon as a call to adventure and exploration. We used her body to enrich our own, both physically and spiritually. We needed her to be alive, limitless and sentient so we could explore our own sentience.

But more recently we've largely done away with this relationship in favour of a more utilitarian and profit driven exploitation of her vastness. Five hundred years of excessive plundering, starting along continental coastlines but roaming ever further offshore, has seen the immensity of the Ocean shrink, the unknowable wildness tamed and the living sentience transformed into so many millions of tons of 'product'. Where once we stood on the shore and felt a sense of wonder, of life, wild and limitless, we now ponder resource depletion, species extinction, dead zones, plastic islands, pollution and rising sea-levels. Since the industrial revolution we have treated the Ocean as little more than a resource bank, forever withdrawing but never repaying, our only deposits the toxic waste of our excess.

And yet, despite our temporary amnesia, the Ocean hasn't entirely forsaken us, nor us her. How can we? We are, in every way, dependent on her life processes. The wisdom of the Ocean hasn't been lost. It resides in every water molecule, every microscopic algae, in the memories of the whale and within the traditional knowledge systems of indigenous Ocean people. It resides still in all who hear the call of the Ocean, feel the salt in their veins and find themselves yearning once again to feel her embrace.

And I have loved thee, Ocean! And my joy of youthful sports was on thy breast to be borne, like thy bubbles, onward; from a boy I wantoned with thy breakers. They to me were a delight; and if the freshening sea made them a terror, 'twas a pleasing fear.
– Lord Byron

* * *

The story of the Ocean is the story of life on Earth, including the colonisation of the land. It is the story of evolution, from our planet's formation to the emergence of life, to the present moment. It would take volumes to tell in any detail and would need continual updating as our knowledge grows and our understanding deepens. My aim here is not to catalogue details but rather to evoke a sense of wonder, awe and connection with the living Ocean. Necessarily I will have to omit much that is both interesting and important, but I hope that by focusing on a few examples of how life expresses itself – as an Ocean-wide, and deep process – I can weave a coherent and worthy overview.

This book is first and foremost a celebration of the Ocean in all her living splendour. It looks at the scientific evidence for a living Ocean as far as we know it, keeping in mind that our knowledge and understanding is continually being revised. The further back in time we go the less sure we can be of the actual events. So much of what we might take to be scientific fact, especially about the distant past, is ultimately based on conjecture, derived from patchy evidence and theory. Nobody was there to bear witness. But this is not just a scientific story.

As an Ocean ecologist, the scientific understanding of how the Ocean works as a complex system fascinates me, but as a practitioner of Deep Ecology, I'm filled with profound reverence for the intrinsic beauty and powerful life-force that is the soul of the Ocean. As a diver and underwater naturalist I'm transfixed by the diversity, peculiarity and habits of her myriad life forms, and as an Ocean sailor I'm seduced by her ever changing moods and the intimacy of her relationship with the atmosphere that gives birth to the winds filling my sails. In telling this story I have drawn on all these facets of my deep connection to the living Ocean.

But no modern story of the Ocean would be complete without addressing the current threats to the Ocean's wellbeing. I have adopted the approach taken by Gaian scientist, James Lovelock, of being a 'planetary physician'. In Chapter 10 we'll pay a visit to the 'Ocean Doctor' for an Ocean-wide check-up and diagnosis. Finally we'll draw on our deepened sense of connection to look at what action we can take to lessen the burden on the Ocean and give her a chance to recover her health.

I have attempted to keep scientific language to a minimum for the sake of narrative flow, but readers with an interest in delving further into the science will find useful references in the chapter notes and bibliography. My writing style is unashamedly 'animistic': imbuing supposedly non-living or inanimate objects with agency and soul. I have deliberately employed this writing style because it best describes my relationship with the Ocean. Another intentional grammatical quirk you may notice is that I have chosen to capitalise Ocean in most situations. I've done this to emphasis the Ocean as a living being, a 'who' rather than a 'what'.

In keeping with the understanding that knowledge leads to meaning through direct experience, I have included some guided visualisations, in italics, on aspects of the living Ocean. Not as a replacement for direct experience, but rather as an invitation to 'imaginary sensorial experience' – a method developed by the 18th century visionary, Johann Wolfgang von

Goethe, for the phenomenological study of living organisms. Ideally though I encourage you to journey to the Ocean and engage with her directly. If this isn't possible there may be a way you can connect with another body of water: a lake, river or stream. After all, all water on our planet is connected and is at various times an integral part of the living Ocean.

Part One

The Living Ocean

1

Is the Ocean Really Alive?

No aquarium, no tank in a marine land, however spacious it may be, can
begin to duplicate the conditions of the sea.
– Jacques Yves Cousteau

When I started my diving career 30 years ago I worked as an aquarium assistant at the world's first acrylic tunnel aquarium on the waterfront in Auckland, New Zealand. The ingenious idea of diving pioneer, Kelly Tarlton, the tunnel creates a 'reality-flip', with the people encased in an acrylic tunnel running through a giant saltwater tank. Fish, sharks and stingrays swim around and over the tunnel, giving the people inside the tunnel a 3D view, an underwater experience without getting wet. From my position inside the tank with the fish, I often wondered just who was on display! But the thing I noticed most was how different it felt diving inside the confines of the tank compared to diving in the Ocean.

When I dive in the Ocean the very water feels alive. Every piece of my exposed skin is being caressed by microscopic phytoplankton, tiny zoo-plankton, larval fish and invertebrates as well as all the faecal matter associated with their metabolism, not to mention all the dissolved nutri-ents continually mixing with the water molecules. Ocean water feels ener-gised. And of course there's a whole community of fish and invertebrates, encrusting life such as corals, sponges, anemones and ascidians, kelps and seaweeds, all going about their business of hunting, foraging, fossicking, filtering and photosynthesising. On the sea floor the benthic community is just as vibrant and busy. Unimaginable numbers of life forms, from polychaete worms and shellfish, to microbes and single-celled bacteria are busy recycling nutrients from the continual supply of faecal pellets and other detritus raining down from above. In the Ocean there is no such thing as waste. In short, the Ocean is a complex living system.

In an aquarium on the other hand, the water is re-circulated through giant biological filtration tanks to remove particulate matter, ozone filters to sterilize the water and high-pressure pumps to re-oxygenate it. Because there is often no direct sunlight, the only photosynthesis that happens is from artificial lighting. Basically much of the life is removed from the water itself. Every other day myself and other divers would vacuum the sand with large suction hoses, removing all the fish detritus as waste, to minimise bacterial build up and reduce the rate of infection in the fish. Despite our precautions we would occasionally have to add antibiotics to their food, as well as vitamin D, to make up for the lack of sunlight. The result of all this was a largely sterile environment rather than a vibrant, complex ecosystem.

For the tourists moving through the acrylic tunnel on a motorised conveyer belt, the aquarium is a fascinating and entertaining window into the underwater world, a journey into the Ocean. But for me it was more like being in a parody of the Ocean. It looked similar but it felt like a facsimile, an abstract representation that the life had literally been sucked out of. The fish, sharks and stingrays swimming around and over the acrylic tunnel watching the passing display of humans, were swimming in a tank full of more or less lifeless water rather than a living Ocean.

Nevertheless, it was at the aquarium where I first encountered individual personalities amongst the population of supposedly unthinking, non-feeling and primitive sharks, rays and fish. Until then, like most people, I bought into the belief that it was only humans and a select band of higher mammals that enjoy the gifts of sentience and individualism. But not only did they have their own personalities, it also appeared that at least some of the sharks, rays and even some of the fish could recognise individual divers and would react differently to each of us. The differences between the divers were often subtle, a slightly different swimming style or breathing pattern perhaps, but nonetheless, we could observe different responses to each diver from those animals who were interested in interacting with us. It wasn't until sometime later that I realised they were probably responding to our different energetic fields and chemical signatures as much as our behaviour and looks.

So, what was this sense of aliveness I could feel in the Ocean but not in the aquarium? Certainly the polystyrene rocks, artificial light and limited diversity played their part, but there seemed to be something else missing, something in the water, so to speak. Is it possible there is something about the Ocean as a whole that can't be replicated: the water, minerals, nutrients, and myriad organisms creating more than the sum of the parts, in other words, a living Ocean?

Just to be clear, I don't mean 'living' in the metaphoric sense favoured by some scientists, who would use the term 'living ocean' to describe the myriad collection of biological life forms inhabiting the Ocean. In this context the ocean is seen as consisting of biological life within a non-living environment. This is the classic separation between the biotic and abiotic, the living and non-living, that has been championed by science for the past four hundred or so years. In fact, so pervasive has this separation become in Western thought that we scarcely pay it any attention, and yet it is an idea that has played a key role in shaping our current relationship with life itself. Before we explore the question of the living Ocean further it's worth briefly tracing how this separation came about.

Changing Perceptions of Life

For most of the two hundred thousand year history of our species we have lived in tune with the rhythms of the planet, our identity grounded firmly within the physical world around us. Our surroundings not only served as a physical orientation, but also provided our spiritual compass with which we began to explore our growing self-awareness. That self-awareness was underpinned by the fundamental acceptance that our very survival depended on maintaining an intimate connection to the life-force around us. We needed to nurture our relationship with our surroundings in order to maintain access to the knowledge of how everything in our world fitted together.

One could not have knowledge about predator or prey without understanding how they also related to, and within the world. We needed to remain sensitive to how those relationships fluctuated with the changing moods of our shared environment. It would have been both counter-intuitive and counter-productive to separate life and environment in any way. The life of the sunbathing lizard and the sun-baked rock, the spawning salmon and the milt-swollen river, the schooling fish and the surging

Ocean; all were part of the same life process, as were we. To be *self*-aware, was to identify and have knowledge of yourself within the larger body of life around you, rather than to imagine yourself outside and separate from the world.

We have largely lost this sense of 'embeddedness' in our modern cultures, and now view it as a naïve belief system held by indigenous cultures that imbue inanimate objects with agency and soul. This worldview has been labelled *animistic* by Western scholars, who themselves are following a philosophical tradition set in motion by Plato in the 4th century BCE. He was amongst the first to articulate the idea that the power of creation lay somewhere outside the material world, thereby giving birth to the notion of an eternal heavenly realm, apart from and superior to the earthly body.

Even though he championed the human intellect as the pathway to this divine realm, he also saw the world as a living embodiment of the creative force, alive with soul and agency. In one of his most important texts *Timaeus* he writes, 'This world is indeed a living being supplied with soul and intelligence ... a single visible entity, containing all other living entities.' This was later translated into Latin as the *anima mundi* the 'soul of the world'. So, even while paving the way for Christianity – and later the scientific revolution – to separate and raise humans above the rest of life, Plato himself it would appear, experienced the world as a sentient living whole.[1]

But even before Plato, we were starting to disengage ourselves from the intimate relationship with place that had nurtured us for so long. The advent of farming and agriculture drove a wedge between humans and the *more-than-human* world. Where once all the land was alive with its own story, we now enforced our will upon some areas, taming the rocks and soil, domesticating the plants and animals. Beyond our fences the land became a threat, full of untamed forces that would encroach upon our newly perceived security. We now had a dual relationship with our surroundings: the safety and relative predictability of our enclosures (the places under our control), and the wild beyond. As our dominance spread across the land so the wilderness withdrew, and along with it our connection to the anima mundi, the living soul of the world.[2]

The scientific revolution of the 16th and 17th centuries introduced a new element to this growing separation: the concept of the world, and indeed the entire universe, as a vast machine whose workings could be understood using the new scientific method of reductionism expounded by

René Descartes. Descartes' belief that any phenomenon could be understood by studying its constituent parts in isolation even extended to living animals, which he saw as nothing more than complex machines without feelings or soul. The subsequent success of Isaac Newton's newly formulated *differential calculus* in predicting the trajectory of moving bodies, such as the planets, seemed to back-up this idea of a mechanistic universe that could be understood and ultimately controlled, using objective measurement and mathematical reason.

So now, not only had we drawn a line between biological life and the non-living environment, but we had also re-defined life into sentient and soulful human existence, surrounded by all other life that enjoyed neither sentience nor soul. In a funny sort of way we then reunited non-human life and its non-living environment by giving it a name – Nature.[3]

Of course not all Western thinkers held this view. Even amongst scientists – Charles Darwin among them – there were those who found the idea of a world in which humans were the only sentient beings deeply disturbing. Nevertheless, with the start of the industrial revolution it seemed that through the rapid development of technology, and the use of ever-more powerful machines, the physical world could indeed be controlled and exploited for the sole benefit of humanity.

The one place that still seemed beyond our controlling reach was the vast open Ocean. Somehow the Ocean beyond the near shore still held the mystery of the unknowable, the untamable. In this context she was still alive to us, capable of exerting her free will upon any who would venture onto her vast body. Survival depended on the intimacy of our relationship with her rhythms and changing moods. The seafarer who neglected this relationship would soon find the Ocean a cruel and heartless mistress; while those who paid heed understood that she held no favourites, dispensing neither punishment nor reward, but rather, embraced all at their own risk.

But as the 20th century progressed even the vastness of the Ocean was succumbing to our relentless drive for domination. Not only was our new oil-driven technology opening up the entire Ocean to exploitation, but it was also driving a stake into the heart of this last bastion of our connection to the anima mundi. Following the global voyage of discovery by H.M.S. Challenger in 1872, when we first put a number to the deepest part of the Ocean, our scientific exploration has replaced much of the mystery with objective measurement and reduced the living pulse of her vastness to a catalogue of resources, there for the taking by those with the capability.

Complex Systems: A New Science of Life

Four hundred years of separatist thinking may have brought us to the brink of ecological catastrophe, but it has only done so through our misuse of knowledge, rather than the knowledge itself. While we must all take responsibility for the way our civilisation continues to abuse the Ocean, and indeed the whole planet, we can also celebrate the incredible advances in our understanding about the nature of life. A giant leap forward in that understanding came in 1859 when Charles Darwin published *On the Origin of Species*. Darwin's theory of evolution by natural selection introduced two hugely important ideas that laid the foundation for science to explore a new direction in its quest to explain life.

The first was that all life, including humans, shares a common ancestry, and the second was that new species come about through a process of natural selection.[4] The more profound implications of Darwin's controversial ideas have only recently started to be realised in the scientific context. That all life is interconnected and that evolution progresses, not in accordance with a grand design, but rather through the emergence of spontaneous and novel adaptations resulting from the life process itself, is now the cornerstone of modern scientific understanding.

Darwin may have laid the biological foundations for this understanding, but advances have come in all fields of science, including our discovery of the quantum universe, the microbial world and the chemistry of life. All have contributed to the shift in our understanding. Despite the reluctance of some mainstream evolutionary biologists, we can now finally move away from the simplistic idea of life as a machine; where competition for scarce resources drives evolutionary change, to one where life is a milieu of complex, cooperative and interactive relationships which continually evoke creative responses to challenges and opportunities alike.

This new science of life is known as the *Systems View of Life*, a term coined by physicist and complexity researcher Fitjof Capra, which is based on the understanding that living systems create networks of relationships, and that these networks have a pattern to them that can only be understood when viewed as a whole.[5] Furthermore, there are networks within networks and wholes within wholes. For example, our bodies are made up of approximately 50 trillion cells.[6] Each cell is a whole within itself, but is also nested as part of a greater whole; for example the liver, heart or brain, and each of these organs is also a whole nested within the whole body. We cannot understand the human organism by studying a single cell, any more than we can understand the Ocean by studying a single fish.

The theoretical framework for studying these patterns of networks is known as *Complexity Theory*, or *Non-linear Dynamics*, which for the first time has allowed scientists to create models of these networks using non-linear mathematical equations. What the models show is that living systems are always in a state of dynamic flow. The patterns we can see are *fractal*, meaning self-similar rather than identical, allowing the system to creatively adapt to ever-changing circumstances. In other words, living systems are contextual: they can only be understood in the context of their surroundings. This also means that living systems are inherently unpredictable.

So how does this relate to our quest to connect with the living Ocean? Can we view the whole Ocean as one complex living system? It would seem so. Indeed, the scientific understanding of the complex dance between biological life in the Ocean and the Ocean medium itself has blossomed in the past few decades. In fact, recent discoveries about the part the Ocean plays in the whole Earth as a single living system are truly remarkable. We now know for example that this tightly coupled interplay is a major player in the planet's various carbon cycles, which we'll examine shortly.

This new Earth Systems view of the Ocean is strongly influenced by James Lovelock's *Gaia Theory*.[7] Lovelock's intuitive understanding, backed up by careful research and empirical evidence, that life itself (in partnership with rocks, air and water) plays a vital role in producing and maintaining environmental conditions within the narrow limits that life can tolerate, and on a planetary scale, is one of the truly great scientific achievements of the 20th century. For Lovelock, Gaia is not just the sum of all life in feedback with the atmosphere, water and Earth's crust (the biosphere), but is rather the emergence of a self-regulating *superorganism* that comes into existence through the process of evolution. In his own words: 'Life and its environment are so closely coupled that evolution concerns Gaia, not the organisms or the environment taken separately.'[8]

Gaia's Ocean

Without water, our planet would be one of the billions of lifeless rocks float-
ing endlessly in the vastness of the inky-black void.
– Fabien Cousteau

The Ocean is by far the largest part of Gaia. Not only does the Ocean cover more than 70 percent of Gaia's surface, but it also accounts for somewhere between 97 to 99 percent of the livable biosphere.[9] So it's not surprising that virtually all of the self-regulating mechanisms she employs involve the Ocean in some way. As far as we know life isn't possible without water, so it's safe to say that without the Ocean, Gaia and therefore all life would not exist. But what if the converse is also true: without life the Ocean wouldn't exist? This may sound far fetched, but from a Gaian perspective there is strong evidence that without the influence of life's metabolic processes, the water on our planet would have literally evaporated into space and Earth would be as desiccated and lifeless as its nearest neighbours, Venus and Mars.[10]

In the next chapter we will travel far back in time to explore how the Ocean first came into being as a living synthesis, but for now we'll focus on the extraordinary fact that, of the three inner planets – Venus, Earth and Mars – it's only Earth that's managed to maintain significant volumes of water in liquid form. To understand the part life plays in this miraculous achievement, let's first look at the elemental properties of water and how they interact with other forces. This will help us understand what may have happened to our planetary neighbours, and what our own planet's fate might have been without life's intervention.

The water molecule (H_2O) is perhaps the most widely recognised symbol in the language of chemistry. Two hydrogen atoms bonded to one oxygen atom to create the life-giving miracle that is water. To really appreciate the beauty of this dynamic relationship let's follow the inspired work of Gaian scientist and Deep Ecology practitioner, Stephan Harding and his beautifully animistic descriptions of these elemental personalities.[11]

All atoms contain positively charged protons residing within their nucleus. Orbiting the nucleus in concentric rings is an equal number of negatively charged electrons. The first ring closest to the nucleus can only hold a maximum of two electrons, the second and third rings eight each and beyond them subsequent rings can hold even more. The magical property of atoms that makes life possible is their intense need to have a full outer ring of electrons. For example, a carbon atom has six protons within its nucleus with six electrons in orbit around them. This means it needs two rings, an inner ring with its full complement of two electrons, and an outer ring with four electrons to equal its six protons. Thus it needs to find another four electrons to fill its outer orbit. This can happen when carbon atoms come together and share electrons with each other in a mutually fulfilling bond of friendship in what chemists call a *covalent bond*. These long carbon chains happily bond with other elementals, such as oxygen, sulphur, phosphorus and nitrogen, to form the complex molecules of life.

The hydrogen atom is the lightest and most abundant element in the universe with just a single proton within its nucleus and one lonely electron in orbit around it. In search of just one more electron to fill its single orbit it can find fulfilment most easily by joining with another hydrogen atom to form a hydrogen molecule (H_2). But so light and fancy free are the hydrogen atoms that they are more than happy to indulge the advances of other elemental beings such as oxygen. This suits the passionate oxygen atom, who with an outer orbit needing two electrons, will bond with just about any other element. When it comes across our hydrogen molecule its passionate dreams are fulfilled and the resulting 'lover's embrace' creates the miracle molecule, (H_2O) water. (Figure 1.1)

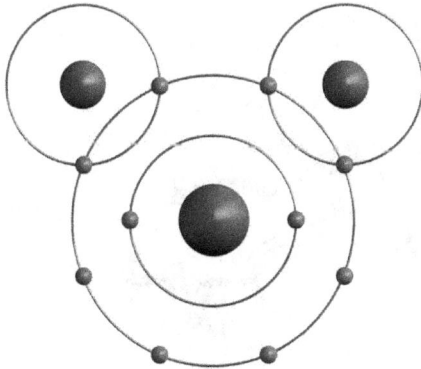

Figure 1.1 The water molecule (H_2O). (Image: iStock)

There's something else we should know about our watery lovers. Our oxygen 'Romeo' puts so much passionate energy into this *ménage á trios* with the two hydrogen 'Juliets', that he is left feeling a bit negative about their flippant ways; while the light hearted Juliets have nothing but positive

tive vibes and an urge for more. So much so in fact, they just can't resist smooching up to the oxygen atom in the neighbouring molecule. In chemistry this is known as a *weak hydrogen bond* and is the reason water molecules have a tendency to stick together. In liquid water each molecule can be hydrogen-bonded to as many as four others.

Water is indeed the miracle molecule. Not only is it the facilitator of life as we know it, but because of its unique and mysterious ability to move easily between liquid, gas and solid states, it plays a key role in the whole climate process. In fact, so mysterious is this *phase-shifting* capability of water, that scientists have until recently been at a loss to explain just how water achieves many of its miraculous feats. But over the last decade a team of researchers, lead by Professor Gerald Pollack from the University of Washington in Seattle, have made a breakthrough discovery that could shake the very foundations of our scientific understanding of life.

They've discovered a *fourth phase* of water that is neither liquid nor solid but is described as '...a liquid crystal with the physical properties analogous to those of raw egg white'. This *liquid-crystalline*, or *inter-facial* water, forms around any hydrophilic (water-attracting) surface, including organic particles, creating an *exclusion zone* between the surface and the surrounding water, hence the nickname, 'EZ' water. As the name suggests this exclusion zone *excludes* other molecules like dissolved minerals. But the really important discovery is that EZ water takes on a different molecular structure: H_3O_2. (Figure 1.2)

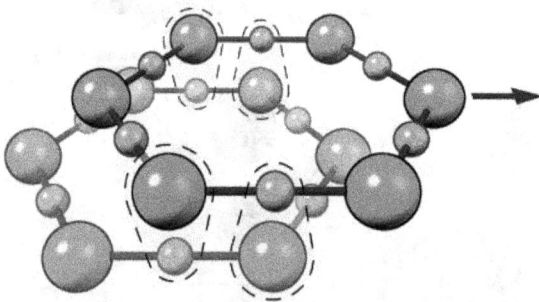

Figure 1.2 EZ water forms lattice like layers, resulting in a different molecular structure (H_3O_2), in which two oxygen atoms become bonded with three hydrogen atoms. (Image courtesy of Professor Gerald Pollack, © Ebner and Sons/Gerald Pollack)

This means that EZ water actually carries a negative charge instead of a neutral charge like ordinary water. A helpful, although not entirely accurate, way to grasp this is to think of two water molecules joined together but missing one hydrogen atom.[12] The leftover hydrogen atoms are transferred to the surrounding water where they latch on to ordinary water molecules, creating positively charged hydronium ions (H_3O). This results in an area of positive charge right next to the negatively charged EZ. (Figure 1.3)

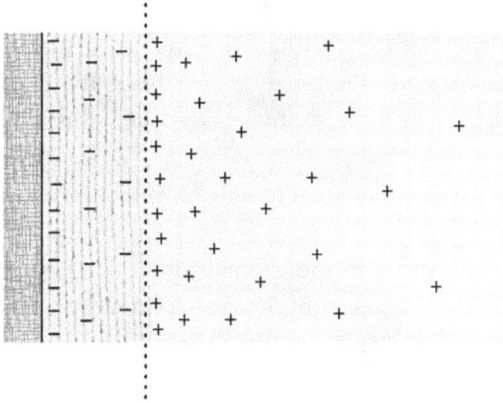

Figure 1.3 The resulting hydronium ions associated with the molecular structure of EZ water creates a positive charge in the surrounding bulk water. (Image courtesy of Professor Gerald Pollack, © Ebner and Sons/Gerald Pollack)

Pollack and his team have made two other key discoveries. EZ water absorbs radiant electromagnetic energy from the sun and uses it, much like plants do during the initial stages of their more complex photosynthesis process. Secondly, EZ water can store potential energy like a battery.[13] Research into EZ water is still in its infancy and, like so many new discoveries, will take time to be digested, tested and either accepted or rejected by the scientific community. However, the implications for the life process are profound, and we'll be exploring some of these in later chapters, but for now we'll just note that the work of scientists like Professor Pollack and others, is starting to provide some of the details for what the great Austrian naturalist, Victor Schauberger, called 'the living nature of water'.[14]

Life to the Rescue

If that is all there was to the elemental story of water we would more than likely be living on a much wetter planet and, if we could look backwards in time through a powerful telescope, we would be able to look upon our nearest galactic neighbours, Venus and Mars, and see vast oceans possibly teeming with life. Instead, we now see barren landscapes devoid of life, but clearly showing the telltale geological features indicating large volumes of water once covered their surface.

So, what happened? The answer lies in the light-hearted nature of hydrogen. So light in fact, that with hardly a backwards glance, it will leave the bereft oxygen behind, slip easily away from the clutches of Earth's gravity and disappear into the vastness of space. One of the processes by which this happens is called *photo-dissociation* – when liquid water evaporates and becomes a gas (water vapour). As it rises into the stratosphere, ultraviolet radiation from the sun breaks the strong hydrogen-oxygen bond, releasing the hydrogen molecules into space forever. Another important process is the sequestering of the oxygen atoms by iron and sulphur, present in the basalt rocks on the Ocean floor, which again frees the hydrogen to escape into space.

When our solar system was young, Venus, with its closer proximity to the sun, was exposed to approximately 40 percent more solar radiation than Earth. This would have caused vast quantities of water to evaporate into the atmosphere, setting in motion a runaway positive feedback loop of warming (due to the powerful greenhouse effect of water vapour), leading to an exponential increase in photo-dissociation and subsequent hydrogen loss to space. This positive feedback loop would have continued until virtually all the water on Venus had evaporated.[15]

The fate of Mars' ocean is probably somewhat more complex. Being further away from the sun it receives some 43 percent less solar radiation than Earth. Even so, there were probably abundant greenhouse gases, such as methane and carbon dioxide (CO_2), capable of generating high enough temperatures to hold water in its liquid state. Some of this water would have been lost through evaporation and photo-dissociation. In addition, vast quantities of carbon dioxide would have been stripped from the atmosphere over geological time, forming carbonate rock. With no plate tectonics to replace the carbon dioxide through volcanic activity, the Martian atmosphere has become thin and lost its greenhouse capability. As the temperature plummeted much of the liquid water on Mars may have frozen, which is evidenced by the large polar icecaps and possibly large areas of underground ice.[16]

The atmospheres of Venus and Mars are now in a state of near equilibrium and are completely at the mercy of the chemical and physical processes described above. Without life, Earth's atmosphere would be in a similar state of equilibrium with 98 percent carbon dioxide and little or no oxygen. Like Venus we would be in an unstoppable greenhouse feedback loop, creating furnace-like surface temperatures and causing massive evaporation of the Ocean. With this and other processes, it's estimated that under these conditions Earth's Ocean would have completely disappeared by about two billion years ago.[17] That I'm sitting here writing this book attests to the fact that this didn't happen! So how has life saved the Ocean and itself?

According to Gaia Theory there are two main strategies by which life sustains Earth as the Ocean planet in our solar system. The first is the various ways in which life maintains atmospheric temperatures suitable for liquid water – neither too hot nor too cold. These include manipulating the ratios of greenhouse gases in the atmosphere, for example through the metabolic process of photosynthesis that removes vast amounts of carbon dioxide from the atmosphere and replaces it with oxygen.[18] Besides providing life with a breathable atmosphere, this free oxygen is responsible for the ozone layer, which vastly reduces photo-dissociation in the stratosphere.[19] Life also plays a major role in the long-term carbon cycle; critical to maintaining the balance of carbon dioxide levels in the atmosphere and therefore planetary temperatures. Life also influences the temperature of the atmosphere and Ocean by helping to form the clouds that reflect some of the sun's heat back into space. (We'll find out how in Chapter 3.)

The second way in which life reduces water loss is by enticing the free and easy hydrogen atoms back into their watery marriage with oxygen before they can escape into space. We have the microbial world of bacteria to thank for this. In the darkest depths of the Ocean, uncountable armies of bacteria have been tirelessly working behind the scenes, conjuring wonderfully imaginative acts of molecular alchemy, blissfully unaware that their metabolic livelihoods were playing such an important role in keeping Gaia moist. Some of these creative strategies include metabolising sulphur, which releases hydrogen to join with the oxygen produced by photosynthesisers. Others react carbon dioxide with free hydrogen to produce methane and water.[20] Of course, like all complex systems, these strategies are so completely interconnected that it is a little misleading to present them as separate processes. Be that as it may, it is useful to have an example, just to illustrate the profound creativity of Gaia. It's also worth reminding ourselves that all of these strategies started with the coming into being of the living Ocean.

The Long-Term Carbon Cycle and the Biological Carbonate Pump

The long-term carbon cycle is recycling on a grand scale, which happens over geological time frames measured in hundreds of thousands to millions of years. The first part of the recycling process is known as *silicate rock weathering*. It involves atmospheric carbon dioxide (CO_2) dissolved in rainwater, reacting with exposed granite and basalt rock surfaces to form water-soluble calcium bicarbonate. The calcium bicarbonate is carried by rivers and streams to the Ocean, where it is consumed by marine organisms, thereby removing carbon dioxide from the atmosphere.

Until the early 1980's this was considered a purely chemical process. However, we now know that life has been enhancing this process for at least hundreds of millions of years. From bacteria and lichens to massive tree roots, life works its way into the rocks, exposing more surfaces to weathering. It's estimated that this life-enhanced rock weathering is ten times more efficient at removing carbon dioxide from the atmosphere than chemical weathering alone, and plays a hugely important role in keeping the Earth cool.[21] The living Ocean is involved in every aspect of this beautiful Gaian process, from the seeding of the rain-producing clouds that dissolve the carbon dioxide in the atmosphere, to the rivers that deliver it to the Ocean, and the carbon sequestering organisms in the Ocean that consume the calcium bicarbonate through a process known as the *biological carbonate pump*.

The current champions of the biological carbonate pump are a group of microscopic algae with the exotic name of *coccolithophores*. Not only are they one of the primary producers in the Ocean, using the sun's energy to convert carbon dioxide and water into sugars and oxygen, but also – as if this isn't enough – they use that sugary energy to perform one of the most important climate control functions on the planet. Extracting calcium bi-carbonate ions from the Ocean, they create exquisitely crafted chalky plates – *coccoliths* – within their cellular structure. Each coccolith plate is in essence a storehouse of carbon that was once carbon dioxide drifting in the atmosphere (Figure. 1.4).

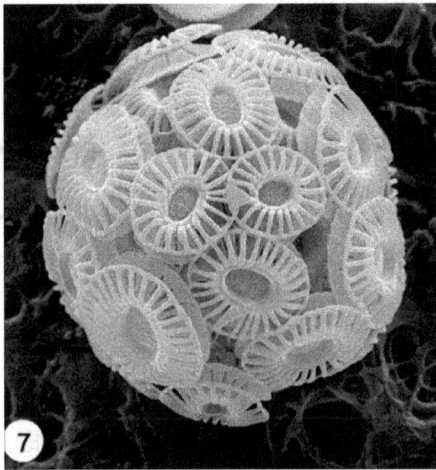

Figure 1.4 Coccolithophores extract calcium bicarbonate from the Ocean to create their exquisitely crafted coccolith plates. (Image Source: Andruleit et al. 2005 JNR Arabian Sea coccos. Image courtesy of University College, London.http://ina.tmsoc.org/Nannotax3)

When they die and sink to the Ocean floor, their chalky skeletons accumu-late in such vast numbers that their combined weight forms solid chalk and limestone rock. Over millions of years these rocks are carried along the Ocean floor by the movement of tectonic plates, until they are finally sub-ducted below the Ocean's crust, where the intense heat melts them into reformed granite. The intense heat also releases the trapped carbon diox-ide, which is spewed back into the atmosphere through volcanic eruptions, thus completing the cycle and contributing to the dynamic balancing act that keeps Gaia habitable. Eminent American geologist Don Anderson, even postulates that the immense weight of the limestone laid down by the coccolithophores and other calcifiers, may be one of the drivers of plate tectonics.[22]

The life-enhanced long-term carbon cycle not only plays a pivotal role in maintaining habitable conditions, but also contributes mightily to the retention of water through its temperature controlling influence. This, and the many other life processes that have contributed to maintaining the Ocean, are only possible because water was there in the first place. But, as we've seen, water is a mysteriously complex, elemental relationship that can only survive in its liquid phase with the help of more than a few 'lively' friends.

From this perspective it makes no sense to impose an arbitrary separation between the Ocean medium and the life within it. If one cannot exist without the other the only sensible option is to view them as one intra-dependent, living entity. The Ocean isn't the background for life; rather it is *life in motion*. Or, as the eminent 19th century Russian scientist Vladimir Vernadsky so eloquently put it, 'Life is animated water'.[23]

Of course this applies equally to the atmosphere and terrestrial life. Every air molecule in every inhalation we take is only possible because of all the breaths that have gone before. In fact, our atmosphere as it exists now, is exactly the breath of life. The 21 percent oxygen in our atmosphere is only there by the grace of all those photosynthesisers in the Ocean and on land, which in turn rely on the planet-wide exhalation of carbon dioxide to help them harness the sun's energy. As terrestrial, air-breathing beings it's perhaps understandable that we identify most strongly with these two minority realms, and yet, without a living Ocean there would be no land plants, no breathable atmosphere and no us! Our very physiology mirrors Gaia's great body and tells the story of our Ocean origins.

It's clear that the Ocean exists the way she does today because of the intricate and complex dance of life within her great body. But if we restrict ourselves to a purely scientific, rational explanation of this complexity we're in danger of losing our newly rekindled connection to her living essence. Science can help us deepen our understanding about how we should behave in our relationship with the Ocean, but it can never explain that deep sense of tingling anticipation, as we stand on her shore ready to dive into her liquid embrace. In that moment, when we leave rationality behind and feel her fluid pressure against our flesh; when we feel ourselves fully alive; that's when the Ocean reveals her true, living nature to us.

And how does the Ocean respond to our plunging body? We feel her watery touch on our flesh, but is she not also feeling our 'fleshy' touch? Our presence is being felt in an active exchange of information. Our body is a mass of electromagnetic and chemical messages and the Ocean is the ultimate interpreter; our own unique, living signature instantly translated into thousands of different languages and available for download by myriad life forms, seen and unseen. This is the living synthesis our sensing body responds to as we push through the water.

Clearly there's more going on here than just the physics of electromagnetic conductivity in seawater. Indeed we can easily replicate a saline solution capable of equal conductivity; we can even put a fish in that water and measure how quickly it receives the electrical impulses. What we can't re-create though, are the complex relationships that give context and meaning to those impulses; only the living Ocean can do that. In the next chapter we'll dive into the depths of time, to the very origins of the Ocean herself, but before we do, let's imagine what it would be like to become part of the living Ocean.

* * *

Becoming Water

If you can, find a place beside the Ocean, or a river, lake or any body of water.

Look into the water. Take a few slow, deep breaths and imagine yourself shrinking down to an infinitesimally small being as you dive in. You are so small that even the single-celled algae floating past seem like giants. You have become the smallest, lightest elemental being in the Universe: a hydrogen atom.

You feel light and spacious as if nothing, not even the pressure of the water, or gravity itself, can hold you. But somehow you feel incomplete, like the beginning of a story, without a middle or end. An irresistible urge to join with your kin comes over you as you're drawn towards another hydrogen atom. Embracing, you feel a great sense of peace and fulfilment, and yet, even together you still feel yourselves floating through the watery expanse towards the surface and infinite space beyond.

Just as you are about to leave the watery realm behind you feel an intense presence. An oxygen atom, newly liberated from its carbon mate by the photosynthesising magic of a passing single-celled algae, is charming its way between you and your partner. You don't want to be separated, but even so, you feel a tingle of excitement as the oxygen atom snuggles in between you.

You feel the weight of its presence holding you in place and your senses become alive to a new consciousness that is so much more than you could have achieved separately. You are now a water molecule, the essence of life itself. Your newly expanded self is thrumming with potential and you sense your ability to move with ease between liquid, gas and solid states.

In your current liquid state, another urge is building within your hydrogen twins, who can't resist the electrifying personalities of other oxygen atoms in the water molecules all around you. Before long you find yourself connecting with your neighbours until you are completely cocooned in a watery embrace.

Nested within your kindred community you feel connection upon connection flowing in all directions, but you are also aware of other life-forces moving within your expanded body; other elemental beings – magnesium, potassium, calcium, sulphate, iron – all adding their unique consciousness to your own. Gradually you start to feel the presence of much larger beings, cellular and multi-cellular forms, dancing through your body and filling your senses with their exuberance. As you vibrate to this living symphony you realise that together you have become part of the living Ocean.

2

Coming Into Being

For deep in the Ocean, lies the first secret.

The living Ocean is an evolutionary synthesis of water and life – four billion years in the making. We experience her now as the vast interconnected and interdependent being that profoundly affects our own existence, indeed that makes our existence possible. But how did the Ocean come into being? What was the nature of her birth? How did life start at all? And why in the Ocean? So complex are these questions and so long ago did it all happen that all we can really do is make educated guesses about the details. However, we know enough to paint across the deep chasm of time with broad brush-strokes to tell a somewhat coherent story.

Our solar system is around five billion years old, fully a third as old as the Universe herself. Earth, along with the other planets, coalesced out of a nebular cloud of swirling, stellar dust, left behind after a supernova explosion that also gave birth to our sun. Over hundreds of millions of years, tiny stellar dust particles came together into larger and larger clumps that eventually formed into mountain sized *planetesimals*, hurtling through space in increasingly defined gravitational orbits around our nascent sun. Time and time again these planetesimals collided with each other, eventually forming the four inner planets (Mercury, Venus, Earth and Mars).

The four outer planets (Jupiter, Saturn, Neptune and Uranus) remained as gas giants, but the inner planets took on a more solid form. After millions of years of this continual accretion, Earth coalesced into a molten cauldron of liquid rock surrounded by swirling clouds of gas. About 4.5 billion years ago a Mars-sized planet smashed into Earth, creating a massive tsunami of molten rock that was thrust out into space. This circling ring of lava slowly cooled and eventually formed into our closest galactic neighbour, the moon. This was perhaps the most important event in the life of the young Earth, for without the moon circling in close consort with our planet, the evolutionary story that has led to you reading these pages would have unfolded in a very different way.[1]

The first important effect of this cataclysmic collision was to create a tilt in the Earth's axis, which to this day gives us our seasons. The moon, which was much closer then, also acted to slow and stabilise Earth's rotation, lengthening the days and providing a gravitational counterbalance to the pull of the sun. The moon's gravitational dance with Earth is critical to our Ocean story, as it is the primary driver of the daily ebb and flow of tides. Although we don't know exactly how big the tides may have been when the moon was so much closer to Earth, it's certain that they would have dwarfed even the largest king tides we see today.[2] These massive tides would have created surging rapids and massive whirlpools as the Ocean was violently pulled from one side of the planet to the other.

There are many other critical factors that allowed Earth to flourish as the Ocean planet and cradle of life in our solar system. For a start, it was just the right distance from the sun to allow water to stay in liquid form, and its mass created just enough gravity to hold that water – along with the atmosphere – in a close embrace. Even the other planets helped the infant Earth by contributing their gravitational forces to the overall mix of emergent stability as the solar system evolved. So, the conditions were just right for our Ocean to come into being, but where did all that water come from in the first place?

In the Beginning There Was Just Water

Water is abundant in our solar system but much of it is locked up in frozen comets, asteroids and meteors. Water molecules were present in the nebular cloud that formed our solar system and at least some of them would have been drawn into the Earth, mixing with the dust particles as they formed into rock. It's estimated that there may be as much as five to ten ocean's worth of water locked-up in the mantle, below the Earth's crust. So it seems most likely that Earth's water is a mixture of this *embedded* water, out-gassed over time through volcanic activity, and galactic water delivered from comets, asteroids and meteors colliding with the young Earth.[3]

Just how much water came from galactic bombardment is unclear, but even two or three large asteroids would deliver an Ocean's worth.

For the first few hundred million years Earth was in a tumultuous state as violent volcanic eruptions spewed molten lava, gas clouds and water vapour into the atmosphere while meteors and comets bombarded the surface. During this period there were probably several episodes of liquid water forming, only to be vaporised back into the atmosphere, before the Earth cooled enough for the liquid water to finally remain permanently. By four billion years ago, at the beginning of the *Archean* eon, most of the planet's surface was covered by water, with perhaps as much as twice the volume as the Ocean today.[4]

The scene would be completely unfamiliar to us. There were no continental landmasses: the only dry land would have been volcanic islands rising above the surface. This water world and the sky above would have looked like an alien planet from some science fiction fantasy. Hues of pink and orange, created by the hydrogen sulphide laden atmosphere, would have painted the water in shades of brown; and no matter where and how we looked there would be no signs of life.

But below the surface a most important geological process was already in motion. The newly formed crust covering the mantle of molten, viscous magma was constantly being remelted and reformed as the young Earth continued to slowly cool. Slowly, the rock making up the Earth's crust separated into heavy, dense basalt and lighter, less dense granite, which was able to float higher on the molten sea of magma. As this granite built up over hundreds of millions of years the continents slowly formed until they finally reached their current landmass some 2.5 billion years ago.[5]

Earth's crust was now differentiated into the lighter but thicker granite continental landmasses, and the heavier, but thinner basalt of the sea floor. On average the oceanic basalt crust is four to ten kilometres thick, while the continental granite crust is 30 to 40 kilometres thick. This means that the oceanic crust is recycled very much faster into the mantle than the granite. This recycling process continues to this day in the form of plate tectonics and in fact, it is the lubricating qualities of water that keep the tectonic plates in perpetual motion.[6] Without plate tectonics Earth would be unrecognisable and as lifeless as Mars appears to be, whose crust fused into a single encircling skin eons ago. But Earth does have plate tectonics and it's at these sub-marine meeting points, where the oceanic crusts are in a continual state of creative renewal, that we may get a glimpse of the Ocean's first secret: the beginning of life itself.

Life Begins

I felt the full breadth and depth of the ocean around the sphere of the Earth, back billions of years to the beginning of life, across all the passing lives and deaths, the endless waves of swimming joy and quiet losses of exquisite creatures with fins and fronds, tentacles and wings, colourful and transparent, tiny and huge, coming and going. There is nothing the ocean has not seen.
– Sally Andrew (2009) *The Fire Dogs of Climate Change: An Inspirational Call to Action.*

Deep below the Ocean's surface the mysterious alchemy of life's beginnings may still be playing out, in the same way it did some 3.9 billion years ago. Along the mid-ocean ridges, where the Ocean crust is continually emerging anew, high-pressure thermal vents spew out super-heated water loaded with life's essential minerals. As this 400°C elemental concoction meets the Ocean and begins to cool, chemical reactions are created that have the potential to cohere into creative and dynamic patterns of behaviour. Usually these patterns are very short lived, lasting only as long as the chemical reaction that evoked them; but at some point in the distant past, at least one of these dynamic patterns persisted with such coherence that it was able to draw energy into itself and use that energy to maintain coherence.

Just how that coherence occurred is mysterious, but a potential answer lies in the newly discovered *fourth phase* of water. If you remember from the last chapter this *inter-facial*, or EZ water, forms around organic molecules, creating a negatively charged, liquid crystalline skin around the molecule, while at the same time sending positively charged *hydronium ions* into the surrounding water. Multiple organic molecules, with their negatively charged EZ skin, are attracted to the intervening positively charged water, bringing them close enough to each other for them to cohere into a condensed mass.

Experiments carried out by scientists at the University of Washington in Seattle, confirmed that molecules surrounded by a skin of EZ water are indeed attracted to each other via the intervening, positively charged water, and that they do form condensed masses (Figure 2.1). Based on this evidence it seems quite possible that this physics-defying property of 'living water' may have provided the physical mechanism for the chemicals of life to come together. If so, the potential energy stored in the EZ water may well have supplied at least the initial energy needed to prolong coherence.[7] Thus the first and most fundamental aspect of life may have come into being – the ability to renew and maintain itself by metabolising energy.[8]

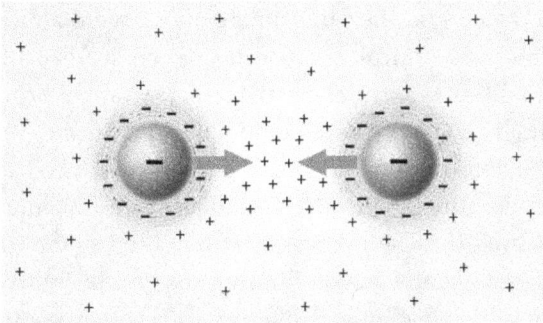

Figure 2.1 Organic molecules surrounded by a skin of negatively charged EZ water are drawn together via the intervening positively charged bulk water. (Image courtesy of Professor Gerald Pollack, © Ebner and Sons/Gerald Pollack)

Chilean biologist, Humberto Maturana, calls this metabolic miracle, *autopoiesis*, which literally means self-making. Autopoiesis is defined as: 'a self-organising system capable of sustaining itself through a network of reactions that continually regenerate its components, within a boundary of its own making'.[9] A cell is a perfect example of an autopoietic system: within the boundary of its *self-made*, permeable membrane, it sustains itself by absorbing energy from its surroundings and using that energy to regenerate its internal structure.

Through autopoiesis it was only a matter of time before one of these chemical beings became a biological being. Perhaps from an oily droplet of complex carbon compounds, autopoiesis worked its metabolic magic and brought forth the first membrane-encased bacterial cell. We'll probably never know the exact details, but once bacterial life had begun in the watery depths of the Archean Ocean, there was no turning back. Even so, it would take hundreds of millions of years before life became a major player in planetary affairs.

These first hardy bacteria dined on a rich soup of organic molecules and sulphides. Very early on some of them started producing methane as a by-product of their metabolism. This was critical, as methane is a powerful green house gas and its accumulation in the atmosphere kept the early Earth warm enough to stop the Ocean from freezing over completely and 'snuffing out' life just as it was beginning. Another early innovation involved using the sun's energy to break down hydrogen sulphide into sulphates. This was a hugely important precursor to perhaps the most stunning and influential innovation life has ever achieved; the magic of oxygen-producing photosynthesis.[10]

The infant Ocean and the atmosphere above were almost completely oxygen-free. This was critical because if oxygen were present it would have interfered with the essential chemical reactions that brought-forth life in the first place. It can't have taken long however, for the early bacteria to exhaust the available organic chemical goodies and need a new energy source to power their metabolism. The challenge was taken up by an innovative group of bacteria who evolved the ability to use the sun's energy to break the strong elemental bonds binding oxygen to hydrogen in water molecules. Using this new style of photosynthesis they combined the carbon and hydrogen atoms to make food as well as manufacturing cellular structures including DNA. The by-product of their autopoetic metabolism was oxygen.[11]

These talented innovators are *cyanobacteria* - named for their blue-green colouration - and over millions of years they populated the sunlit Ocean shallows. Cyanobacteria are the ancestors of all modern photosynthesisers in the Ocean and on land, and even today they are abundant. In fact, recent research shows that cyanobacteria are still the dominant photosynthesisers in the nutrient-poor tropical areas of the Ocean.[12]

To start with, any free oxygen was immediately sequestered by oxidising agents in the Ocean such as iron and sulphur, but over time vast colonies of cyanobacteria started to produce more oxygen than could be absorbed. By about 3.5 billion years ago there is evidence of local accumulation of oxygen and 200 million years later there were trace amounts of oxygen gas (O_2) in sediments and in the atmosphere.[13]

As continental landmasses started to develop, the cyanobacteria took advantage of the shallow continental slopes to build solid platforms on which they could bask in the light of the young sun. Over millions of years they secreted carbonate skeletons, building up massive structures that supported other types of bacteria, creating complex microbial communities that thrived in the sun-drenched shallows. Known as *stromatolites*, these were the first barrier reefs, billions of years before our familiar coral reefs existed. Living stromatolites still exist in a few locations, such as Shark Bay in Western Australia, where they continue their traditional livelihood, unchanged almost since life began (Figure 2.2).

Figure 2.2 Stromatolites, such as these in Shark Bay, Western Australia, represent a visible, living link to the Archean Ocean. (Image: dreamstime)

James Lovelock speculates that Gaia as a living, planetary system didn't manifest until bacteria covered most of the planet.[14] If this is so, then that slow awakening took its first tentative steps at life's beginning nearly four billion years ago somewhere in the Ocean. For the next billion years or so, the cyanobacteria ruled the planet and quietly went about the business of co-creating a living, breathing Ocean. As the living Ocean awakened Gaia became possible.

The Great Oxidation Event

The runaway success of photosynthesis created the first life-induced environmental crisis, some 2.5 billion years ago. Over a relatively short – 150 million year period – cyanobacteria became so prolific that they oxygenated the top layer of the Ocean as well as the atmosphere. Not only was oxygen lethal to some of the other bacteria, but also the new oxygen gas (O_2) readily reacted with the methane gas in the atmosphere, reducing the greenhouse effect dramatically. Even before the cyanobacteria had a chance to consume the remaining carbon dioxide, Gaia was plunged into a severe ice age that may have lasted for millions of years before she managed to steady herself.[15]

With ice covering vast areas of the planet's surface, more of the sun's warmth was reflected back into space, cooling the planet even further. If this had carried on, Earth might have frozen permanently. Luckily, some areas of the Ocean remained ice-free, while volcanic activity introduced more carbon dioxide into the atmosphere.

Slowly the living Ocean reached a happy balance, with the photosynthesisers metabolising carbon dioxide to produce oxygen, and myriad other bacteria feeding on the decomposing organic leftovers, producing carbon dioxide and methane.[16] This was self-regulation on a grand scale! The Ocean as a living system had survived her first big test, and now the stage was set for an evolutionary masterstroke that would eventually lead to the staggering diversity of today's Ocean, and indeed all multi-cellular life on the planet.

Evolving Ocean

The first two billion years of the living Ocean belonged to the bacteria; who represent the first 'Kingdom of Life'. The second Kingdom emerged out of the bacterial equivalent of a marriage of convenience, somewhere between two and 1.7 billion years ago, during the *Proterozoic* eon, which stretched from 2.5 billion to 542 million years ago. From the 'bacteria eat bacteria' watery jungle, a sort of benign cannibalism emerged that eventually lead to mutually beneficial symbiosis. Through multiple mergings a new kind of cell evolved, the *eukaryotic*, or nucleated cell, which incorporated the various skills and talents of individual bacteria within its expanded body.[17] The evolution of eukaryotic cells ushered in the second Kingdom of Life: *protoctista*, meaning 'first beings'.

These free-swimming organisms were responsible for the development of some of life's more familiar innovations such as sexual reproduction, speciation and even aging and dying. Some would later go on to become the other three Kingdoms of life - the animals, fungi and plants. For at least a billion years the protoctists concerned themselves with exploring their own creative potential, diversifying into a stunning array of planktonic beings that carpeted the surface of the living Ocean, gently reorganising the chemical makeup of the entire planet. Others took up a more sedentary life, inhabiting the Ocean floor and feasting on the continual organic smorgasbord of dead bodies raining down from above – recycling on a grand scale. All life today is either *prokaryotic* (bacteria and Achaea) or eukaryotic (plants, animals, fungi and protoctists) but without the symbiotic bacteria living in our eukaryotic cells none of us would be here. In fact, we are the result of the greatest act of coordination and cooperation life has ever seen.

Today there are thousands, perhaps millions of species of Ocean protoctists. Just like the bacterial kingdom, the protoctists include both primary producers (the photosynthesisers) and consumers: those that eat the primary producers and/or other consumers. Most of them are far too small for us to see unaided, but with the help of a microscope a world of unparalleled beauty and intricate design is revealed. From the photosynthesising *diatoms*, *coccolithophores* and *dinoflagellates*, to consumers such as the *radiolarians* and *foraminifera*, these tiny beings join the bacteria at the very foundation of the Ocean as a living presence (Figure 2.3).

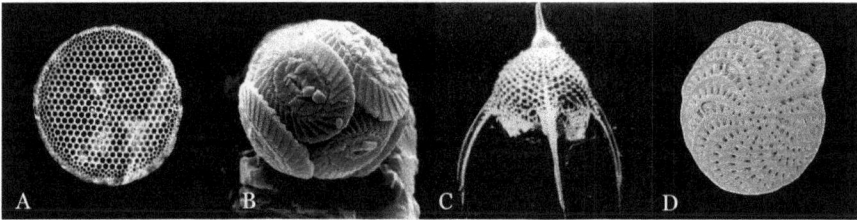

Figure 2.3 Representative protoctists, showing the internal structure of A: Diatom *Thalassiosira ferelineata* (Jouse), B: Coccolithophore *Watznaueria barnesae* (Black in Black and Barnes, 1959) Perch-Nielsen, 1968, C: Radiolarian *Elphidium macellum* (Fichtel and Moll), D: Foraminifera *Pterocanium praetaxum* (Ehrenberg). (All images courtesy of University College London Micropalaeontology Unit http://www.ucl.ac.uk/GeolSci/micropal/index.html

We'll revisit them when we explore the planktonic surface layer of the Ocean in Chapter 5, but for now, there's one other very important point to make about the protoctista kingdom. Not only did it revolutionise single-celled life with the development of the eukaryotic cell, but it also introduced multi-cellular life into the evolutionary mix. In the primordial shallows, perhaps as long as ago as a billion years, the first tentative multi-cellular life forms appeared.[18] What we now call seaweed started its swaying dance into the future. All of today's algae, from the microscopic phytoplankton to the giant kelp forests, are in fact not plants at all but the modern descendants of those early protoctists.

As I snorkel out from a beach in South West Devon, England I can see vast mats of kelp and seaweed slowly undulating back and forth in the gentle Atlantic swell. Diving down I find a clear patch of sand amongst the ancient rocky reefs, where I can float at eye level to this swaying forest of life. While my breath lasts I caress the broad rubbery fronds of kelp, with their root-like holdfasts clinging tenaciously to the rocks, and gently squeeze the more cylindrical, sponge-like branches of the seaweeds stretching towards the surface (Figure 2.4).

Figure 2.4 The extraordinary kelp and seaweed gardens of the south- western Devon coast in England.

The creative exuberance of shape, colour, texture and movement is mesmerising and it's only my aching lungs that force me back to the surface. As soon as I get my breath back I dive down again, for here amongst this swaying mass I can experience a tangible, visible link to the very first multi-cellular beings large enough to be seen with the naked eye. If we could somehow dive 700 million years back in time, we might glimpse ancient kelps and seaweeds, not entirely dissimilar to the Ocean forests of today.

Kingdom of the Animals

As we've seen, the first two Kingdoms of Life toiled for three billion years, creating, refining and maintaining a living home for themselves; but they were also putting the building blocks in place for an explosion of creative expansion. The secret ingredient that took life from primordial soup to extravagant banquet was oxygen, or more precisely, oxygen gas (O_2). Only in a living, breathing Ocean could this have been achieved. Sometime around 700 to 800 million years ago, long before the so-called *Cambrian Explosion* of hard-bodied animals that produced such a treasure trove of fossils, life was undergoing its next major metamorphosis that would give birth to our own animal kingdom.

In the Ediacara Hills in southern Australia, fossil remains of bizarre, soft-bodied beings preserved in 650 million year old sandstone, may well represent life's first foray into an animal way of being. These *Ediacaran* beings were mobile jelly-like organisms inhabiting shallow sunlit waters. Most were probably multi-cellular protoctists, harvesting the sunlight, or feeding on floating bacterial pastures.[19] But it's here that some of the fundamental aspects of being animal may have emerged, including the adoption of the sperm/egg way of reproducing and a distinctively 'animal' approach to embryonic development. So, rather than the sudden arrival suggested by the Cambrian Explosion, the animal way of being evolved slowly through a creative exploration of life's possibilities in a supportive living environment. The ancient ancestors of today's *ctenophores* – comb jellies – may have been amongst these earliest of animals.[20]

The first definitive fossil records of early animal life date back 635 million years, where there is clear evidence of abundant and continuous presence of sponges in the salty basins of The Sultanate of Oman.[21] Sponges are the most un-animal-like animals imaginable! They are simple souls, with only a few different cell types taking care of all their needs, from physical form to feeding and reproduction. Yet they have persisted and prospered through time, surviving violent geological upheavals, numerous ice ages, even massive meteor impacts. The five great mass extinctions passed them by with hardly a raised *spicule* (the exquisite, interlaced glass-like fibres they craft from silica or calcite) and today they inhabit all Ocean realms, from shallow tropical reefs to frozen polar seas and deep Ocean trenches. They are the Buddhas of the Ocean: less is more. Respected Gaian scientist, Tim Lenton, suggests that they may have even helped oxygenate the deep

Ocean through their filtering lifestyle, thereby setting the scene for more complex beings to evolve.[22]

From these humble beginnings the animal Kingdom very quickly blossomed into a period of creative energy, the likes of which had never before been seen. By the time of the Cambrian Explosion, 540 million years ago, fossil records contain examples of virtually every major animal group we see today, as well as many that didn't make it. One hugely successful group brought forth by this evolutionary spike was the *arthropods*. With their external skeleton and jointed legs they thrived and diversified. Crabs, lobsters and shrimps are their living descendants in the Ocean, but they also spread on to the land in the form of spiders and other insects.

Around this time appearances were made by the first ancestors of our modern *cnidarians*: jellyfish, anemones and corals, as well as the *echinoderms*: starfish, urchins and sea cucumbers and also the *cephalopods*: squid, cuttlefish and octopus. The first *vertebrates*, animals with backbones, also appeared, probably resembling modern day hagfish or eels.[23]

Of the creatures that didn't make it, perhaps the *trilobites* best exemplify this period of evolutionary creativity. Never before had the Ocean seen anything remotely like these armour-plated creatures scuttling across the bottom in search of easy meals. But their articulated body armour and ornately adorned helmets weren't just for looks; this was also the period when predators capable of swallowing large prey evolved. Over the next 100 million years or so, the Ocean became a cosmopolitan and complex web of lifestyles that laid the foundation for the diversity of life present in the Ocean today. However, towards the end of this period many beings besides the trilobites 'fell by the wayside', possibly as a result of a temporary drop in the amount of oxygen in the ocean.[24]

Despite these setbacks life continued to diversify. Around 460 million years ago fish divided into two major groups: the bony fish with a hard skeleton, and the cartilaginous fish with softer skeletons made of cartilage. The cartilaginous group would eventually develop into the sharks and rays of today's Ocean. Some 20 million years later the bony fish again split into two major groups: the lobe-finned fish with bones in their fleshy fins, and the ray-finned fish with softer cartilage in their fins. The ray-finned fish are the direct ancestors of most modern fish species while the lobe-finned fish would go on to evolve into amphibians, reptiles, birds and mammals. In a wonderful evolutionary twist one group of lobe-finned fish, the *coelacanths* diverged from the rest of the lobe-fins around 425 million years ago and have remained virtually unchanged to this day (Figure 2.5). They are the oldest known living 'fossil' fish species in the Ocean.[25]

Figure 2.5 The coelacanth is a member of the lobe-finned fish group that eventually evolved into amphibians, reptiles, birds and mammals. They are the oldest known living example of lobe-finned fish. (Image: iStock)

Unsteady Progress

After three billion years of life's evolution in the Ocean the scene was finally set for substantial colonisation of the land. By 400 million years ago much of the land was covered in forest, and finally terrestrial life could give something back to the Ocean, in the form of even more oxygen to dissolve into her fluid body. For another 150 million years life flourished. Coral reefs came into being, sharks and other large predators prospered and marine reptiles including turtles roamed far and wide. Amongst the sediment an unparalleled diversity of crawling and burrowing creatures continually recycled nutrients raining down from the surface.

Then, 250 million years ago the largest mass extinction Gaia has ever experienced wiped out more than 95 percent of Ocean life and two thirds of life on land. Just what caused this cataclysmic event at the end of the Permian Period isn't fully understood, but it coincided with a time of intense volcanic activity that spewed forth two million cubic kilometres of molten, basalt rock over what is now Siberia. Massive amounts of carbon dioxide were released into the air, initiating a warming phase that brought Gaia out of a stable glacial period that had lasted at least 60 million years. Recent research suggests this may have led to a drop in oxygen levels in the deep Ocean, causing the release of poisonous hydrogen sulphide gas. This may have been due to a combination of the warmer water holding less dissolved oxygen, and an increase in hydrogen sulphide production by the bacterial decomposition of massive plankton blooms, triggered by the warmer conditions.[26] All of this drama coincided with the beginning of the breakup of Pangea, the planet's most recent supercontinent.

The *Permian Extinction* was the biggest of five mass extinction events to befall Gaia. The next largest, the *Cretaceous*, 65 million years ago, not only wiped out the dinosaurs, but also decimated the vast majority of the Ocean's plankton species. What's surprising is that life bounced back relatively quickly after each of these extinction episodes. Not only did life recover; it did so with renewed vigour and diversity. The Ocean became the place of giants: predatory sharks three times the size of today's biggest great whites patrolled the *Miocene* seas up until five million years ago; enormous squid; fierce sperm whales with teeth three times the size of today's sperm whales; and massive predatory fish, all attest to an Ocean at least as productive as todays.[27]

We now enter the evolutionary recent past and the 'coming into being' of today's Ocean. By 30 million years ago modern *cetaceans* - whales, dolphins and porpoises - had evolved and split into their two distinct groups, the *mysticetes*: those whales that filter krill and small fish through comb-like baleen, and the *odontocetes*: all the toothed whales including the smaller dolphins and porpoises. The Ocean started filling with all the familiar fish families we know today; the coral reefs and other shallow habitats took on their modern kaleidoscope of colour and form; the open Ocean thrummed to the pulse of mega-schools of baitfish, hunting tuna, sailfish and sharks, one and all supported by the uncountable, microscopic descendents of those first intrepid explorers of life's potential. The old and the new enmeshed in an evolutionary expression of complex vibrancy nearly four billion years in the making and still in progress today. This is the living Ocean that greeted our ancestors as they spread out from the savannah and discovered the boundless shore about 130,000 years ago[28].

Physical Transformation

But what of the Ocean's liquid body? Over all this time, stretching back almost to the very beginning of Planet Earth, the Ocean has been a constant presence. And yet, just like her ever-changing surface, her liquid body seems to have been in a state of constant, slow motion change. We've seen that she may have started with as much as twice the volume she has now. In her early years there were no continents to interrupt her continuity, no shores to break her wind-born waves, except on those few volcanic islands. She had to bide her time while deep below her surface the Earth's molten interior slowly formed continental landmasses to keep her company.

For the past 2.5 billion years these landmasses have been on a ponderous journey of their own, coming together as supercontinents, only to slowly break apart time and again. The most recent of these great supercontinents (Pangea) formed around 270 million years ago with the coming together of ancient Gondwanaland – Antarctica, Australia and the Indian sub-continent – and most of what is now Europe, the Americas and Africa. But almost as soon as Pangea had formed, the ever-moving tectonic plates forced a slow, inexorable separation.

First Africa and the Americas moved apart, forming what we now call the South Atlantic around 180 to 140 million years ago. Not long after, India drifted away from Antarctica and Australia, creating the Indian Ocean. Between 100 and 80 million years ago North America and Europe separated to form the North Atlantic, while at about the same time Australia drifted north, and Antarctica headed south, putting the finishing touches to what we now call the Southern Ocean. Of course the continental movements didn't stop there. A mere 50 million years ago India, having broken her long embrace with Madagascar, collided head-on with Eurasia with such force that the Himalayan mountains were thrust skyward. The vast expanse of the Ocean's body not bounded by these newly formed continents is of course the great Pacific.

And still the tectonic plates continue their water-lubricated, sliding dance with each other. Today the continents are coming together again. Already the continental slopes of North Africa and Southern Europe have begun to collide and the Australian plate is colliding with South East Asia. In another 50 million years or so, Africa, Australia and Eurasia will become the next supercontinent.[29]

While all this continental drama was playing out, the Ocean was continually adjusting her response to the ever-changing landscape. Her never ending sculpting of emerging shorelines, either moving further inland or receding down continental shelves, depended on how much her liquid body was warmed by the sun, or morphed into solid ice during the numerous glacial and interglacial periods. What we call sea-level has always been a fluid dance between land and sea, which at least in part, is choreographed by the climate-controlling influence of the Ocean's own abundant life-force. Of course, human induced climate change is now playing a not insignificant role in this sea level dance, but we'll leave that for a later discussion.

Of most interest to our living Ocean story now, is how her great body moves around the various landmasses, and indeed how she circulates, distributes and regulates all the vital ingredients for life throughout her vast expanse. Respiration, circulation and metabolism are key processes in any living body. They are fundamental aspects of physiology, common to all living beings so it's entirely appropriate (although perhaps unconventional) to consider these processes of the living Ocean in the same way. This is not to deny the critical importance of external physical and geological processes. But as we shall see in the coming chapters, life weaves its influential way through these primarily geophysical processes, transforming them into the dynamic, responsive, self-regulating and self-sustaining physiology of the living Ocean. So, let's now turn our attention to Ocean physiology.

3

Respiration: The Ocean's Breath

*With every drop of water you drink, every breath you take, you're con-
nected to the sea. No matter where on Earth you live.*
– Sylvia Earle

The Ocean's breath. How can we imagine such a vast process? Perhaps we
can start by focusing on our own breathing for a moment. As you breathe
in, imagine the life-giving oxygen flowing into your body from every part
of Gaia's atmosphere. Pause for a moment. Savour the feeling of Gaia's
presence within you. As you breathe out, imagine your breath reaching out
into her vastness, connecting you with all other life. You are no longer
apart from this living atmosphere, but rather you are a part of it, you are in
it just as it is in you.

The Ocean and the atmosphere enjoy the same kind of relationship.
They are in each other, their breath mingling in a bond of perpetual renewal. As we'll see, the boundary between the surface and the atmosphere
above is only a very small part of the story. In truth, the Ocean's watery
breath permeates the atmosphere for thousands of metres, while the atmosphere can't resist the Ocean's invitation to spread its molecular consciousness throughout her vast body. It's this mingling of breath that we
are going to explore.

The Ocean's breath is the story of the relationship between water and
air, liquid and gas. But it's much more than just a story about chemistry
and physics; rather, it's the story of how life interacts with these chemo-
physical processes, working with them, so that like a skilled craftsman
working in harmony with the raw material, something beautiful, func-

---
57

tional and life enhancing emerges. It's worth reminding ourselves that the Ocean and atmosphere only exist in their current state because they are a single, interconnected living process, rather than just the backdrop to life.

Before we start our journey it's important to acknowledge and clarify a common misunderstanding about the term respiration. Even though we think of breathing as respiration, the term only refers to the chemical process of releasing the stored glucose energy in an organism's cells. Breathing is in fact a 'three act play': inhalation, respiration and exhalation. The inhalation simply provides the oxygen necessary to facilitate the respiration process, and the exhalation releases the resulting carbon dioxide and water vapour - we only have to breath out on a cold day to see the water vapour in our breath. So in this chapter we are going to stretch our use of the term respiration even further as we celebrate the 'breathing' Ocean.

Air

Air: 21 percent oxygen, 78 percent nitrogen - and about 1 percent comprised of other trace elements, including a mere 0.04 percent carbon dioxide. How easily we can reduce the breath of life to a few dispassionate numbers, and yet, hidden behind those numbers is a vastly complex symphony of living interactions that are quite simply 'breathtaking'. Let's explore a little of how the Ocean breathes new life into the air around us.

Today the Ocean provides about half the oxygen in the atmosphere through the respiration of countless photosynthetic beings. As we learned in the last chapter, photosynthesis was first championed long ago by ancestral cyanobacteria, and even today they account for a significant percentage of the air we breathe. Over time, they were joined by the protoctists who eventually evolved into the microscopic floating algae – the phytoplankton – as well as the kelps and seaweeds. Together they are the lungs of the Ocean's sunlit surface, inhaling carbon dioxide (CO_2) and exhaling oxygen gas (O_2) through the miraculous biochemical alchemy that is photosynthesis.

Let's just take a moment to pay homage to this gift of life the Ocean bestows upon us, by joining one of her photosynthesising champions as it goes about its daily routine. Allow me to introduce Thalassiosira ferelineata, just one of the many thousands of marine diatom species (Figure 3.1). Thalassiosira ferelineata is a microscopic, single-celled algal being with an exquisite silica skeleton protecting its internal organelles. One of these organelles - the chloroplast - itself a descendant of once free swimming cyanobacteria, is what actually does the photosynthesising.

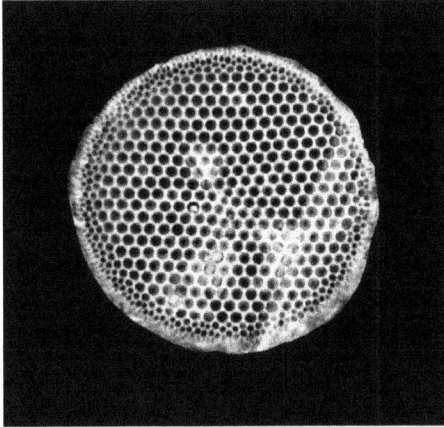

Figure 3.1 Thalassiosira ferelineata. Size: 30 microns, (Image courtesy of University College, London. http://www.ucl.ac.uk/GeolSci/micropal/diatom.html)

Within the chloroplast reside a multitude of green chlorophyll molecules, along with some golden brown carotenoids, cousins to the orange beta carotene, which gives carrots and pumpkins their vibrant colour. Together, it's their job to absorb photons from the sunlight and use that light energy to fuel the photosynthesis process. Firstly, they split the passionate marriage between the two hydrogen atoms and their oxygen lover in the water molecules flowing through the diatom's latticed body. The bereft oxygen atom consoles itself by bonding to a fellow divorcee to create oxygen gas (O2), which the diatom releases into the Ocean. The Ocean of course, then happily shares her oxygen store with the atmosphere above. This is the photo part of photosynthesis.

The remaining light energy is used in the synthesising phase, a complex process in which carbon dioxide and the newly acquired hydrogen atoms are processed and transformed into carbohydrates, which are then combined to make energy-rich glucose molecules. Our dynamic diatom uses this sugary glucose to fuel all the metabolic processes within its intricate silica body.[1] It takes six of these carbon dioxide/hydrogen processes to make a single glucose molecule, so for every glucose molecule our tiny diatom produces, it releases six oxygen molecules into the surrounding Ocean.

Without them, and all the other phytoplankton, not only would we be severely short of oxygen, but we'd also be in grave danger of overheating through excess carbon dioxide in the atmosphere. And the Ocean herself would also be bereft of the most fundamental part of her entire metabolism because phytoplankton are the primary producers on which the whole Ocean food web depends. As if that isn't enough, they're also responsible for processing huge quantities of other essential life ingredients such as nitrogen, sulphur, phosphorous and iron. We'll explore this further when we look at the Ocean's metabolism, but for now let's just breathe and give thanks to the humble photosynthesisers of the living Ocean.

And as you breathe in remember that respiration is a two-way action. Without the in-breath there can be no out-breath. Without the rest of life's combined exhalation of carbon dioxide there would be a grave shortage of CO2 for the phytoplankton to 'inhale'. Respiration is in essence, recycling. To maintain a healthy balance, more or less the same amount of CO2 must be exhaled back into the breathing cycle.[2] And this is exactly what's achieved, on a massive scale. But of course it's much more complex than simply breathing in and out.

The Ocean, through all of her respiring animals, 'breathes out' huge quantities of CO2, which helps to keep the whole system in balance, ensuring that both the Ocean and atmosphere don't become depleted. However, there's a twist to this gassy tale. Every year about 500 million tons of new carbon dioxide is introduced into the system from volcanoes, organic decomposition and various other sources, excluding human-induced ones. Somehow this extra CO2 needs to be removed from the system to keep it in balance. The Ocean and her phytoplankton play a vital role in this balancing act, which has helped to keep carbon dioxide levels steady for millions of years.[3]

We can now see how fundamental the respiration of carbon dioxide is to the whole life process. We can also see that keeping CO2 levels in a dynamic steady state is a living process. Our own physiological response to a build up of carbon dioxide in our body is to take a deep breath of the oxygen rich air. The photosynthesising Ocean responds by breathing more deeply of the CO2 dissolved within her body. But like us, there are some metabolic limitations as to how deeply she can breathe.

Water

Now let's turn our attention to the Ocean's other respiratory medium: water. Perhaps this conjures up images of fish 'breathing' the water, but even though they might appear to be, they are of course, extracting the oxygen gas dissolved in the water. But what we are really interested in here is the role of the Ocean's breath in the planetary water cycle, otherwise known as the hydrological cycle.

The hydrological cycle represents the movement of water between the various water reservoirs of Gaia: the ocean; atmosphere; surface water; (in the form of rivers, lakes and ground water), along with all the frozen water locked up in glaciers and icecaps. As a way of connecting to the water cycle, just think of the water vapour that condenses from your own out-breath on cold mornings. With every breath, we are all of us, involved in the planet's water cycle, but it's the living Ocean that dominates the process.

Before we explore the Ocean's physiology as it applies to the water cycle, it's worthwhile giving some context to the scale of her involvement. The Ocean contains a staggering 1.33 billion cubic kilometres (km3) of water, which is about 97 percent of all the water on, or near, the surface of the planet. To put that into some sort of perspective, consider that it would take approximately 400,000 Olympic sized swimming pools just to fill a single cubic kilometre!

Gaia's fresh water reserves amount to around 38 million cubic kilometres, almost all of it either frozen in glaciers and ice caps, or deep underground, with less than 1 percent in lakes, rivers, swamps and soil. The atmosphere holds around 13,000 to 15,000 cubic kilometres as water vapour, at any given time. This is a tiny, but critical percentage of Gaia's total water, when we consider how important water vapour is as a greenhouse gas.

Now let's consider the movement of water between the Ocean, atmosphere and land. In purely physical terms, the water cycle is powered by heat from the sun. As surface water warms, huge quantities evaporate into the atmosphere – around 500,000km3 annually. As this water vapour cools it condenses to form clouds and is then precipitated back to the surface as rain or snow.[4] The vast majority of evaporation and precipitation happens over the Ocean (Figure 3.2), which isn't surprising considering the Ocean covers so much of the planet's surface. Only about ten percent of her evaporated body makes landfall, but that's enough to account for nearly half of the overall precipitation over the land. This water subsequently cycles through rivers, lakes, soil and ground water until it eventually returns to the Ocean as run-off. But the living Ocean plays a much bigger role than this. In fact without her influence, along with substantial help from all the green life on land, the water cycle would be but a trickle, and most of Gaia's landmasses would be deserts.

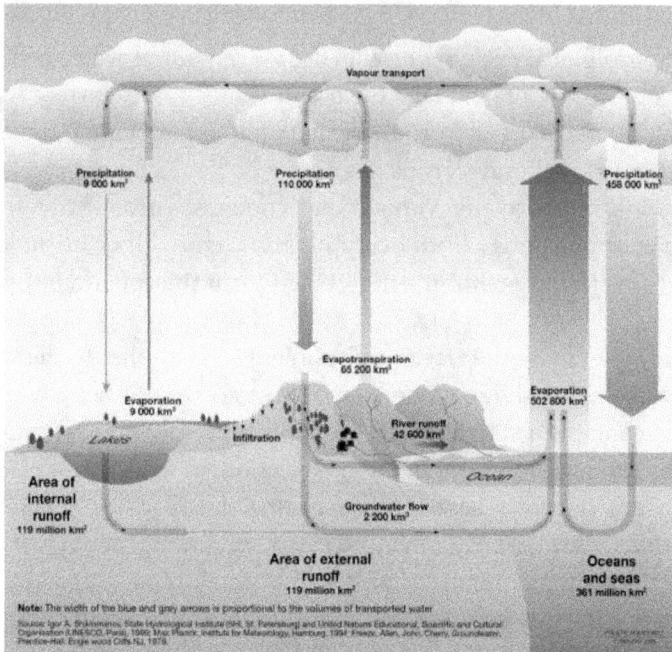

Figure 3.2 The hydrological cycle includes precipitation, vapour transport, evaporation, evapo-transpiration, infiltration, groundwater flow and run-off, but as the graphic shows, the Ocean influences the vast majority of the cycle. Image credit: Philippe Rekacewicz, UNEP/GRID-Arendal. http://www.grida.no/graphicslib/detail/the-water-cycle_171f

How does the living Ocean influence the water cycle? Well, initially by supporting suitable climate conditions in the first place. If too much of the sun's heat gets through to the Ocean's surface, more water would be evaporated into the atmosphere. Water vapour is a powerful greenhouse gas in its own right, so too much of it in the atmosphere could lead to runaway global heating – the same positive feedback loop that probably occurred on Venus. Conversely, if there aren't enough other greenhouse gases to keep the warmth in, not enough water will evaporate, leading to less rainfall.

less rainfall. We've already touched on how the living Ocean contributes to maintaining carbon dioxide at optimal levels through her respiration, as well as the biological carbonate pump, that we explored in Chapter 1.

But there's an even more tantalising relationship between the Ocean and the atmosphere that really evokes the sense of life as one great inter-connected process, one in which we can literally see the Ocean breathing its watery body into the atmosphere. All we need do to experience this, is to look up at the billowing clouds, rising in great columns above the Ocean.

Clouds are critical to maintaining global temperatures. High up in the atmosphere cirrus clouds restrict the loss of heat radiating from the planet's surface. Lower down, the cumulus and marine stratus use their dense white upper-sides to reflect enough of the sun's light back into space to keep things comfortably cool. This reflective trick affects the albedo – reflectivity of surfaces – of the whole planet, keeping the global average temperature a massive 4°centigrade cooler.[5] But what has the living Ocean got to do with cloud formation, apart from supplying the water vapour in the first place?

We know that water vapour rising off the sun-warmed Ocean condenses once it reaches the cooler air, hundreds of metres above. But meeting the cold air alone isn't enough for clouds to form, as the water molecules need something to condense around. Wind-blown salt spray, surface organic particles, as well as dust particles from the land provide a substantial percentage of these nucleating particles, but our humble phytoplankton also play a role in forming the billowing clouds that rise above the Ocean. They provide an essential ingredient, that not only contributes to the water cycle, rainfall and albedo, but also plays the starring role in one of life's other essential processes; the sulphur cycle.

The magic ingredient is an aromatic gas called dimethyl sulphide (DMS); the tangy seaweed smell, so familiar to us when we visit the beach at low tide, is thanks to the sulphur in this gas. DMS is produced in huge quantities by a wide range of algae, including the large seaweeds, but especially the very tiny phytoplankton that congregate in massive blooms near the sunlit surface. Rising into the air like an aromatic sigh, DMS is immediately seduced by that other great exhalation from the Ocean's surface: oxygen. The resulting sulphate aerosol particles are irresistible to the surrounding water vapour molecules, who cluster around them eagerly, and before long, dense marine stratus clouds literally materialise out of thin air![6]

But this is just the beginning of what we might call a living cloud story. As water vapour condenses into clouds, it gifts some of its accumulated warmth into the surrounding air. This acts like a booster pump, lifting the clouds even higher into the cold air above, where they ride the atmospheric thermal currents, sometimes for hundreds of kilometres. Eventually the condensed water vapour in the clouds cools to the point where it becomes too heavy to remain aloft and falls back through the atmosphere as rain.

The ten percent of these clouds that release their watery load over the land, also deposit the sulphur that helped them form in the first place. This is the main source of sulphur essential for terrestrial life, without which we can't produce the amino acids that build proteins in our cells. We get most of our sulphur from the plants we eat; they get it from the rain delivered by the clouds that brought it from the Ocean, via the combined effort of countless microscopic algae. The Ocean is a storehouse for sulphur and is continually resupplied by rivers, delivering freshly liberated sulphur from rock weathering, which in turn relies on the dissolved carbon dioxide within the raindrops falling from those very same clouds.

Let's just ponder this remarkable flow of interconnected relationships for a moment. Without the cloud-forming, chemical artistry of phytoplankton in the Ocean, terrestrial life as we know it would be impossible. The water cycle would be severely disrupted and global climate would be radically affected. This is but one, very simplified, example of the complex web of relationships that keep our living planet functioning.[7] Hopefully by now it's becoming clear that Gaia is the emergent evolutionary synthesis of all these relationships; a living whole that's more than just the sum of her parts and the Ocean as the largest part, is herself an emergent whole within the greater whole.

But why do the phytoplankton produce DMS in the first place? What purpose does it serve them? Surely they're not expending all that energy just for the greater good of the whole planet? Initial research pointed to DMS being a mere by-product of a more complex molecule dimethylsulphoniopropionate (DMSP) that protects the tiny algae from the dehydrating effects of their salty realm. Further research showed that the algae also use an enzyme to break down DMSP into DMS and acrylic acid, which acts as a foul tasting deterrent to predators.[8] Both of these processes are obviously beneficial to the algae, but evolutionary biologists kept searching for any clues that would point to a direct benefit from DMS gas itself. Well, it turns out that there may be a direct benefit to our tiny unicellular algae, and it's so fantastic that we can but wonder at the exquisite creativity of life.

For reasons that will become clear in the next two chapters, our hordes of oxygen-producing, cloud-seeding, albedo-influencing phytoplankton can become victims of their own success. When conditions are right – plenty of sunshine and abundant nutrients – they undergo phenomenal population explosions, resulting in massive blooms covering hundreds of square kilometres of ocean. Unfortunately though, unless there is a continual supply of fresh nutrients, these enormous blooms of productivity can quickly turn into a 'bloom and bust' for our intrepid heroes.

But like true heroes, instead of just giving up they take matters into their own hands. If the nutrients won't come to them, they'll just create some clouds, hitch a ride and surf the skies in search of richer waters! As implausible as this sounds, it seems that this may indeed be a reality.

When nutrients reach a critical level, a bloom-wide chemical conversion of DMSP into acrylic acid and DMS is triggered, resulting in a rapid release of huge plumes of DMS into the air above the bloom. Water vapour quickly condenses around the resulting sulphate particles, creating massive, dense clouds. Remember that as water vapour condenses it gifts some of its stored energy as heat, causing the clouds to rise. Air beneath the clouds is sucked up, creating an updraft strong enough to carry the tiny phytoplankton with it.

Once in the clouds, the anti-freeze properties of the remaining DMSP within the algae's cell protects it from the intense cold, so that they can remain aloft for days. Eventually the water vapour condenses back into a liquid phase and the algae are returned to the Ocean within falling raindrops. If they're lucky they'll end up in a patch of Ocean with abundant nutrients and be able to carry on their heroic work.[9]

Considering that there are at least 600 million years of evolutionary history behind many of today's phytoplankton species, it would appear that it's a strategy that works. And it seems they can successfully travel great distances. Scientists working in Antarctica collected algae from an air mass that had travelled 1,500km from South America.[10]

Next time you're out on the Ocean or near the coast, look up at the billowing clouds and give thanks to the humble phytoplankton. They might just be 'looking down' on you from within the Ocean's visible 'breath in the sky'.

Now let's finish our exploration of the Ocean's respiration, by joining our algal heroes, the coccolithophores, on a journey into the clouds.

* * *

Breathing the Ocean

Imagine yourself as a tiny coccolithophore, floating serenely in the sunlit Ocean. Inside your single cell's chloroplast, the alchemy of photosynthesis is transforming the sun's light into energy to power your metabolism. Oxygen molecules flow from your minute body into the surrounding Ocean and in return she supplies you with a rich soup of essential nutrient – carbon, nitrogen, phosphorus, sulphur and iron, as well as calcium – that you transform into the exquisite calcite discs surrounding your delicate cell membrane.

All around you trillions of your brothers and sisters are feasting on the nutrient bonanza brought to the surface by the springtime coastal upwelling of deep Ocean water. You are happily producing everything you need to satisfy your life's purpose, including DMSP to protect you from the dehydrating effect of your salty home. A complimentary enzyme transforms some of your DMSP into acrylic acid to ward off predators. DMS slowly wafts from you into the surrounding water and then into the air above, enabling water vapour to form gently billowing clouds as it rises.

For several days the feasting continues and you are amazed and delighted by the incredible diversity of life forms being supported by the massive bloom you are a part of. You become lost in reverence for the powerful continuity of life, until your reverie is interrupted by an uncomfortable feeling within your organelles: a growing ache you recognise as hunger pangs, and with dismay you realise that the nutrients which brought you all together are running out.

A ripple of unease runs through the bloom, quickly followed by a collective sense of urgency and purpose. You realise that together you have the ability to respond to this life-threatening situation. You start to feel the response in your own body as your DMSP digesting enzymes go into overdrive and start producing large quantities of DMS gas, which immediately gets propelled into the surrounding Ocean. All around you billions of others are doing the same, causing an intense pulse of DMS to rise from the Ocean, triggering a condensation of dense white clouds above you.

The rising clouds draw up warm air, creating a breeze that soon stirs the Ocean's surface into motion. Before long you feel yourself being jostled towards the choppy surface and then quite suddenly you are air-born, riding an updraft into the very cloud you helped create. Millions of your kin are already here and as more arrive you all release another pulse of DMS gas, lifting everyone higher until you are drifting en masse, a dense living cloud, high above your Ocean home.

For days you float suspended within the water vapour of your cloud, protected from the intense cold by your personal reserves of antifreeze. As your cloud merges with others, you get a sense of how you're helping to reflect enough of the sun's light back into space to keep your Ocean home comfortably cool.

Finally, just as your energy reserves are running out, you feel the water vapour around you condensing back into liquid form, encasing you in a protective raindrop, which carries you safely back into the Ocean below. As your raindrop merges with the Ocean's surface, you taste the familiar saltiness of your surroundings and gratefully join your fellow travellers in feasting on the abundant nutrients you have been lucky to land in.

4

Circulation

Thirty metres from the shoreline of Manado Tua Island, Indonesia, the reef plummets almost vertically for 2000 metres. Descending onto this underwater cliff face I'm immediately caught in a flowing 'river' of water rushing along the wall. It's like being on a transparent conveyor belt with the kaleidoscopic colours of the reef passing by me. I'm gliding in liquid space, effortless and serene. Four hundred metres below me I can visualise metre long coelacanths lurking under dark ledges. Manado Tua is one of only two places in the world where these living fossil fish have been filmed.

Suddenly I'm jerked out of my daydreaming. There's danger ahead. The wall juts out into the current, disturbing its flow. I can see fish swimming hard towards the surface, but they're not making much progress; they're caught in a down-welling, caused by the convergence of different water flows at the point.

The island and its siblings sit on an Ocean plateau that rises from the abyssal depths. Deep Ocean water rising up onto the plateau is forced through narrow channels winding their way between the islands. Colder and denser than the surface waters, this deep water rushes through the narrow channels, creating vortices of swirling currents as it displaces the warmer surface water. Tidal flows add to the mix to form complex and unpredictable currents, like the down-welling on the point. Drifting closer I see the telltale shimmering where the cold and warm water is mixing, creating a thermocline. Sometimes these down-wellings can descend a hundred metres, well beyond safe diving limits, so it's important to negotiate them carefully. Despite the risks though, it's a special privilege to dive

here amongst these currents and physically experience the coming together of these different aspects of Ocean circulation.

Several processes are involved in maintaining the Ocean's circulation:
the thermohaline and the major surface currents (we can think of these as
the Ocean's large-scale circulation); the daily ebb and flow of the tides, ensuring localised circulation of essential life processes; and finally, the
strange phenomenon of the Ocean's thermocline. Let's take a 'ride'
through these processes and get a sense of how they all interconnect to
keep the Ocean circulating.

Thermohaline

If there's any phenomenon that truly illustrates the living Ocean as one
interconnected being it has to be the thermohaline, also known as the
Ocean conveyor belt. It weaves its way from pole to pole, from surface to
abyssal depths and back to the surface again. It's the lifeblood of the
Ocean, flowing to the pulse of geological time and driven by the ultimate
source of the life process itself, the sun. At its core is the sun's heat, warming the surface waters in tropical latitudes, and infusing the very water
molecules with light energy so that they literally expand, becoming less
dense, lighter and warmer. This lighter, warmer water floats on top of the
colder, dense water below, creating a thermal barrier (thermocline) between the two layers. Over time, surface currents carry this warmer water
away from the tropics towards the poles. In the Atlantic it's carried by the
Gulf Stream as it flows up the east coast of the United States before crossing the Atlantic to caress the western shores of the United Kingdom and
northern Europe.

On its journey from the tropics, much of its warmth is gifted back to
the atmosphere through evaporation, keeping the above coastlines sub-
stantially warmer than they would otherwise be. This also makes it saltier
than Northern waters, where there is more fresh water mixing from rivers
and ice melt. By the time the Gulf Stream delivers this tropical water to the
Arctic Ocean around Greenland, it's so much denser and saltier than the
surrounding water that it plunges towards the Ocean floor as powerful
down-wellings. Our 'ex-tropical' water is joined by dense cold water, produced locally when sea ice forms at the surface releasing dissolved salts
and making the water underneath denser and saltier, so that it too sinks.
Just to give you some idea of the volume of water involved – imagine if all

the rivers of the world flowed into the same basin, it would still only be one twelfth of the Arctic downwelling.[1]

Meanwhile, a similar pattern plays out in the Ross and Weddell Seas in Antarctica, although here it's the intense cold of local conditions that produces the bulk of the down-welling water. In both cases the sinking water joins a slow and steady flow of cold, dense water on a journey that spans many thousands of kilometres, across entire Ocean basins, over mid-Ocean ridges, abyssal plains and deep Ocean trenches. Eventually, the North Atlantic deep water flows into the Antarctic basin, where it streams along just above the slightly more dense Antarctic deep water. Both slowly wend their way back into tropical climes, where they eventually re-surface to be warmed by the sun once more (Figure 4.1).[2]

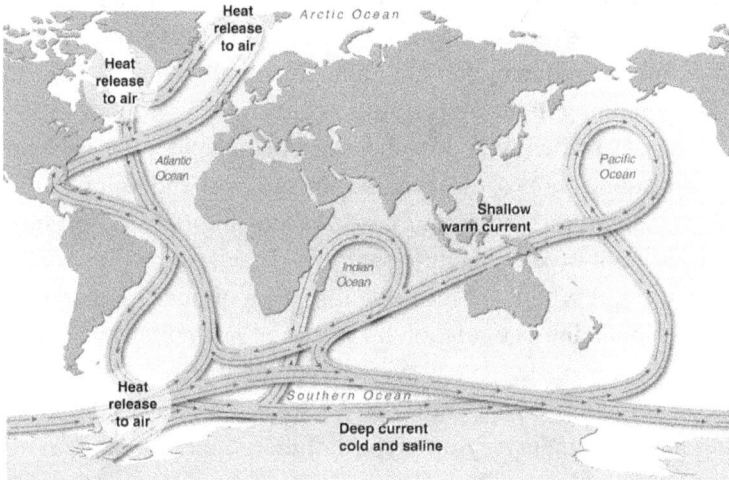

Figure 4.1 The Ocean's thermohaline circulation. Note the stored heat released to the atmosphere in the north Altlantic, Arctic and Antarctic regions. Graphic credit: Hugo Ahlenius, UNEP/GRID-Arendal
http://www.grida.no/graphicslib/detail/world-ocean-thermohaline-circulation_79a9

The thermohaline not only moves water around the Ocean, but also distributes heat from the sun around the planet, from the equator to the polar-regions and delivers a refreshing coolness back to tropical waters. It is perhaps the most important circulatory process in maintaining a global temperature balance that prevents large areas of the northern hemisphere from freezing over permanently.[3]

But the thermohaline does much more than just act as a global thermostat. It's also the primary distributor of oxygen to the deep Ocean. The

Ocean's surface waters gladly receive the gifts of oxygen exhaled directly from the multitudinous photosynthesising beings near her surface, as well as absorbing oxygen gas (O_2) from the atmosphere. As surface water descends into the depths it shares some of its O_2 with mid-Ocean water, but still has enough to replenish the deep Ocean so it can support all the oxygen dependant beings living far below the surface.

The thermohaline performs the same physiological trick with carbon dioxide: transporting dissolved CO_2 directly from the atmosphere as well as carrying uncountable carbon-rich planktonic corpses to the Ocean floor. This physical pump temporarily removes vast quantities of carbon dioxide from the atmosphere, which in turn contributes to maintaining the right balance of greenhouse gases in the atmosphere. Without the thermohaline much less carbon would be transported to the chill of the deep Ocean, leading to a positive feedback loop of hotter atmosphere and warmer surface temperatures, reducing her CO_2 absorbing ability and leading to even more CO_2 remaining in the atmosphere.[4]

So, far from being just a geo-physical phenomenon, the thermohaline is also a physiological process. Just like the arteries and veins of our own circulatory system, the thermohaline is the pulsing flow of 'plasma', distributing life-giving oxygen, nutrients and heat around the core of the Ocean's body. But where we measure the pulse of our circulation in minutes, the thermohaline's circulation takes more than a thousand years.

Just like our own circulatory system though, it is in a continual state of dynamic relationship with all other physiological processes, responding to changing needs, influencing and being influenced by internal and external conditions. Our pulse quickens or slows, our blood surges or meanders, depending on our needs. So too the thermohaline, and just like us, there are limits to the extremes the system can handle.

Analysis of historical data has led climate scientists to generalise the thermohaline as having three primary states, cold, warm and off. In the cold and warm positions, the thermohaline is in a state of dynamic, non-linear relationship with the prevailing climatic conditions, in which the location of the down-welling moves between north and south positions. The off state seems to be triggered by rapid changes such as dramatic warming over a relatively short period.[5]

Scientists debate the often confusing and sometimes contradictory data as they strive to unravel the non-linear complexities of the thermohaline. But if we again invoke the analogy of our own circulatory system, we can perhaps see a similar pattern in the way it responds to extremes. When we become hypothermic our circulatory system retracts to our core, protecting our vital organs with any remaining heat it can muster. Conversely, when we overheat our system opens itself to allow heat to escape. In both cases there is a threshold – a tipping point – beyond which our system switches to the off state. The thermohaline, when viewed from this perspective, seems to respond in a similar way.

But the thermohaline doesn't operate in isolation; it needs a way to bring deep water back to the sunlit surface, to be re-energised and keep the circulation moving. In the tropics some of this deep water gently rises to replace the surface water as it starts its journey toward the poles. The rest is thrust towards the surface as powerful upwellings, but this only happens in a few special places and is largely dependent on the circulation of the Ocean's surface currents.

Surface Currents, Gyres and Deep Water Upwellings

The Ocean's surface is her most familiar aspect to us. We experience our relationship with her primarily through our interaction with the first few metres of her great depths and the overriding sense we experience is one of perpetual movement. It's never still, even on the calmest of days there's always motion, and that motion is nothing less than the physical expression of the intimate relationship between the Ocean and her Gaian partner, the atmosphere.

As soon as even the gentlest breeze blows across her surface we can see the Ocean respond with rippling excitement. It may be hard for us to equate this to Ocean-wide circulation, but it is exactly the combined effect of all the gentle breezes, trade winds and howling gales across her surface that drive the major surface currents. To understand even a little of this complex relationship we need to explore, in very basic form, how the wind blows in the first place.

Wind is the sun's energy manifest as movement. This movement begins imperceptibly as the equatorial Ocean warms under the sun's gaze and water molecules are drawn up into the air as water vapour. Air and water molecules mix happily together, creating the humid tropical air familiar to anyone who has spent time in the tropics. This warm humid air is less dense and so creates a low-pressure area known as the equatorial low. As this tropical air rises into the atmosphere it starts to cool, allowing the water vapour to condense and release its own stored heat as a parting gift to the rapidly cooling air. This extra energy boost helps our tropical air reach new heights, until it finds a satisfying equilibrium with the surrounding atmosphere. Finding itself sandwiched between even less dense air above and more dense air below, the only direction it can travel is sideways.

As our tropical air flows outwards from the equator towards the poles, it continues to release heat until, at approximately 30° latitude north and south, it becomes too cold and heavy to remain aloft and so sinks back toward the surface as a dense down-draft, thereby creating the sub-tropical high pressure area. Air, like all gases, just can't abide inequality and so our dense high-pressure air now rushes back towards the equatorial low-pressure area it started from. The result is a more or less continuous circular flow of air between the equator and the subtropical regions of both hemispheres in what we call the easterly trade winds. A similar pattern operates between latitudes 30° and 60°, except the flow is in the reverse direction, resulting in the mid-latitude westerlies. Between 60° and 90° the flow reverses again to create the polar easterlies (Figure 4.2).[6]

GLOBAL ATMOSPHERIC CIRCULATION

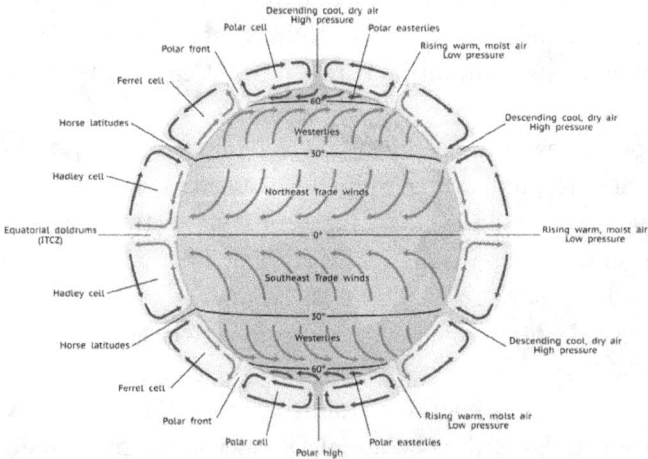

Figure 4.2 Global atmospheric circulation is intimately connected to the Ocean through her ability to absorb and store heat from the sun, then release it back into the atmosphere through evaporation, creating updrafts and pressure gradients. (Image: dreamstime_m_53769579).

This is of course a very simplified picture. There are seasonal variations, complex, localised weather systems, winter storms, tropical cyclones, typhoons and hurricanes, even decadal oscillations such as El Nino and La Nina, not to mention the enormous impact life has on these climatic processes. But perhaps this is enough to enable us to explore how the Ocean's major surface currents work. Before we do though, there are two other very important components to consider: the Coriolis effect and the continental boundaries.

Named after the nineteenth century French mathematician, Gaspard Gustave de Coriolis, who was first to calculate the forces acting on rotating objects. The Coriolis effect explains how the Earth's rotation affects both the atmosphere and the Ocean. As the planet rotates it exerts a deflecting force on any moving body, on or near its surface. At the equator this force is zero, but gets progressively stronger towards the poles. The deflection in the northern hemisphere is to the right and to the left in the southern hemisphere (Figure 4.3). Without the Coriolis effect the northern hemisphere trade winds would flow from north to south, but under its influence they flow from northeast to southwest, while in the southern hemisphere they blow from southeast to northwest.[7] This has profound implications for the Ocean's surface currents, as we shall see.

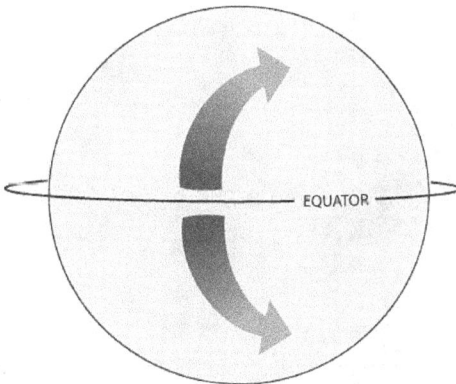

Figure 4.3 The Coriolis effect explains how the Earth's rotation affects both the Ocean and the atmosphere. (Image courtesy of NOAA)

Continental boundaries also play a vital role in Ocean circulation. The major Ocean basins – the Pacific, Atlantic and Indian – are separated by continental landmasses, which form barriers to the east-west/west-east flow of the wind driven currents, effectively forcing them into basin wide circular movement. We now have all the physical ingredients for understanding the Ocean's surface currents.

As wind blows across the surface of the Ocean it creates friction between the air molecules and the surface water molecules, who are literally pulled along for the ride. The stronger the wind blows the greater the friction and the thicker the layer of water being moved. As the depth of the current increases, friction between the layers of water molecules slows it down until it eventually fades out, usually less than 100m below the surface.

The Coriolis effect, already influencing the wind direction, now weaves its deflecting spell on the moving water so that surface currents actually move perpendicular (90°) to the wind direction. This is known as the Ekman transport and is critical to Ocean circulation (Figure 4.4).[8] The Coriolis effect and associated Ekman transport, combine with the continental boundaries to create the circular movement of the Ocean's surface currents, which in turn form the great Ocean gyres. You may have heard of the Ocean gyres in relation to plastic pollution in the Ocean – we'll revisit this in Chapter 10 – but for now, let's look at the very important role the gyres play in Ocean circulation.

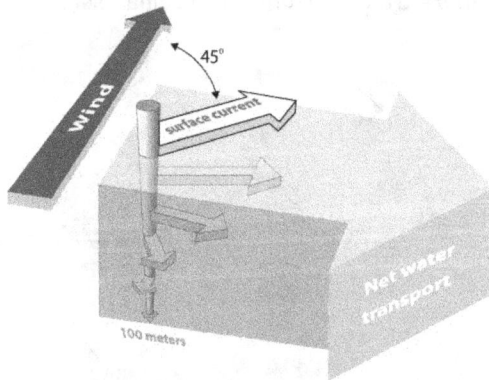

Figure 4.4 The Ekman transport results from the Coriolis effect and deflects surface water away from the wind direction in a spiral, causing surface currents to run perpendicular to the wind direction. (Image courtesy of NOAA)

There are five sub-tropical gyres, two in the Pacific, north and south, likewise in the Atlantic and one in the Indian Ocean. There are also polar gyres in the Arctic and Antarctica, which are hugely influential to global climate balance.[9] As you can see from Figure 4.5, Ocean surface currents flow in a clockwise direction in the northern hemisphere, while those in the southern hemisphere rotate counter clockwise. Under the Coriolis influence, the western boundary currents flow faster than eastern boundary currents, while the Ekman transport results in a general flow towards the centre of the gyres. There's a surprising twist to this story though – the Coriolis effect increases the faster an object is moving – which means the faster flowing western boundary currents tend to veer more sharply than their eastern counterparts, resulting in the centre of the gyres being much further west than the actual centre of the Ocean basin.

As the wind driven boundary currents of the sub-tropical gyres flow along continental coastlines, the Coriolis effect and the Ekman transport encourage surface water to move seaward away from the coast. Deep Ocean water that's found its way to the continental slopes can't resist the invitation to take its place, and is pulled towards the surface as upwelling. For reasons that will become clear when we meet the thermocline, the eastern boundary upwellings are often richer in life-enhancing nutrients than their faster flowing western counterparts. Consequently they're also some of the most productive and busiest parts of the living Ocean. They include the year round coastal upwellings off the coast of Peru in South America and the west coast of Africa.

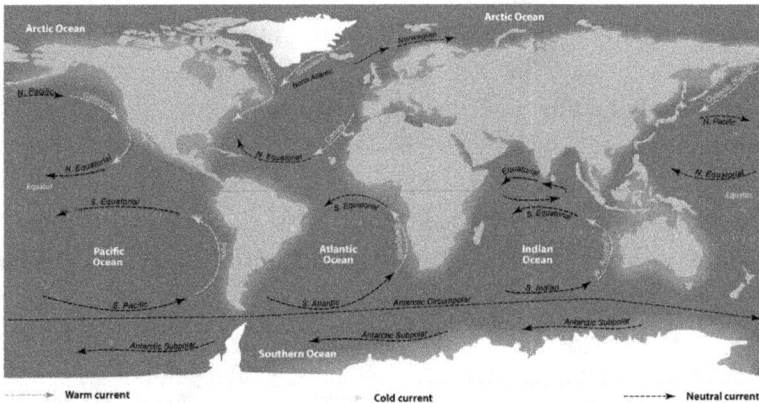

Figure 4.5 The major Ocean surface currents flow in a clockwise direction in the northern hemisphere, while in the southern hemisphere they flow counter clockwise. Continental boundaries combine with the Coriolis effect and the Ekman transport, causing the surface currents to move in a circular direction and creating the great Ocean gyres. (Image: dreamstime)

Other coastal upwellings are more seasonal, usually only occurring in the spring and summer, when prevailing offshore winds flow in unison with the boundary currents, thus enhancing the upwelling effect. Most temperate coastal areas, like New Zealand and the west coast of the United States, experience seasonal upwellings. We'll delve into this phenomenon further when we explore Ocean metabolism in Chapter 5.

Before turning our attention to the tides, there are two other very important upwellings relevant to Ocean-wide circulation, which need mentioning. One operates near the equator and helps bring deep Ocean water back to the sun's warmth. The other occurs in Antarctica and involves two surface currents: the Antarctic circumpolar current, flowing west to east and the Polar current flowing in the opposite direction. In this latter case it's nutrient rich water that has travelled all the way from the Arctic that is pulled to the surface. However, instead of being warmed by the sun, it actually gets even colder in the freezing Antarctic conditions and sinks back to the Ocean floor once more, but not before depositing its nutrient load at the surface.[10]

Tidal Currents

The ebb and flow of the tides... what could be more peaceful than sitting by a tidal harbour in meditative silence, witnessing the slow inward and outward movement of the Ocean as it caresses the rippling sand flats, playing hide and seek with fields of seaweed and barnacle-encrusted rocks...? It's easy to imagine this movement as the Ocean's slow, rhythmic breathing and in a way it is. With every flood tide fresh supplies of oxygenated water replenish shallow rock pools, mangrove forests and mud-flats, while the ebb carries nutrients from the land back to the Ocean.

Tidal currents support vast communities of stationary filter-feeding beings, who rely on the current-borne smorgasbord of nutrients and tiny planktonic organisms streaming past their open mouths. By flowing in and out of harbours and estuaries, inlets and bays, the tidal currents are the 'public transport' system of the coastal Ocean, connecting diverse living communities and creating bustling, energetic hotspots of activity around prominent headlands and underwater landmarks.

The tide's part in Ocean circulation though is more than just a supporting role. The surface turbulence caused by the flowing tidal currents vastly enhances thermal mixing of shallow coastal waters, which in turn contributes enormously to the wind-driven upwellings of the boundary currents, and therefore to the overall productivity of coastal regions.

Thermal mixing, as the name suggests, is the mixing of surface water warmed by the sun, and the layer of colder water beneath. As we've already learnt, warm water is less dense and floats on top of the denser, colder water below. It's this temperature-derived density difference, along with salinity variances, that drives the thermohaline. It's also what causes a thermocline. And as we're about to learn, the Ocean's thermocline performs an intricate and complex balancing act, not only in terms of circulation but also, and perhaps most importantly, in the Ocean's overall metabolism.

Thermocline

Anyone who's dived or snorkelled in temperate seas in the late spring or summer will have probably experienced the chilly reality of a thermocline. Descending through the comparatively warm surface layer the first sign of the looming thermocline is usually a visual shimmering, much like the hazy heat waves rising from a road, roasting in the summer sun. As soon as you enter this shimmering field you feel an abrupt temperature change, like stepping from the heat of a sweltering summer's day into an air-conditioned room.

The thermocline may not be so comfortable for us, unless of course we're cocooned in a thick wetsuit or drysuit, but without it the Ocean's physiology would be entirely different, with potentially disastrous results. To understand why, let's first take a closer look at how the thermocline forms and how it varies in different parts of the Ocean. As we've already learnt, the thermocline separates warm surface water from the cold, dense, saltier water below. Scientists call this the two-layered Ocean and across vast areas of the open Ocean there is very little mixing between the two layers.

It seems pretty obvious that the tropical areas of the Ocean, exposed as they are to year round warming by the sun, would have a thicker layer of warm water, resulting in the thermocline being deeper than it is in colder climes. In general this is the case. In the tropical Ocean it may be as deep as 200 metres or more, while in seasonal seas it ranges from about 30 to 100 metres. But these are only averages and don't tell us much about the complex relationship between the Ocean's other circulatory processes. This isn't the place to go into a detailed explanation, but let's look at a couple of examples of this complexity from the perspective of Ocean-wide circulation.

We already know that the thermohaline, with the help of the surface currents, transports the sun's warmth around the Ocean, ensuring the tropics don't overheat and the polar regions don't freeze over permanently. Through this interplay the Ocean-wide thermocline emerges as the mechanism that maintains the density and salinity differences necessary to keep the circulation functioning.

A very important 'emergent property' of the thermocline's role is known as the basin-wide tilt.[11] As you can see in Figure 4.5 the wind-driven currents all flow to the west near the equator, which results in warm water accumulating on the western boundaries of the Atlantic and Pacific basins. The thermocline descends to about 200 metres here to accommodate these 'warm pools', which in turn provides a greater volume of warm water for the fast flowing western boundary currents to carry towards the poles. The opposite effect happens on the eastern boundaries where the thermocline is closer to surface, thanks to colder water being delivered by the surface currents.

It's easy to see how the basin-wide tilt of the thermocline enhances the circulation of the sun's warmth around the Ocean. What's less obvious, but no less important, is the role it plays in the Ocean's metabolism. As you may recall, upwellings occur along the continental boundaries where surface water is drawn offshore by the combined influence of the Coriolis effect and the associated Ekman transport, making room for the underlying water to take its place. In western Ocean boundaries, because the thermocline is deeper, quite a lot of the upwelling actually occurs above the thermocline and only a relatively small amount of nutrient-rich, deep Ocean water is drawn up towards the surface. In the east, where the thermocline is much closer to the surface, a lot more nutrient-rich deep water is drawn up – explaining why the eastern boundary upwellings support some of the most intensely productive areas of the Ocean.

In temperate coastal regions, the seasonal upwellings coincide with relatively shallow thermocline positions, often only 30 to 50 metres below the surface, sometimes even shallower. The result is really well mixed water that's nutrient-rich, which is further enhanced by tidal currents. In polar regions the combination of cold surface temperatures and strong turbulent mixing often results in an almost complete absence of the thermocline. When the longer days of spring and summer bathe these nutrient-rich waters in light, everything is in place for an exuberant celebration of the Ocean's life process.

A question you may be asking at this point, is why the deep water below the thermocline is so nutrient-rich, while the surface water above appears to be lacking in essential life-giving nutrients? The very short answer, which we will expand on in the next chapter, is that the uncountable organisms living near the surface consume the nutrients and the thermocline restricts their replenishment. This being the case it would seem that the thermocline, far from being helpful, is actually a hindrance to life in the Ocean.

Many oceanographers and marine biologists do indeed consider the thermocline to be a major barrier to productivity in the Ocean. Some call it, 'the dilemma of the two layered ocean' and even go as far as describing the Ocean as '…a really lousy system for supporting life'.[12] This is a perfectly understandable response if the thermocline is viewed in isolation, but when we embrace the Ocean as a living system we can instead see the thermocline as an essential part of a complex physiology, actively responding to changing conditions and needs, while maintaining the dynamic balance of the whole system.

* * *

Riding the Ocean's Circulation

If you can, find somewhere to sit comfortably and look into the Ocean. Begin by focusing on a wide view, noticing in particular the continual movement of the Ocean's surface. Slowly bring your attention down into a smaller area and now notice how this continual movement changes from moment to moment; each moment a completely unique expression of the Ocean's life process.

As you contemplate this movement, imagine the water molecules in your own body joining with their brothers and sisters in the Ocean and becoming part of this dynamic, ever-changing movement. Allow yourself, in your wholeness, to become one of those water molecules, nestled amongst your kin and feeling the flow of life moving through you. Feel the presence of other elemental beings: dissolved carbon, oxygen, calcium, magnesium, sodium, nitrogen, iron and many others. Together you experience them as a salty presence within your very being.

As you float near the surface you feel the sun's warmth infusing you with light-hearted energy. You feel expanded and free. Some of your kin floating just above you abandon their liquid form and float into the air as vapour, but you remain in your fluid embrace. Slowly you start to feel a change in the movement around you. There is a gentle but irresistible pull from the trade winds whispering above and an equally gentle push from below, urging you forward, so that you start to feel yourself a part of a flowing river of movement, alive with purpose.

As this sense of purpose builds you're joined by other water molecules, energised by the tropical sun, eager to contribute their exuberance and anticipation for the journey ahead. You feel the pace quicken as you leave the Indian Ocean behind and join the jostling tidal race around the Cape of Good Hope and into the South Atlantic Ocean. Your journey is measured, not by time, but rather the timelessness of experiencing yourself as integral to the flow of life.

You now join the mighty Gulf Stream as it surges powerfully along the coast of North America. You start to feel some of your pent-up energy dissipating as warmth into the surrounding Ocean and air above, but it feels more like a gift rather than a loss. Your sense of life's circularity is heightened as you feel the Earth's rotation bending the Gulf Stream away from the coast of North America towards Europe.

Continuing your northward flow you feel even more warmth dissipating and the first chill of the Arctic Ocean starts to permeate your consciousness. The cold allows you to absorb much more oxygen, but nevertheless you feel sluggish and heavy, as you taste the saltiness becoming more concentrated in your liquid body. By the time you reach the frozen shores of Greenland, you feel so dense and heavy that you can stay afloat no longer and sink into the powerful down-welling that signals the start of your return journey.

Descending into darkness, you feel the immense pressure of all your watery kin above driving you on. Continuing downwards you contribute some of the oxygen within your body to sustain the myriad luminescent life forms flashing around you, and in return receive a storehouse of life-giving nutrients. Reaching the Ocean floor, you feel a sense of deep awareness and wisdom as ancient as life itself, and experience waves of peaceful continuity as you join the silent pilgrimage across abyssal plains, mountainous ridges and plunging depths.

Deep in the Southern Ocean an even more intense river of densely cold water flows below you, pushing you towards the surface, where wind-borne fingers of upwelling momentum reach down and draw you ever upward until you find yourself amongst massive blooms of plankton, eager to consume your reservoir of essential nutrients. Before long though, the irresistible force of the Antarctic down-welling takes hold and plunges you downward towards the last leg of your global journey.

Once again you experience the oxygen/nutrient exchange as you negotiate the undulating Pacific Ocean Basin. As your pace slows you have time to ponder the continual renewal of the Earth's crust along oceanic ridges and wonder at life's beginnings where plumes of superheated water spew forth from mineral rich vents. Gradually a deep longing for the warmth and light of the sun builds within your fluid consciousness, and you sense the same anticipation amongst your kin.

You start to experience a gentle pull from above, reminiscent of your journey's beginning, even as those below urge you on. Finally, after a one thousand year odyssey, you emerge into the sunlit surface of the tropical Ocean once more. As you float basking in the warmth, you reflect on the deep sense of connection and participation in this vast circulation of the life process. Even as you ponder this deep connection, you start to feel that light, energetic expansiveness once more, and a tingle of excitement runs through you with the invitation of that first gentle, but irresistible pull from the trade winds and that flowing river of movement bringing you alive with movement.

5

Metabolism

The Poor Knights Marine Reserve on the east coast of the North Island, New Zealand, is one of my favourite places on the planet. Snorkelling ten metres out from the vertical cliffs I can look down into the blue depths of these protected waters and witness an entire food chain in progress. My imagination must supply the details of the planktonic scene, too microscopic for my eyes to discern, but its reality is proven by the intense activity of myriad larger forms.

Directly below me, a shaft of sunlight reflects off the iridescent blue carapace of a tiny *copepod* as it scurries through the water column grazing on phytoplankton; comb jellies and salps sieve the water through translucent bodies; clouds of two-spot demoiselles pirouette with outstretched pectoral fins as they delicately pluck tiny zooplankton morsels; a school of koheru, mouths agape, sift the planktonic soup in perfect unison. Against the cliff-face a swarm of pink-fleshed krill are corralled into a corner and devoured by hungry snapper; below them reef fish move away from the rocks and kelp to feast on the morsels raining down from the orgy above. Nearer the surface a mixed school of trevally and blue maomao form a wall of mouths, driving swarms of tiny shrimps before them. Prowling amongst them all are the predators: kingfish, kahawai and occasionally sharks, watchful and patient, biding their time and secure in their apex role.

While my classifying brain attempts to dissect the scene into ecological niches, my sensing body is filled with great joy at being immersed in such vibrancy! Eventually my senses win out and the niches dissolve into a deeper understanding of life as process; the individuals before my eyes resolving into the moving parts of a larger being, the ecosystem itself. The mechanistic and linear concept of food chain is replaced by the reciprocity of an interconnected web of relationships within this larger ecological being.

The Poor Knights ecosystem is the living whole, emerging from all the myriad lives, being lived in relationship with each other and the physical body of the reef. It is a local example of what happens on an Ocean-wide scale. The living Ocean coheres as an emergent whole through all the various ecosystems – large and small, deep and shallow, Oceanic and coastal, tropical and sub-polar – all contributing their unique qualities.

Life in the Balance

So far we've seen how the Ocean's respiration balances two of life's most fundamental elements – carbon and oxygen. We've also touched on how she circulates both throughout her vast body. We can appreciate the vital role she plays in global climate, influencing the amount of sunlight reaching her surface through cloud formation and maintaining the delicate balance of greenhouse gases so that both the atmosphere, and her own body, remain at comfortable temperatures for life to flourish.

We've followed her circulation as she transports much-needed heat from the tropics to the poles and returns with refreshing coolness to equatorial seas. Along the way we've learned that maintaining a balance between energy production and nutrient flow is a dynamic process involving both respiration and circulation; and it's this balance that we should keep in mind as we look at the Ocean's metabolism of life's nutrients, because it too plays a crucial role in balancing the whole Gaian system.

In Chapter 3 we discovered how phytoplankton use photosynthesis to combine hydrogen and carbon dioxide into carbohydrate molecules of sugary glucose, some of the which is used to fix other essential nutrients (phosphorous, nitrogen, iron and sulphur) into useable organic compounds. Organic compounds are the building blocks of life and phytoplankton are the primary producers of organic compounds in the Ocean. The limiting factor in their production is the availability of nutrients; in particular phosphorous, nitrogen and iron. These are critical to phytoplankton growth and reproduction, and their finely tuned availability ensures that just the right amount of phytoplankton exist to breathe a suitable balance of carbon dioxide and oxygen.

Every year their carbon-rich bodies provide around 45 to 50 billion tons of nutritious food for all other Ocean life.[1] The living Ocean's digestive system that metabolises all this food is nothing less than the combined livelihoods of all her myriad organisms; and it's this metabolic process that fine-tunes the whole physiological system, tweaking the flow of nutrients as they're needed to maintain a dynamic living balance. The ability of the living Ocean to recycle all these nutrients is critical; for even though a steady supply of fresh nutrients arrives via flowing rivers and deep-sea vents, they're only a trickle compared to what is required to keep her whole system in balance.[2]

The vast majority of this recycling occurs in the sunlit surface layer, where the primary producing phytoplankton and myriad consumers perform their perpetual nutrient dance. In fact about 85 to 90 percent of the Ocean's metabolism happens here, especially around upwelling hotspots. The other 10 to 15 percent happens in the vastness below the thermocline.[3] Just as with the water cycle, and the tiny but critical percentage of water residing in the atmosphere, the metabolic processes of the deep Ocean are pivotal to maintaining overall balance.

It would take volumes to describe the many and varied ecosystems that contribute to Ocean metabolism as a whole, so we'll confine our exploration to a more general overview. This will nevertheless give us a taste of the beautifully complex web of relationships inherent in such a dynamic and vast body as the living Ocean. Let's start with a brief explanation of the ecological theory behind the flow of energy and nutrients within a living system.

Traditional studies of ecological systems usually revolve around the food chain. Often these are pyramid shaped, with the primary producers making up the broad base; the primary consumers, those animals who feed directly on the primary producers, form the next layer, and the remaining layers are populated by all the carnivores. Each layer represents an ecological niche that gets smaller and smaller until we reach the apex predators right at the top of the pyramid. In ecology these are known as *trophic levels*, and there are seldom more than five trophic levels in any given ecosystem. Each level represents a step in the transfer of energy and nutrients with both decreasing from base to top, hence the pyramid shape.[4]

The useful aspect of these ecological pyramids is the visual representation this gives us of the energetic biomass at the different levels. Unfortunately, it also has a tendency to lead us into a linear way of viewing the relative importance of each layer, and gives the impression that the relationships between the layers are more or less one way. The reality is that these relationships are non-linear and reciprocal. While energy is indeed a one-way transfer, nutrients actually flow back and forth in complex and surprising ways that ultimately form a continual cycle (the essence of recycling). Energy is continually injected into the cycle through the process of photosynthesis, but without the reciprocity of all the beings involved in the nutrient flow, the whole living system would quickly break down.

On an Ocean-wide and deep scale, this nutrient flow encompasses the *biological organic pump*, (Figure 5.1) which works alongside the biological carbonate pump and the physical pump to keep atmospheric carbon dioxide levels stable. The concept of the biological pump is a useful way to get a feel for the Ocean's metabolic cycle, but it would be easy to get lost in an 'ocean' of detail and lose sight of the her as a living whole. So let's just 'swim' with the general flow of the cycle, stopping off here and there for a closer look at some of the many intriguing and surprising complexities that contribute to its continuity.

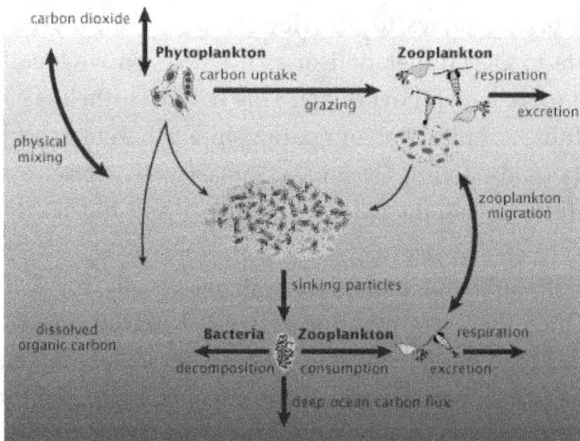

Figure 5.1 The Biological organic pump, which works alongside the physical pump and the biological carbonate pump to keep atmospheric carbon dioxide levels stable. (Image courtesy of NASA, www.earthobservatory.nasa.gov)

Phytoplankton: The Primary Producers

Few sights can fill the soul with such a sense of expansive freedom as standing on a coastal cliff top staring out to the horizon. On calm, clear summer days the horizon appears endless, the mirrored blue of Ocean and sky merging seamlessly into each other; the air seems completely still, yet some unfelt breeze ruffles the Ocean's surface with barely discernable ripples, creating a dappled texture to her sun-drenched skin.

On days like this a mosaic of tendrilled patterns snake lazily across her surface, defining otherwise imperceptible currents with an oily smoothness, hinting at a kind of bodily coherence, reminiscent of the fractal branching of capillaries visible beneath our own skin. The mesmerising tranquillity of the scene belies the intense activity of countless microscopic phytoplankton transforming sunlight into energy, but the oily current lines are a visual clue that there's more going on than just photosynthesis!

As tiny as phytoplankton are, they're still heavier than their salty home, and are in constant danger of sinking below the surface layer beyond the reach of the sun's light energy. Not being good swimmers, they must employ clever strategies to buoy themselves up. Some cyanobacteria alter their buoyancy by creating an internal gas bubble, but many of the larger phytoplankton produce oil droplets that accumulate inside their cells. As oil is less dense than water, this enables them to float happily in the light zone. The current lines we see on the surface are made visible as excess oil leaks from their bodies, especially when they die or get eaten.[5] This oily residue signals the beginning of another cycle in the continual flow of nutrients through the Ocean's body.

The Primary Consumers: Ocean Vegetarians

The exquisite microscopic world of phytoplankton is matched by an equally fantastical plethora of single-celled consumers, from the microscopic to the comparatively massive. With tiny vibrating hairs called cilia, armies of ciliates filter cyanobacteria from the water with ruthless efficiency. Non-photosynthesising dinoflagellates swarm amongst their sun-loving cousins scooping up vast quantities in their wildly swinging flagella arms. Shell-building foraminifera and radiolarians extend amoeba-like *psuedopods* beyond their shells to entrap passing diatoms and coccolithophores.

All of these single-celled consumers have the ability to reproduce themselves in a matter of hours, or days, to match their equally prolific sun-loving prey. Some of them even become minute farmers, housing smaller photosynthesising beings within their bodies, providing shelter and transport in exchange for a share of their sugary glucose production.[6]

But more than just single-celled vegetarians feast on the sun-loving phytoplankton. Multi-cellular beings abound, tiny to our squinting eyes, but giants compared to their prey. They are the zooplankton, an all encompassing term that includes animals who spend their entire lives in the plankton layer, as well as the countless species of fish and invertebrates who spend only their first days or weeks floating with the currents. During their brief stay in the plankton layer these visitors are omnivores, feasting on both phytoplankton and other zooplankton, whereas many of the permanent residents are primarily herbivores, only occasionally snacking on other consumers.

Most abundant amongst them are the *copepods*, miniscule crustaceans only a few millimetres long (Figure 5.2). These teardrop shaped, armour-plated cousins to shrimps and lobsters propel themselves through the water with their jointed legs. Long antennae sense the surrounding water for prey, but also warn of approaching predators, which the copepod can avoid with surprising bursts of speed. Most copepod species are *diurnal*, taking advantage of the cover darkness offers, feeding near the surface at night then descending into the relative safety of deeper water during the day.

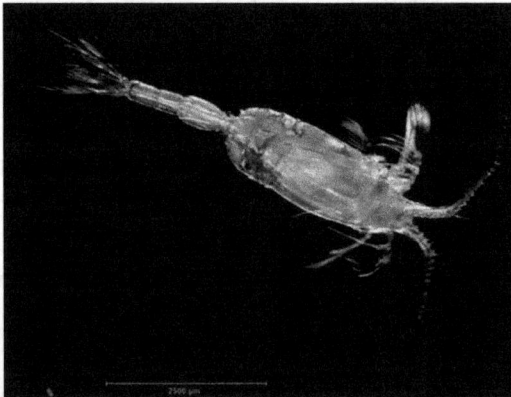

Figure 5.2 Copepods are the most numerous and arguably the ecologically most important members of the zooplankton primary consumers Ocean-wide. (Image courtesy of R. Hopcroft, UAF).
http://oceanexplorer.noaa.gov/explorations/12arctic/background/biodiversit y/media/copepod.html

Another group of crustaceans that often take part in daily vertical migrations are krill (Figure 5.3). Much larger than copepods, they are nevertheless primarily vegetarians sieving the water for phytoplankton with their modified front legs. Krill are a common species in many parts of the Ocean, but are particularly abundant and important around Antarctica where they are the primary food source for everything from fish, to penguins, seals and whales (we'll come back to this when we look at some of the ways nutrients are recycled in the Ocean).

Southwest Fisheries Science Center, NOAA Fisheries Service

Figure 5.3 Antarctic krill, *Euphausia superba* are the primary food source for many species and are the keystone species for the entire Antarctic food web. (Photo courtesy of NOAA, photo Credit: Wayne Trivelpiece), https://swfsc.noaa.gov/ImageGallery/?moid=3437

An equally important and abundant species of primary consumers are the *pteropods* – commonly known as sea butterflies. These tiny planktonic snails swim through the water column by flapping their wing-like foot, dragging a mucus membrane behind them to catch their lunch (Figure 5.4). So abundant are they in some areas that when they die their fragile calcite shell makes up the bulk of the sediment layer on the Ocean floor.

This is just a 'taste' of the rich and diverse world of the plankton layer.

Secondary Consumers: Filtering the Plankton Soup

Such a rich plankton soup provides a veritable feast for our second level of consumers, many of whom use a variety of techniques to filter huge quantities of water through their bodies as they feed.[7] All manner of soft-bodied, jelly-like creatures waft through the water sieving algae and animal alike; colonial salps band together into pink funnels, sometimes many metres long, and capable of sieving hundreds of litres of water per hour; stunningly beautiful comb jellies create iridescent light-shows with their eight rows of beating cilia, catching zooplankton as they go; jellyfish pulse through the water trailing deadly 'nets' ready to ensnare any unwary prey. Of course there are also all the stationary creatures, shellfish, corals, sponges and a host of others who make their home wherever the Ocean provides a suitable base from which they can extend their filtering bodies into the nutrient flow.

It's here also that fish enter our metabolic story, firstly as floating membrane-encased eggs – themselves a tasty feast for others – then as tiny translucent *fry*, filtering the riches around them until they're big enough to venture beyond the plankton layer. A surprisingly wide variety of fish species make their fulltime living by filtering the plankton soup. They feed by swimming, mouth agape, forcing water through sieve-like *gill-rakers* that catch their tiny prey and direct it straight to their gullet, at the same time as extracting oxygen from the water as it passes through. Some species, herring and menhaden among them, have very fine gill-rakers, allowing them to feed directly on phytoplankton. Others like sardines, mackerel, pilchards and anchovies dine solely on zooplankton. All of them are pivotal species within Ocean food webs, especially where seasonal upwellings create massive plankton blooms.

Figure 5.4 Pterapods, commonly known as sea butterflies, are tiny planktonic snails swim through the water column by flapping their wing-like foot, dragging a mucus membrane behind them to catch their food. (Photo courtesy of NOAA)

But it's not just these diminutive fish that enjoy the plankton riches. Whale sharks and basking sharks, up to 15m and 12m long respectively, are the largest and second largest fish in the Ocean. They shortcut the usual ascending size scale of the trophic levels by feeding directly on the primary consumers, where they're joined by giant mantas and devil rays. But none of them come close to the real filter-feeding giants.

They are of course the baleen whales, including the largest of all: the blue whale. Baleen whales filter tons of water at a time through hair-like baleen plates hanging from their upper jaw. As they close their mouths the water is squeezed out, leaving their prey to be licked from the inside of the baleen plates. Baleen whales filter a variety of prey this way, but in the Antarctic their favourite food is krill, which they consume in enormous quantities. However, there's a fascinating twist to this relationship that we'll explore shortly.

Predators

Strictly speaking, many of the beings mentioned above could be called predators, as even amongst the primary consumers feeding on passing algae, there are those that employ predatory techniques to ensnare their prey. To help us make the distinction between those and the truly 'predatory' predators, we can think of the former as the large volume grazers of the Ocean's surface, while the following are generally the fast moving and more individually focused hunters.

An enormous variety of predators have evolved as the Ocean's metabolism has matured, and they've filled every niche within the varied ecosystems that make up her body. From open-Ocean hunters like tuna, sharks and marlin to the bottom-stalking moray eels and grouper, a plethora of fish species make a living by eating each other. Joining the feast is a host of other beings, such as squid, octopus and cuttlefish, who use their dextrous arms to engulf the unwary. All sorts of other mobile invertebrates, from lobsters and crabs to starfish, roam the Ocean's reefs in search of prey.

Marine mammals play their part as well. Tied to the surface for breath they may be, but that doesn't stop them roaming far, wide and deep in search of their favourite meal. Seals and other *pinipeds* mostly stay close to the coast so they can haul-out to breed, but the toothed whales, including the small dolphin and porpoise species, are found throughout the Ocean.

Individual groups often specialise in highly refined hunting techniques that require astute planning and coordination. In many cases toothed whales are the apex predators within their own particular ecosystem, with orca and sperm whales being without doubt the Ocean's top two predators.[8]

And just to emphasise the intimate relationship between the Ocean and Gaia's other realms – the land and the atmosphere – we must include the massive contribution of all the seabirds to Ocean metabolism. Whether it's the streaking gannet, the diving cormorant, the ubiquitous gull or the majestic albatross, birds on the wing are indispensable servants to the recycling of nutrients across the Ocean's surface. Their nitrate and phosphate-packed guano provides an instant fix for a new generation of phytoplankton, whose energy-rich bodies will eventually contribute to a future meal for the birds themselves.[9] Likewise with those diving specialists the penguins, whose plankton-seeding guano is an integral part of the Southern Ocean's nutrient flow.

In terms of the flow of nutrients the role of the predator is to fine-tune the balance between the primary producing phytoplankton and all the myriad consumers. Their diversity, mobility and longevity are the key ingredients. They're like mobile storehouses, moving through the Ocean defecating parcels of nutrient 'goodies' wherever they go. Their diversity means that nutrients are also continually being passed from one to another, as predator becomes prey and eventually, food for myriad scavenging and decomposing organisms. Without them the Ocean's metabolism would slow to a mere trickle.

That Sinking Feeling

And what of the vast body of the Ocean below the sunlit surface? How does she feed the myriad beings of her inner body? Deep diving submersibles have given us a glimpse of the mindboggling array of creatures living in the blackness beyond the twilight zone of the sunlight's reach. Their strangeness only seems to emphasis the unfathomable, alien world they inhabit. Below the thermocline theirs is a nutrient-rich world, but without the photosynthesising algae, there is no one to transform those nutrients into useable organic compounds, and they must instead rely on leftovers from the surface.

Imagine floating in liquid space, 300 metres below the surface. Looking up through the inky twilight you follow the gradual transition from dark to light, like the shaded promise of sunrise. As your eyes adjust, you discern the dim light reflecting off tiny particles raining down from above. Below you the blackness is sparkling with an unparalleled bioluminescent light display as thousands of strange beings feast on this marine 'snow'!

We've already learned that of the 45 or so billion tons of carbon photosynthesised in the Ocean each year, about 85 to 90 percent is recycled in the *euphotic* zone above the thermocline. This leaves about five billion tons to be shared out amongst the denizens of the deep, most of which needs to eventually find its way back to the surface, in order to close the carbon cycle and ensure the continuity of the whole system.

A sizeable proportion of this five billion tons is already second hand in the form of faecal pellets – a polite term for planktonic poo – or locked up in the dead bodies of planktonic beings that slip through the net of hungry mouths near the surface and sink through the thermocline. This part of the biological pump relies on gravity to carry the faecal feast into the depths, and the larger the particles are the faster they will sink. Waiting for them is a plethora of talented recyclers, ready to extract the leftover nutrient goodness.

So efficient are they, that only about one percent makes it to the deep Ocean floor where another army of recycling organisms is ready to mine the last scraps of goodness. By the time they're finished less than 0.1 percent of the original carbon gets buried in the sediment layer as part of the long-term carbon cycle. The result of all this recycling is the release of dissolved carbon dioxide and other life-giving nutrients into the water, where they either join the slow procession of the thermohaline, which eventually delivers them back to the surface, or they fast-track their return journey via upwellings.

Vertical diurnal migration supplies the remaining carbon load to the waiting mouths below the thermocline. We've already met the migrating copepods and krill who feast on phytoplankton at night, then ride the 'gravity train' into the depths during the day, where they're joined by a procession of secondary grazers of the fishy kind. The diminutive *lanternfish* make up the vast bulk of this migrating mass, and are so prolific that in many parts of the Ocean they may account for up to 80 percent of fish biomass (Figure 5.5).[10]

Lanternfish are named for the light-emitting *photophores* along their bodies that provide bioluminescent counter-shading, making them almost invisible to predators from below. At night they feast on a banquet of zooplankton near the surface, then descend into the depths just before dawn. Their faecal excretions at depth provide a 'fast food' service to all the waiting organisms below, while the lanternfish themselves provide a tasty meal for deep Ocean dwellers such as squid and deep diving whales. Even so, they're safer in the dark depths than at the surface, where they're also a favourite with tuna, salmon, sharks, marine mammals and seabirds.[11]

Figure 5.5 Lanternfish are named for the light-emitting *photophores* along their bodies that provide bioluminescent counter-shading, making them almost invisible to predators from below. (Photo courtesy of NOAA)

This vertical migration of beings ranges from the surface down to depths of 1,500m. Below this the really deep Ocean belongs to profoundly strange creatures that survive as scavengers, or predators of scavengers. But they all play vital roles in the Ocean's metabolism, storing and recycling carbon and other essential nutrients, eventually returning them to the surrounding water, ready for the return journey to the surface.

But the Ocean has a few tricks up her sleeve that enable her to fine-tune these cyclical processes. Over eons, her living metabolism has evolved into the most exquisitely diverse collection of life forms that enjoy equally exquisite and complex relationships. Let's look at some examples to illustrate the importance of balance in a healthy, living Ocean system.

The Biological Pump in Reverse

For decades marine scientists have puzzled over how the Ocean maintains enough nutrients in the surface layer to support the intense abundance of life there. Given the 'dilemma' of the two-layered Ocean, most scientists have looked to the physical processes of surface currents, turbulent mixing and upwellings to explain the nutrient flow back to the surface layer. But new research has uncovered some truly remarkable physiological processes that highlight just how important the complex web of relationships that make up the Ocean as a living system are to her overall wellbeing.

It appears that the biological pump not only transports carbon and nutrients into the depths, but it also plays a critically important role in returning nutrients to the surface. It does this in such highly refined and targeted ways that in many situations, it is the key player in the flow of nutrients determining the makeup and abundance of species within particular ecosystems. The biological pump works in three ways to return nutrients to the surface: active transport, biological turbulent mixing and targeted recycling.[12] Of course they aren't really separate processes at all, but rather the emergent mechanisms by which the Ocean's metabolic cycle maintains dynamic balance.

Active transport happens when animals consume carbon and nutrient-rich food below the thermocline, then swim up towards the surface where their excreta returns much needed nutrients to the water. It was always assumed that animals involved in diurnal vertical migration were only feeding near the surface, but it turns out that many of them also feed in the depths during the day then defecate at the surface at night. For example, krill have been observed feeding on sedimentary goodies on the Ocean floor 3,500 metres below the surface.

Larger Ocean beings also play an important role in transporting nutrients back to the surface. In what scientists have called the *whale pump*, many species of whales actively feed below the thermocline then return to the surface to breathe (Figure 5.6).[13] While resting on the surface they urinate and defecate, releasing huge quantities of highly concentrated nutrients, including nitrogen, iron and phosphorous. In the Gulf of Maine humpback whales feed in the rich surface waters of Stellwagon Bank during the day, then as darkness falls they dive down to the bottom for a tasty snack of sand lance, a small but numerous fish species who bury themselves in the sandy bottom at night. In other areas of the Gulf, fin whales dive below the thermocline to feast on krill during the day, while right whales scoop up tasty copepods hiding below the thermocline.

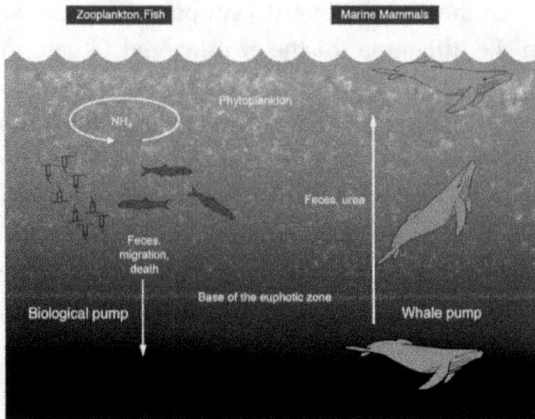

Figure 5.6 A conceptual model of the whale pump. In the common concept of the biological pump, zooplankton feed in the euphotic zone and export nutrients via sinking fecal pellets, and vertical migration. Fish typically release nutrients at the same depth at which they feed. Excretion for marine mammals, tethered to the surface for respiration, is expected to be shallower in the water column than where they feed. (Image and caption from: Roman J, McCarthy JJ (2010) The Whale Pump: Marine Mammals Enhance Primary Productivity in a Coastal Basin. PLoS ONE 5(10): e13255. doi:10.1371/journal.pone.0013255)

It's estimated that even today's remnant population of whales excrete more nutritious nitrogen back into the surface waters than all of the rivers flowing into the area combined! Some scientists believe that prior to the decimation of whale populations by commercial whaling, the Gulf of Maine may have been twice as productive as it is today.[14]

In Antarctica, baleen whales are more like Ocean farmers than predators. Not only are they returning nitrogen and phosphorous to the surface layer, but their poo contains an enormous storehouse of essential iron. Without iron, phytoplankton can't grow, and without the phytoplankton there would be no krill. As it happens, Antarctic waters are low in iron, because there's no run-off from the land to replace what the phytoplankton consume. But over millions of years a naturally amplified, biological recycling system has evolved to compensate.

Phytoplankton absorb the iron-rich whale poo; krill graze on the phytoplankton, accumulating iron in their muscles; whales then consume vast quantities of iron-rich krill, but because they're primarily growing a nice fat layer of blubber, they don't need all the iron so excrete most of it back into the water in highly concentrated bursts. In fact the iron in Antarctic whale poo is ten million times more concentrated than in the surrounding water. This provides the iron-rich fertiliser phytoplankton need to bloom, which in turn leads to an explosion of krill, which of course means more krill feasts for the whales! Over time this amplified recycling boosted the whole metabolism of Antarctica to the point where it was not only supporting millions of whales, but many other marine mammals, fish and birds that rely on the vast swarms of krill for their survival.[15]

We might intuitively think that a large population of whales would end up eating all the krill. But tragically, we have proof that this amplified recycling of iron by a large population of whales actually lead to a greater abundance of krill rather than less. Since the 1960's, when industrial scale whaling decimated the whales in their Antarctic feeding grounds, the krill population, rather than increasing, has actually plummeted, perhaps by as much as 80 percent.[16] Without the whales and their iron-rich poo the whole Antarctic metabolism has been impoverished (we'll return to this discussion in Chapter 10).

It's not just in iron-poor Antarctica that whales perform this essential metabolic service. The mighty sperm whales, one of the deep diving champions of the cetacean world, hunt iron-rich giant squid over a thousand metres below the surface, where the immense pressure of the Ocean depths postpones their bowel and bladder movements until they return to the surface, where their whale-sized, iron-laden poo is most needed.

And more than this, with every thrust of their mighty tails the whales create whirlpools and vortices in the water column. As they pass up through the thermocline this living turbulence actually mixes the two layers of water, literally pulling dissolved gases and nutrients back up into the surface layer, where they can once again nourish the phytoplankton.[17] The decline in whale populations may well have had unforseen impacts on the entire Ocean's metabolism.

Interestingly, it's not only whales that perform this biological turbulent mixing. Many large beings: seals, tuna, sharks, squid and others add to the mix as they cross the thermal threshold. In fact, scientists are now investigating the possibility that even tiny organisms like copepods, lanternfish and krill may have a significant influence on thermal mixing when they make their daily mass vertical migrations.[18]

More than the Sum of its Parts

We can now see that the Ocean's metabolism relies on tightly coupled feedback loops involving intricately complex relationships, not only between the myriad life forms that manifest her living essence, but also with her other physiological processes. Our journey through the Ocean's respiration, circulation and metabolism has given us glimpses of a profound interconnectedness, a vast presence, whose life processes even reach beyond her own physical, fluid body and permeate every aspect of this living planet.

These are of course bodily functions – the physical manifestation of the flow of energy – familiar concepts adapted for the purpose of presenting the Ocean as a living presence. There are obviously significant differences between the physiology of a single biological organism, such as you or me, and the vastness of the bodily Ocean; not least of which is the fact that we are open systems in terms of nutrient flow. We require a constant supply of oxygen and new nutrients, which we metabolise, extracting the stored energy and goodness, then excreting the waste that's leftover.

The Ocean on the other hand is more of a semi-closed system. Certainly, she receives a continual supply of energy from the sun, but the supply of new nutrients is a mere trickle compared to her needs. Instead, she continually recycles what she already has through the combined metabolism of all her myriad children, which in no way diminishes the hugely important role the trickle plays in her overall physiology. In fact it's this very trickle of new nutrients that proves the reality of an Ocean-wide metabolism.[19]

The Ocean is a super-organism; a global, living ecosystem; a self-regulating whole, more than the sum of her physiological parts. If this Ocean-wide physiology is the emergent property of a four billion year living journey, what other life processes should we consider as emergent and universal? We have thankfully moved on from the dangerous and conceited idea that humans are the only sentient beings within life's family, but how far are we prepared to go in our reconciliation with our evolutionary brothers and sisters? We can clearly recognise kindred spirit amongst the whales and dolphins, our air-breathing mammalian cousins. But can we also acknowledge sentience, intelligence, self-awareness and community amongst other Ocean dwellers? Indeed, can we recognise these qualities as inherent to the Ocean herself? The rest of our living Ocean journey is devoted to exploring these questions.

6

Sentient Ocean

(From the Latin, sentire: 'to perceive or feel')
Sentient: adjective, 'ability to feel or perceive, responsive to or conscious of
sense impressions' (Merriam-Webster Dictionary)
Sentience: noun, 'the state or quality of being sentient; awareness'
(Collins English Dictionary)

Looking down through the Ocean's translucent skin I can see the reef five metres below. The hulls of our catamaran slowly give up their momentum to her viscous insistence as we glide up to the mooring buoy and tie off. This is Lafalafa, an undulating coral reef plateau three nautical miles from our base on Foa Island. Lafalafa rises from the sand 200 metres below, creating a raised platform that brings the Ocean floor within range of the sunlit surface. It provides a solid foundation for coral reef communities to flourish. Tidal currents wash deep, nutrient-rich water across its flanks, continually nourishing the sun-drenched reefs. The reef pinnacle below me reaches almost to the surface. It has built up over tens of thousands of years, its living surface supported by uncountable coral ancestors, whose limestone skeletons provide structure, solidity and continuity.

Standing at the stern of the catamaran scuba equipment in place, I pause to enjoy that exquisite sense of anticipation of leaving the gravity-bound terrestrial world behind and entering the weightless, multi-dimensional universe of liquid space. Step out into the momentary heaviness of falling, then almost immediately the feel of the Ocean's embrace, immersed, transformed into an Ocean version of myself.

Breathing in through the regulator's mouthpiece, I'm comforted by the familiar 'Darth Vader' sound-effect, as air from the scuba cylinder fills my lungs; then exhaling a stream of carbon dioxide bubbles that rush towards the surface to merge with their air-born kin. Ahh, it's good to be underwater again! A temporary Ocean dweller, clumsy and slow compared to the real thing, but weightless and elegant of movement beyond anything I could achieve in the gravity-bound world above.

There's always a period of sensual adjustment: the insistent, fluid pressure pushing against stretched air-drums, reminding my body to gently equalise itself to this denser *watersphere*; feeling that viscous, watery caress on exposed skin; a little taste reminding my tongue of the Ocean's elemental vibrancy. Now tuning in to the Ocean's soundscape beyond my own noisy breath, amplified surround sound, from all directions simultaneously, thanks to the quadrupled speed of soundwaves travelling through the Ocean's more dense body.

Clearing my fogged mask I focus on this visible watersphere. Vision too has a different quality in the Ocean. My analytical brain knows that the refractive qualities of water combine with the flat lens of my mask, making everything appear 25 percent closer and a third larger than it actually is. But my sensing body isn't fooled by this 'trick of the light' and automatically compensates, tuning in my spatial awareness to the physical reality of the reef. Even in this clear, tropical water my horizontal view extends only about 40 metres before dissolving into a blue haze. But within this visual field, light leaps and dances in exalted union with the watersphere, piercing the depths with shimmering rays, converging into a single point of intensity, or splashing the shallow reef in dappled extravagance.

After a few minutes my body feels attuned, transitioned as much as possible into a state of Ocean sentience. This transition time's important, part physical part mental, but mostly energetic, a movement from terrestrial consciousness into an Ocean way of being. On land it's easy to forget sometimes that we are in the world. We often walk through places, unaware of their sensual presence. Underwater though it's impossible not to feel in the Ocean!

Gliding closer to the reef I feel its living presence permeating my senses, probing me for a response. This is a bodily communion: subtle communication far too complex for my brain to compute. This is communication at a molecular level, involving billions of chemical and electromagnetic signals every second. I experience this as a feeling, or more precisely, a whole bunch of feelings at once. My brain follows along behind in what neuroscientists call the 'the half second rule', attempting to interpret meaning from my felt experience.[1] But this isn't just my experience; I'm also being *experienced* by individual organisms, as well as the reef as a whole.

Thirty metres away a school of batfish subtly incline their disk-shaped bodies in my direction (Figure 6.1). The whole school shifts in one fluid movement, fifty bodies acting as one. We are aware of each other, momentarily connected, but experience tells me that if I try to fin closer they'll probably move away, maintaining a constant distance between us. But if I can tune into their collective network, they may allow me to join the school for a short time.

To do this I need to focus all my senses in a different way: more peripherally, almost slightly out of focus, so that I'm not tempted into any preoccupation with a single fish. This singular focus is exactly what a predator does just before attacking. But it's not just the single fish that takes fright. The whole school responds as one body, turning or inclining so that the predator literally loses sight of its intended target. The school is sensing the energetic intentions of the predator, not as individuals, but as one body. It has its own sensory perception, its own sentience, which is more than just the sum of the combined sensory organs of each individual fish within its body. Indeed, the school is an emergent superorganism.

Figure 6.1 Batfish above Lafalafa. The school moves as one body, each individual turning or inclining their bodies simultaneously in one fluid movement.

Even if the school perceives no threat from me there's no guarantee it will let me get closer. Its response isn't simply blind instinct, 'fight or flight'. There's decision-making involved and the decisions are contextual. There's always a lot happening on the reef; no two moments are the same. I may have benign intent, but the school may also be interacting with grey reef sharks further down the reef slope, or maybe it's preoccupied with the school of plankton-grazing fusiliers, twenty metres to their right. Anyway, I have my own decisions to make and today I'm more interested in getting a sense, a feel, for the reef as a whole.

Gliding effortlessly with the current I follow the contours of the reef as it cascades downwards to thirty metres. Here colonies of billowing soft corals, their bodies engorged with water, waft their tentacled polyps into the flowing current, ensnaring passing zooplankton. A large grouper senses my approach and comes out of his daytime lair to satisfy his curiosity. Further down the slope I see the resident gang of grey reef sharks patrolling lazily, their presence eliciting hardly a murmur amongst the reef community: everyone knows it's not lunchtime. This 'knowing' is in the very water itself. It's alive with information, chemical signals, electromagnetic pulses, sounds and vibrational messages – intensely complex but subtle, and virtually all beyond our own sensual comprehension. And yet every fish, every tiny shrimp, every coral polyp can instantly discern meaning from this sensual milieu and then make responsive decisions. Every decision adds yet another piece of information to a never-ending reciprocity of lived experience.

Out of this melting pot of interactive and non-linear reciprocity, a self-organising system emerges: a living reef community, whose emergent property is sentience. Just like the school of batfish, functioning as one sentient body, so too the reef becomes one pulsing, feeling, perceiving being. How can we explain this self-organising, emergent living being? The reality is, we can't. We have no way of dissecting emergence into constituent parts. It's simply not reducible – it just, well, emerges. But there is a pattern to the way sentient behaviour emerges in living systems.

A Sense of Place

To approach any kind of understanding of sentient behaviour we need to remind ourselves about one of the most fundamental aspects of life: it is contextual. To understand sentience in any living system, be it a single-celled amoeba, or an entire ecosystem, we must view it in the context of the ever-changing conditions, both within itself and its external surroundings.

Let's use our own sentience as an example. Our living essence emerges from the totality of fifty trillion individual cells, each with their own story, within the larger story that is our body. But we are much more than just this totality. Each and every cell is in a continual flow of energetic communication with its surroundings, receiving and interpreting electromagnetic, as well as chemical, information. Each cell is sensing its world and responding to it and the world responds back. It's the cell's participation in this energetic communication that evokes its state of sentience. In other words, the cell is sentient because there is something other than itself to be aware of, to interact with, and decide how to respond to. The cell's level of sentience is contextually appropriate for its needs.

Through billions of these individual interactions every single moment, we each emerge as a coherent, sentient living system that is more than just the sum of all these individual interactions. If we study any of the cells in isolation we can't find anything we could identify as containing a blueprint for this 'whole body' sentience, it comes into existence as a consequence of our interaction with the world, but it also requires the world to interact back. In other words, it's not possible to be sentient in an insentient world.[2] And of course, groups of cells differentiate into our sensory organs, amplifying and refining our sensual experience into a highly personalised perceptual awareness.

Sentient Beginnings

So, sentience begins with the ability to sense the world around us. But to glimpse the emergence of this sentient behaviour we must journey all the way back to our evolutionary beginnings, to those first oceanic, bacterial adventurers. Remember in Chapter 2 we learned about autopoiesis, the self-making and self-maintaining process that brought life into being? The very first autopoietic bacterial beings maintained and renewed themselves by absorbing tiny, energy-rich food molecules through the multitude of tiny pores in their semi-permeable cell membrane, then excreting their metabolic waste through the very same pores.

But here our intrepid bacterial ancestors were faced with several life-defining challenges. The first was finding new sources of food to keep their metabolism going. Their ingenious response to this challenge was to develop chemical sensory receptors on their cell membranes to 'smell' the surrounding Ocean for clues as to where they might find a new source of tasty molecular treats. Once they had located a new food source they could then use their flagella to move themselves towards it.

Equally important though, was finding a way of monitoring their internal processes. Unless they could develop internal senses there would be no way to *feel* hungry and therefore no imperative to search for a new food source. This internal sensing, or 'sense of self', is known as *interoception* and is fundamental to all life. In our own bodies, interoception not only signals us when it's time to eat by providing us with hunger pangs, but also lets us know when it's time to breathe, urinate, defecate and so on.[3]

And here's where we see the emergence of sentient behaviour, because not only were our ancestral bacteria sensing themselves and the world around them, but they were also discerning meaning from the chemical signals pouring in through their cell membrane. They could decide whether the sensory information they were receiving meant a tasty treat or a noxious poison, and then choose an appropriate course of action. The two Chilean biologists who developed the theory of autopoiesis, Humberto Maturana and Francisco Varela, realised that these cognitive skills are inseparable from the life process. Without this fundamental level of cognitive sentience there can be no autopoiesis, and therefore no life. As they put it: 'to live is to know'.[4]

Biologist and early pioneer of systems thinking, Gregory Bateson, described this cognitive sentience as 'mental process' or more directly, 'mind in nature'. Like Maturana and Varela, he saw these mental processes as inseparable from the physical structure of life. For him, mind was the essential process of life long before the development of higher nervous systems or brains. In his words: '...mind is the essence of life'.[5] He also emphasised that mind isn't limited to individual organisms, but is also manifest in social systems as well as whole ecosystems.

This leads us on to the next essential step in our understanding of sentience as an emergent property of self-organising systems. Life is communal, nothing lives in isolation and in order to live communally there must be a reliable and contextually appropriate way to communicate with each other. We're used to thinking of communication in human terms, but in fact it's as old as life itself and has its origins, once again, in the world of bacteria.

Bacteria are the ultimate networkers. They are outstandingly successful at living in communities because long ago they mastered the art of communication! Their language is chemical, but far from being the mindless automatic response to external stimuli it was once considered, it turns out that it's highly complex and entirely contextual. In other words, the meaning of a particular molecular signal depends on the context in which each bacterial cell receives it, and their response is triggered by their internal state as well as the state of their external environment.

The result is the emergence of highly co-ordinated group behaviour, far beyond anything individual bacteria could achieve. Acting as one superorganism, microbial colonies (sometimes made up of many different species) pool their sensing skills into a higher level of sentient ability known as *quorum sensing*. So sophisticated is this emergent sentience and resulting social cohesion, that some scientists compare it to the social intelligence displayed by animals such as swarming insects, birds, fish and even primates.[6]

Microbiologists from MIT and Monterey Bay Aquarium used an ingenious, drifting robotic sampler and cutting edge genomic technology to observe 'a day in the life' of surface bacterial communities. They discovered that not only were different bacterial colonies sharing information, but they were also coordinating differentiated gene expression to optimise environmental conditions. In other words they were working cooperatively as one body, to get the most out of their shared home.[7] In his ground-breaking book *Animate Earth*, ecologist Stephan Harding describes bacteria as: '...deeply sentient creatures that live in a rich, meaningful, communal world, partially of their own making, to which they respond creatively and with exquisite sensitivity.'[8]

In an unexpectedly emergent way, a team of scientists, led by microbiologist Yuri Gorgy at the Marine Environmental Biology Department, University of Southern California, are investigating the networking capabilities of marine bacteria and have discovered that they use electrically conductive *nanowires* to transfer electrons in respiration: communal breathing.[9] Gorgy speculates that these bacterial nanowires may also act as a global communication network in much the same way that neural networks work in animals, including us. A vast electrical network covering the Ocean floor, capable of processing and sharing information a thousand times faster than our own neural networks could be at work: '...an Ocean mind, possibly billions of years in the making and capable of deep thought radically different from our own.'[10] If this is the case it could have profound implications for the way we view Ocean sentience.

This also raises some interesting questions as to the role of the Ocean's watery body in this emergent sentience. We've already learned that water's liquid crystalline fourth phase carries a negative electron charge, while at the same time gifting a positive proton charge to the surrounding water. If, as seems likely, these bacterial nanowires are surrounded by a skin of electron-packed fourth phase water, this could act as a naturally amplified conduit in much the same way as inter-facial water facilitates instantaneous cellular communication in our body's connective collagen tissue.

Quantum biologist Mae Wan Ho calls this cellular quantum coherence *quantum jazz*, and describes it as a 'body consciousness' that probably evolved long before the development of a central nervous system. She believes that, '…this body consciousness is the basis of sentience, the prerequisite for conscious experience that involves the participation of the intercommunicating whole of the energy storage domain.'[11]

This water-facilitated body consciousness then represents the fundamental sentience common to all, from amoeba to jellyfish to humans. As life has become ever more complex, this fundamental sentience has evolved into highly refined and contextually appropriate sensory perception, including self-awareness. Our own self-awareness is highly developed and yet, over the past few hundred years we've been playing out a dangerous 'thought experiment' that's resulted in us losing touch with the sentience of the rest of life.

Science has only recently started to embrace a more inclusive approach to sentience. While the biological sciences have long realised the sensing abilities of other organisms, they are on the whole, still reluctant to acknowledge conscious, perceptive awareness in any but the so-called 'higher' life forms such as some primates, dolphins and whales, elephants and perhaps a few clever parrots. But now, more and more research is indicating that highly developed perceptual awareness, as well as self-awareness, is the norm rather than the exception. In other words, fully-fledged conscious sentience is not just a gift bestowed upon humans, like some kind of evolutionary crown, but is instead widespread.

It's from this perspective that we'll continue our Ocean journey.

7

Sentient Beings in a Sentient Ocean

So far we've looked at how sentience began, and how it self-organises into a contextually appropriate level of sentient ability and social coherence. Now let's turn our attention to the complex and highly evolved way in which some of today's Ocean dwellers sense their watery world. First though, it's worth taking a moment to appreciate just how different the Ocean is from the atmosphere as a sensual medium.

Perhaps the most important and obvious difference between the Ocean and the atmosphere is its density, and of course we feel this difference as soon as we dive through her viscous surface. Density is the ratio of mass to volume, and at sea-level the atmosphere's density is approximately 1.2 kilograms per cubic metre, whereas the Ocean's surface density is over 1000 kilograms per cubic metre. The Ocean's density though isn't uniform; it's affected by a combination of temperature, salinity and pressure. These relationships are complex, but in general density increases as salinity and pressure increase and decreases as water temperature rises.

Density profoundly affects the way light, sound and vibrations travel through the Ocean. Sound and vibrations form pressure waves that travel much faster and further in the dense Ocean medium than in the air. This not only makes the Ocean an acoustic 'utopia', but also opens up an intense vibrational world for those who can tune-in. Sound travels approximately four times faster in the Ocean than in the air. Its exact velocity depends on the dynamic balance between temperature and density. In warm water it travels faster but slows down as the temperature drops, however it speeds up as the water becomes denser. This has profound implications for long distance acoustic communication, which we'll explore later in the chapter.

Light on the other hand, as the visible part of the electromagnetic spectrum, reaches its maximum velocity in the weightless vacuum of space. It slows only imperceptibly as it travels through Earth's atmosphere, but much more dramatically once it meets the dense Ocean; so much so in fact that we can actually see the effect as the 'bending' of light, known as *refraction*.

The Ocean absorbs the sun's light into her dense body as soon it penetrates below her surface. The first wavelengths to be absorbed are ultraviolet and infrared, hence the first colours to disappear from sight only a few metres down are red, violet and orange, followed soon after by yellow. Only the blue-green wavelengths penetrate to any significant depth, which is why the Ocean appears blue or green to us from above, depending on the amount and colour of suspended particles, phytoplankton and dissolved substances reflecting the light back to the surface. Even in clear tropical waters only about one percent of the sun's light reaches below 150 metres, and even that meagre illumination has disappeared completely by 1000 metres.

But it's not only the visible part of the electromagnetic spectrum that's affected by the Ocean. Her salty body is also a highly effective conductor of electrical impulses – 20 billion times more efficient than the atmosphere – thanks to the dissolved sodium, chloride, magnesium, sulphate and other ions that contribute to her saltiness. The Ocean is a wondrous world, full of pungent smells and exotic tastes in the form of chemical signals that can remain 'readable' even in minute concentrations, due to the viscous connections between water molecules.

Let's get a 'taste' of what it's like to live in this intensely aromatic soup.

Chemoreception

Smell and taste – *olfaction* and *gustation* – are the senses that have evolved to perceive the rich chemical language of life, hence the name, *chemoreception*. We know from our own experience how closely linked these senses are; how different our food tastes for instance, when a cold or hayfever blocks our sinuses and deadens our sense of smell. They are the evolutionary refinements gifted to us from those early chemoreceptive pores adorning the cell membranes of Archaen bacteria. Our sense of smell not only points us in the direction of a tasty meal, but also alerts us to a wide range of chemical signposts related to virtually every aspect of life, although most of us remain blissfully unaware of the pungent, pheromone-filled world we live in!

In the Ocean taste and smell are even more intertwined, so much so that in some situations it's more a case of smelling tastes and tasting smells! This is because many of the chemical *bio-molecules* associated with smells that waft easily on the breeze to waiting noses are actually hydrophobic, meaning they aren't very water-soluble and therefore don't travel very far in the Ocean. Consequently organisms have to be in very close proximity, if not actually touching these bio-molecules with their olfactory receptors to smell them. The bio-molecules responsible for the primary tastes (sweet, sour, salty, bitter and umami (savoury)) on the other hand, easily spread far and wide. In other words, the saying 'sniffing out a tasty meal' takes on a whole new meaning in the Ocean.[1]

A really good example of this is a group of animals known as *nudibranchs* (Figure 7.1). These colourful, shell-less sea slugs have two antennae-like *rhinophores* – meaning 'nose bearing' – on top of their heads that they use to 'taste' the surrounding water, while their *oral tentacles* are in continual contact with the odour-rich substrate.

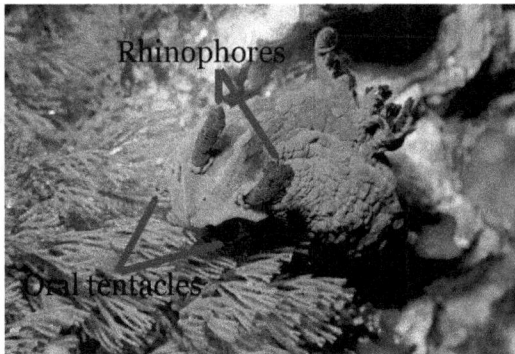

Figure 7.1 *Tambja verconis* nudibranch showing the rhinophores and oral tentacles. Also note the external gills anterior of the rhinophores.

So important is the ability to taste the water around them that fish not only have taste buds in their mouths, but also have taste receptors on other parts of their bodies; in particular, the outside of their lips, gill cavities, flanks and even tail fins. Some species, such as rock cod and goatfish, even have special *barbels* on the underside of their jaws that they use to taste the water-soaked sand. All these taste receptors are connected to the same three cranial nerves in their brains. But there are also other individual chemoreceptor cells connected directly to nerves in other parts of their bodies, suggesting the possibility that it's not just the brain involved in taste-related decision-making.

Of course this is not to say that smell isn't important, or is only used for close-up sensing. There are many other chemical signals dissolved in the water that a keen sense of smell can detect from afar. Sharks have some of the most sensitive noses in the Ocean. Some species can detect blood molecules as low as one part per million, and can even determine the direction of its source based on the split second difference in the time it takes to reach each nostril. Sharks also have a 'nose' for the different chemical signatures of fish intestines.

But it's not just the smell of lunch that's important. Many Ocean beings use chemoreception to locate and choose mates, care for their young, identify and avoid predators and even to navigate home. For example, researchers have discovered that some fish species are able to smell particular genes known as *MHC genes*, important to the healthy functioning of the immune system. Choosing a mate with differing MHC genes ensures offspring will have a stronger immune system.[2] This is bodily intelligence we can but marvel at.

Salmon use their extraordinary noses to smell their way home. As they make their way down their natal stream towards the Ocean, they imprint the unique chemical signatures of each tributary they pass along the way until they reach the river mouth and the open Ocean. When their return journey brings them within range, they home in on each signature smell until they reach the very tributary they were born in. This same extraordinary sense of smell allows them to recognise salmon from their own stream, as well as neighbours from other populations.[3]

Vision

In a world where light barely penetrates the surface we might expect vision to be the forgotten sense. While it's true that in many cases other senses take the lead, vision is nevertheless an important portal into their Ocean world for many of her inhabitants. And of course, as if we need reminding again, like so many other aspects of life, vision evolved in the Ocean.

The eye slowly evolved from the earliest single-celled organisms, who developed simple *photoreceptors* that could do no more than perceive the amount and direction of light reaching them. The pinhole eye enabled basic shapes to be discerned, but lacked any detail. The first true image-forming eye, the compound eye, came along during the Cambrian period and is still the way crustaceans such as lobsters, crabs and shrimps see their world. Image clarity depends on how many segments – called *ommatidia* – the eye has, but even the best compound eyes are only good for seeing things at close range. Compound eyes however, are excellent at detecting movement and in some crustaceans there is highly developed depth perception as well as colour vision.

A great example is the mantis shrimp, whose enormous protruding eyes can swivel in opposite directions at the same time (Figure 7.2). Mantis shrimp not only have excellent colour vision, but they can also do something that we can only achieve with the help of technology: they can see polarised light. This is a huge advantage as much of the light reaching below the surface is polarised due to the reflective and refractive qualities of water. Mantis shrimp eyes are divided into three hemispheres, which gives them outstanding *trinocular* depth perception. The middle hemisphere has highly specialised ommatidia, with up to 12 different colour receptors (compared to our three) enabling them to see the full spectrum of polarised light as well as ultraviolet light. Theirs is a colourful world indeed.[4]

Figure 7.2 Mantis shrimps have compound eyes divided into three hemispheres, giving them trinocular depth perception and the ability to see the full spectrum of polarized and ultraviolet light.

In a remarkable example of convergent evolution two quite different, but equally sophisticated, single-lens eyes have emerged from those first simple photoreceptors. And the owners of these two eye types couldn't be more different. On one side of this visual divide we have the vertebrates: fish, sharks, reptiles and mammals, including all land mammals; on the other a special group of invertebrates: the cephalopods, represented by squid, cuttlefish and octopi. For both these groups the basic function of their single-lens eyes is the same: light enters through the pupil and is focused by the lens onto the photoreceptor cells of the retina. The differences are in how they achieve these fundamentals, and also in some of the neat tricks each has developed to make the most of the limited light available to them.

Looking into the eye of a cuttlefish or octopus can be disconcerting. The clearly intelligent, questioning look responding to your own gaze seems entirely alien. In place of our more familiar round pupil is an elongated and somewhat rectangular slit (Figure 7.3). Like our pupil though, it expands and contracts to control the amount of light reaching the lens. The lens of a cephalopod eye focuses much like the lens of a camera, by moving in and out to focus at different distances, whereas we use muscles around the eye to change the shape of the lens.

Figure 7.3 The elongated pupil of cuttlefish and octopus eyes seem entirely alien to us, and yet they represent a remarkable example of convergent evolution that has produced two distinctly different but equally efficient single-lens eye forms.

Cephalopod eyes have totally different photoreceptor cells to us. While our retina is covered with rods and cones (rods for low light conditions and cones for bright light, as well as colour reception) cephalopods have receptors called *rhabdomeres* that enable them to see both polarised and unpolarised light. Some fish take advantage of polarised light by reflecting it off their silvery bodies, creating a glare that confuses potential predators, but the cephalopod's polarised vision lets them see straight through the glare and onto a potential meal.

Even more intriguing is that the *iridophores* on their skin, which they use to instantly change colour and create intricate patterns, also reflect po- larised light. Not only does this enable them to instantly camouflage them- selves against any background, but also, these eye-catching costume changes may actually be a cryptic language, invisible to predators such as sharks, seals and cetaceans, none of whom are believed to have polarised vision.[5] So the next time you put on your polarised sunglasses think of these soft-bodied masters of light.

On the vertebrate side of this convergent visual evolution, there is a long list of spectacular innovations, which as mentioned earlier, were the forerunners of virtually all terrestrial visual specialisations. For example, colour vision is common amongst many fish species, as is the ability to see ultraviolet light, while some have even emulated the cephalopods and can see polarised light. Night vision was developed in the Ocean, and refined by sharks, who have better night vision than cats.

Marine mammals are children of both worlds, and as vision underwa- ter is paramount for many of them, they have a *fisheye* lens enabling them to focus light correctly onto the retina. But as fisheye lenses can't focus properly above water, some whales have compensated for this with an irregular shaped cornea, which acts like a bi-focal lens, allowing the whale to focus above water. Others have special muscles that bend the lens giv- ing them a clear view above water.[6]

But when vision alone is insufficient, other senses have evolved to take over.

Electromagnetic Sensing

What would it be like to 'see' the electrical fields generated by the smallest muscle movement, even the heartbeat of a fish hiding amongst the rocks or under the sand, or 'feel' the subtle magnetic fields of the Earth, running beneath the Ocean floor? For some Ocean dwellers *electroreception* and *magnetoception* constitute a sixth, and in some cases, a seventh sense.

Electroreception, as the name suggests, is the ability to perceive elec- trical fields pulsing through the water. Like the other senses, electrorecep- tion is primarily a passive receiving sense, used mainly for hunting. There are a few species that have developed active electroreception, whereby they generate a weak electric pulse that can be used for *electro-communication* as well as *electro-location*. There are several species of fish, including the ancient coelacanths, and at least one species of dolphin that use electroreception. But the 'electrifying' champions are the sharks, skates and rays, otherwise known as *elasmobranchs*.

These creatures have evolved a completely unique sensory organ known as the *ampullae of Lorenzini* (Figure 7.4). The ampullae are made up of small clusters of electrically sensitive receptor cells just under the skin on their heads, and are connected to pores on the skin's surface via small jelly-filled tubes. They have several thousand of these pores, but the highest concentration is usually around the mouth, giving us the clue that they are particularly important in tracking the movements of prey in the last moments of attack. In fact, electroreception is most definitely a close-range sensing tool, as the electrical fields they are sensing are incredibly small, which is why some species have gone to great lengths to maximize their sensitivity. Research on sharks' brain response shows that they can detect electric fields as low as 15 billionths of a volt.[7] That's so low we barely have the technology to measure it, yet sharks and rays have this built into their body consciousness.

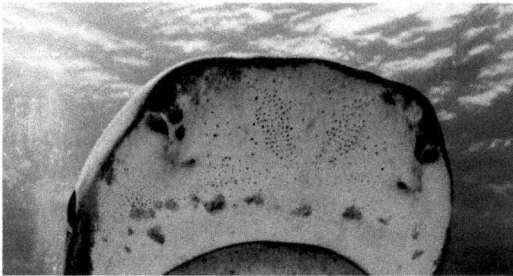

Figure 7.4 The ampullae of Lorenzini are clearly visible on the underside of the nose of this tiger shark *Galeocerdo cuvier*.
(Image: AlberKok, https://commons.wikimedia.org/wiki/File:Lorenzini.jpg)

Some shark and ray species that live in deep or murky water have either larger pores, or more of them, to compensate for the poor visibility. Hammerhead sharks take full advantage of their widely elongated heads. Not only do they have super-wide vision and widely spaced nostrils giving them stereoscopic directional smell, but they also have three thousand ampullae of Lorenzini pores on the front and underside of their head, perfect for hunting over sand or mud bottoms.

One group of rays has taken active electroreception to extremes! Electric rays are not only highly sensitive to electrical fields, but are capable of generating massive electrical pulses up to 220 volts through two large electric organs on either side of their head. They use this incredible firepower to stun prey and as a highly efficient defensive weapon.[8] Having been zapped while trying to rescue an electric ray that was washed up on a beach, I can attest to its 'shocking' efficiency. Luckily for me the poor thing was in such a weak state that it probably couldn't produce its full voltage.

Magnetoception

Magnetoception may be an awkward word to pronounce, but understanding the sensing mechanisms that make it possible has proved even more awkward. Scientists are, on the whole, still baffled by the astounding magnetoception abilities of a wide range of beings: from sharks and rays to turtles, whales, salmon and even some invertebrates such as lobsters. The best understood are probably the sharks and rays who use their staggeringly sensitive ampullae of Lorenzini to sense minute fluctuations in electrical currents as they swim through magnetic fields. It appears that the magnetoception abilities of other Ocean dwellers may be due to a particularly magnetic iron oxide in their brains, known as *magnetite*, which allows them to sense changes in the magnetic field.[9] Whatever the actual mechanism, it seems that magnetoception plays a significant role in the impressive navigational abilities of many of them.

For example, it's believed that turtles may use their magnetic abilities to plot their position on an inbuilt 'magnetic map' of the Ocean, which helps them navigate back to the very beach they were born on.[10] Salmon are believed to use magnetoception to get themselves close enough to their natal river for their keen sense of smell to pick up the friendly aromas of home. There's also growing speculation that humpbacks and other whales may use magnetic fields as part of their navigation 'tool box' on the long migrations between feeding and breeding grounds.

Satellite tagging has uncovered the 'secret lives' of other long distance travelers. Tuna, marlin and swordfish are known to cross entire Ocean basins as they hunt or gather for spawning, and it's thought that the Earth's magnetic fields may help them find their way. Great whites and tiger sharks have been tracked meandering for thousands of kilometres from one favourite 'restaurant' to another. Whale sharks and giant manta rays arrive at precise locations with pinpoint accuracy and impeccable timing to feast on billions of fish eggs, released en masse by spawning fish.[11] Hammerhead sharks with their extra headspace packed with ampullae of Lorenzini, are thought to be particularly skilled in magnetic navigation, and use it to find their way to hammerhead cleaning stations, as well as mass mating rituals.[12]

Hearing and Pressure Sensing

When Jacques Yves Cousteau wrote *The Silent World* in 1953 humanity had no idea about the importance of sound in the Ocean realm. But as Cousteau and the legions of underwater explorers that followed have discovered, the Ocean is in fact a world full of sound, an acoustic paradise for those with the sense-ability to 'tune-in'.

Hearing, whether in air or water, works by sensing pressure change, but because of the unique properties of the Ocean's watery medium, the pressure waves created by sounds act in virtually the same way as pressure waves caused by vibrational movement, such as swimming. Water is only very slightly compressible, which means that pressure gradients are much more subtle than in the air. However, the water's particle velocity, created by sound and pressure waves as they speed through the water, takes on more importance. In this way we might say that hearing underwater is a *felt* experience. And indeed many Ocean dwellers have evolved an integrated, whole body approach that is highly sensitive to both sound and movement.

In most fish species this integrated, *hydrodynamic* approach includes not only the ears, but also the highly sensitive *lateral line* system. The lateral line is made up of rows of receptor cells running around the head and along the body of the fish. Each cell has a fine hair, called *cilia*, embedded in a jelly-like cup, or *cupula*, which is attached to a nerve ending (Figure 7.5). The tiniest pressure change causes the hair to bend, triggering a signal that travels through the nervous system, creating a kind of hydrodynamic 'image'.[13] Some fish also have a direct connection between their inner ear and their gas-filled swim bladders, which are able to detect subtle pressure changes in the surrounding water.

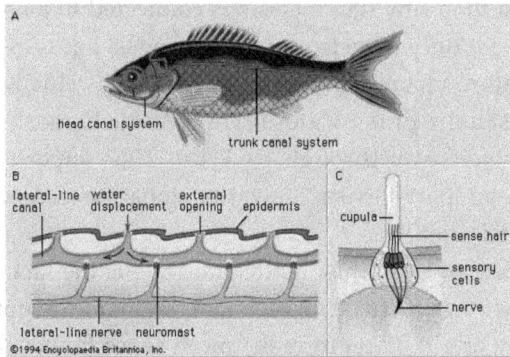

Figure 7.5 The lateral line system showing the subcutaneous lateral line canal and cupula. Image: Encyclopædia Britannica (2016) retrieved from: http://www.britannica.com/science/lateral-line-system

Unlike fish, whose inner ears are closed off from the outside world, sharks have cilia lined openings on either side of their head that lead directly to the inner ear. They also have similar open pores along their lateral line that further enhance hearing ability. It's estimated that some sharks can hear low frequency, pulsating sounds, such as those made by a sick or wounded fish, from several kilometres away.

Not only is the lateral line part of a fish's sense of hearing, but its pressure-sensing capabilities may play a physical role in performing the tightly coordinated and synchronous ballet of schooling behaviour. The lateral line of a schooling fish can feel the minute pressure changes caused by its neighbour's movements, allowing its own bodily intelligence to instantaneously adjust its movements to match.

The importance of hearing and pressure sensing in the Ocean is further highlighted by the convergent evolution of lateral line type systems in strikingly different animals, such as cephalopods, crustaceans and even some marine mammals. Although cephalopods have no ears as such, they do have rows of ciliated receptor cells on their heads and arms that provide them with the same hydrodynamic image of their world. Some crustaceans have similar *mechanoreceptor* cells on their widely separated antennae, providing them with 'stereo sound'.[14]

Even though most marine mammals have excellent hearing, some of them enhance their hydrodynamic capabilities with highly sensitive hair cells around their heads, which they use to detect current and pressure changes. Perhaps the strangest of all is the Arctic dwelling narwhal. This 'unicorn' of the Ocean grows a hard tusk, actually a modified tooth, covered with ten million tiny nerve endings connected to a central nerve. The narwhal's tusk not only detects pressure changes, but is also acutely sensitive to temperature change and particle gradients. This helps them sense changes in the salinity of the water in their Arctic home, a very useful tool for navigating their way through pack ice. This 'super-tooth' also helps them detect water particles carrying the signature characteristics of fish that make up their diet.[15]

An intriguing twist to this 'toothsome' tale is the fact that it's primarily only males who grow tusks, which may seem a little unfair considering how useful they are. It starts to make more sense however when we consider the tight social cohesion of their nomadic lifestyle – following the seasonal advance and retreat of the Arctic pack ice. Lone individuals may sometimes venture further afield, but for the most part they live communal lives where individual talents and skills are pooled together for the benefit of all. It may well be that the male's role in the pod is more focused on foraging and navigating, leaving the females more time and energy to put into caring for calves.

With so much evolutionary genius devoted to hearing and pressure sensing, it goes without saying that they must play a hugely important part in the lives of many Ocean dwellers. But some of the remarkable ways in which the Ocean soundscape influences and informs their lives is truly astounding. So let's immerse ourselves and tune-in to a few examples.

* * *

Home Calling

Imagine for a moment that you're a tiny larval fish, newly hatched from your floating egg cocoon, which was released into the Ocean, along with thousands of sibling eggs, by your mother just a few days previously. You're surrounded by a smorgasbord of tasty planktonic treats even smaller than you are. Your newly awakened chemoreceptive senses point you in the right direction, and you discover that you already have the ability to swim awkwardly towards your first meal. Over the coming weeks you feast continuously on the intensely nutritious plankton, until you have developed beyond your larval stage and are ready to settle down into life on the reef.

The only problem is that while you've been floating around at the Ocean's surface, you've drifted on her currents and are now a long way from the reef your parents launched you from; so you must search for a new reef to call home. While these unsettling 'settlement' urges are occupying your thoughts, you slowly become aware of strange, yet somehow familiar, vibrational sounds entering your consciousness. Amongst the cacophony of noise you can discern a wide range of sounds: crackling, scraping, whoops, whistles, thumps, booms, grunts and clicks. All these sounds are coming from reef inhabitants going about their daily business of feeding, cleaning, communicating and socializing. At first all this'noise makes no sense, but slowly your whole being starts to respond and a sound image forms in your mind, which resonates through you until its meaning becomes clear; 'Home'! And you start swimming purposefully in the direction of this homely 'music'.

As it turns out it's not just larval fish that find their way home using the sounds of the reef. Researchers have so far discovered that a wide range of other beings including lobsters, crayfish, shrimps and even the humble oyster, use the same strategy.[16, 17] Amazingly, even larval coral polyps use the sounds of the reef to find suitable settlement areas. They don't have any kind of specific hearing senses, but it seems they can use the tiny cilia on the outside of their bodies to pick up the particle motion of the sounds, and then use the same cilia to swim in the direction of the sound.[18] Just how far away this strategy works isn't yet clear, but indications are that, for some species at least, it could be up to several kilometres away.

It's not only coral reefs that produce this home-calling music. Rocky reefs, sea-grass beds, mangroves, even sandy beaches have distinctive soundscapes that are recognizable to the beings that call them home. As if that weren't enough, it appears that individual locations of similar kind might have unique signature soundscapes, different enough for the discerning 'home buyer' to overlook one neighbourhood in favour of another more desirable address. And what makes the difference seems to be who's already living in the neighbourhood. A healthy, vibrant community including adults of your own kind is more likely to get your fins flapping or your cilia beating in their direction.[19] This of course has very serious implications for the successful larval settlement of damaged, degraded or overfished ecosystems, where there simply aren't enough voices left to make the right music.

Long Distance Call

The music of the reef might only travel a few kilometres, but there are some Ocean dwellers whose voices can be heard for hundreds and sometimes thousands of kilometres, across entire Ocean basins. Those voices belong to Ocean giants, the great whales, in particular the blue whale and the slightly smaller and sleeker fin whale.

Their deep, sonorous voices emerge mysteriously from deep within their massive bodies, saturating the water, with no visible clue as to how they're formed. Whales don't have vocal chords, but it may be that they force air through their larynx via a series of valves and resonating chambers branching off their respiratory tract. They somehow recycle the same air over and over again as they hold their breath and descend to the depths, all the while producing the most achingly soulful music, whose meaning and purpose we can only guess at.

The blue whale has the deepest voice in the Ocean with seismic rumblings as low as 5 Hertz, way below our hearing threshold. The fin whale also sends out extremely low sound pulses of only 20 Hertz, so what we hear are basically just their high notes. Their voices aren't just deep though; they're also extremely loud. When a blue whale booms out his rhythmic, haunting moan you wouldn't want to be too close, because at 180 decibels it would be like standing next to a jet engine.[20] Even at a safe distance we would feel it more than hear it, like standing next to a speaker stack at a rock concert! But even with the combination of deep and loud, these whales need to employ the help of the Ocean herself to make sure their voices reach those long distant destinations. To understand how they achieve such incredible acoustic feats, we need to delve just a little deeper into how sound travels through the Ocean.

As we learned earlier, the actual speed of sound in the Ocean is affected by the relationship between temperature and density. Surface water warmed by the sun quickens the pace of sound waves, but below the thermocline the temperature drops and so does the speed of sound. Eventually the temperature levels off and instead it's the Ocean's density that becomes the dominating influence. As density increases it overtakes the slowing effect of the cold, and sound starts to speed up again. In between there's a 'sweet spot' where sound waves travel more slowly than either above or below. That sweet spot sits between 600 and 1200m below the surface and is known as the *deep sound channel*.[21]

The deep sound channel acts like a tunnel, keeping sounds produced in the channel from dissipating or diffusing. In this way sound waves, especially ones produced by low frequency tones like those of the blue and fin, can travel unimpeded for thousands of kilometres, with hardly any loss and at breakneck speed (Figure 7.6). The ultra-low pulse of a fin whale can travel 5000 kilometres, from one side of the Atlantic to the other in little more than an hour.[22] Blue whales send out a deep resonating moans in a perfect rhythmic pattern, sometimes for days on end. So, not only do these whales have a voice like no other, but they also know just how and where to use it to full advantage. That they understand their Ocean home so well should come as no surprise. The question to ponder, is why they make these long distance calls in the first place?

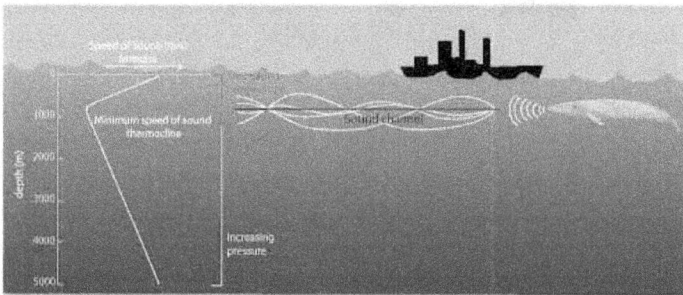

Figure 7.6 The deep sound channel (also known as the SOFAR channel) keeps sounds produced in the channel from dissipating or diffusing. (Image courtesy of NOAA)

David Rothenberg is professor of philosophy and music at the New Jersey Institute of Technology. He is a long time whale 'music' enthusiast and has written a book called, *Thousand Mile Song*. He's gathered together four decades of research on whale acoustics by many of the world's leading whale researchers, as well as teasing out their intuitions, gut feelings and just plain speculations, in an attempt to try and answer that very question. And the answer, at least so far, is that we have very little idea beyond educated guess work and intuition, what this long distance calling is for. Amongst the speculation is the idea that whales may sometimes be using their voices as low frequency, long distance sonar for navigation. Another is that these long distance calls enable mates to find each other in the vast expanses of the Ocean.

But perhaps the most useful and thought provoking idea comes not from scientists, but from a musical perspective. Music is all about rhythm, but perhaps we are listening at the wrong speed. As David Rothenberg says:

> No human musician could stay in time counting as slowly as these whales do. These incredibly low thumps and moans are rhythms at so lax a pace that they are barely perceivable by human beings. Speed a blue whale song up ten times, and thirty minutes becomes three. Move the pitch up to the realm of a cello, bowhead or human moan and exactly every three seconds comes the same soft moan. Only at this slow sense of time do we hear the thousand mile song, a great sigh in the deep sound channel, echoing from one end of an ocean to the other.[23]

Bio-Sonar

While the great whales make full use of the extreme low end of the sound spectrum, their toothed cousins exploit the high frequency world of ultrasound. All the toothed whales use *bio-sonar*, otherwise known as *echolocation*. From the mighty sperm whale to the river dolphins of the Ganges, each species has evolved a three-dimensional 'sound system' to suit their acoustic needs. The fresh water river dolphins use a close range midfrequency pulse that perfectly suits their murky living conditions, while the sperm whale sends powerful long-range pulses into the midnight depths in search of deep-water squid. Orca use high frequency, ultra powerful sound bursts to stun their prey, while others seem to use their sonar primarily for navigation. So, how does it work? To find out, let's take a look at a species that's been studied more than most – the bottlenose dolphin.

Inside the head of every bottlenose dolphin is a 100% organic, biological sonar system far more sophisticated than anything we have been able to conjure to-date. Through a complex arrangement of bones, air sacs and tissue in their skull they produce a stream of high frequency clicks. This *click-train* then passes through the *melon*, a special lipid-filled organ at the front of their head, which acts like an acoustic lens, modulating the clicks into a highly focused beam (Figure 7.7). Depending on how much detail the dolphin wants, the beam may contain a staggering 600 or more clicks per second. The returning echo is received through fatty channels in their lower jaw and highly specialized inner ears. This echo provides the dolphin with an acoustic image that we can only guess at, but considering how much of their very sizeable and complex brain is devoted to processing the returning signal, it's reasonable to assume that it's at least the equal of the three-dimensional visual images we get from devoting so much of our own brain to vision.[24]

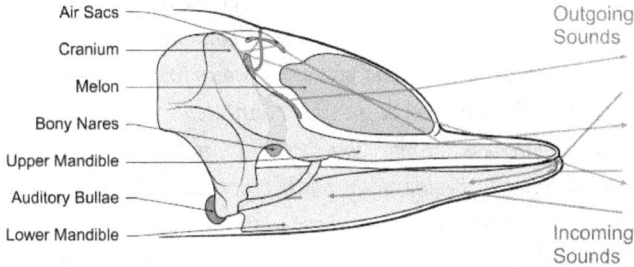

Figure 7.7 Schematic drawing showing the internal cranial structure of the bottlenose dolphin *Tursiops truncates*. (Image courtesy of: Emoscopes https://commons.wikimedia.org/wiki/File:Toothed_whale_sound_production. png)

Given the enhanced qualities of sound in the Ocean and the fact that it easily passes through solids, including living tissue, the dolphin's acoustic imagery is likely to be far more sophisticated than our visual images, perhaps more akin to high-definition x-ray vision. Research conducted primarily on captive dolphins, is certainly suggestive of very detailed acoustic imagery, and even points to this image-making being a form of communication, which may be the dolphin equivalent of language.[25] Field studies of wild bottlenose and Atlantic spotted dolphins by renowned dolphin researcher, Denise Herzing, have given us glimpses of their astounding acoustic skills. With sublime precision they *sound-probe* the sand for invisible tasty treats, or use perfectly focused click-trains to scan each other during a wide range of social interactions.[26] But perhaps there's more to this highly sophisticated sense than meets the ear, so let's leave the slightly dry, scientific dissection of bio-sonar and journey into the more intuitive realm of what it might be like to be a dolphin immersed in three-dimensional sound.

* * *

Imagine yourself newly born into the sleek and supple body of a young dolphin. Swimming right next to you is your mother. Pointing her head towards you she emits a streamed pulse of ultrasonic clicks along the entire length of your body. As she scans you from the head to tail you feel a strange, tingling sensation, followed by a deep sense of wellbeing. Your mother seems satisfied as she sends a final sound pulse directly towards your head. Immediately an image forms in your mind of a dolphin, almost a perfect miniature of your mother floating serenely by her side. It takes a moment for you to realize that the image is of you, streamed by your mother in perfect, moving clarity. This gives you your first sense-of-self and at the same time it makes you feel even more connected to her.

As your awareness grows you begin to notice a huge variety of sounds, and swimming beside your mother you start to identify many of them as belonging to the strange and wonderful sights she's showing you: the boom of rolling Ocean swells spending themselves upon the near shore; the high speed popping of raindrops splashing onto the surface and the low, background thrum of the current flowing swiftly along the reef. On the reef itself you start building a catalogue of sound images to match the visual extravaganza.

Suddenly your senses are overwhelmed as your family pod gathers round to introduce themselves. First your siblings, then aunts, uncles and grandparents welcome you with their own signature whistles. Finally a large male dolphin swims up beside your mother and with gentle strokes of his pectoral fins, introduces himself as your father.

It's now time for you to learn the intricacies of using your own bio-sonar. You were born with the most advanced sound imaging anatomy in the Ocean, but it will take time and practice to build your skills. You start by practicing moving air around your nasal sacs and through your internal phonic lips to produce high-speed clicks. Next you play with modulating the click-trains through your melon into different frequencies. Your mother directs a sound pulse towards a beautiful orange vase sponge and shows you the returning image. Now it's your turn. Aiming at the sponge you stream your first ultrasonic sound pulse into the Ocean, but unlike the perfect image created by your mother, the returning echo is a jumble of meaningless noise. Your older siblings are amused, but with gentle encouragement from your mother you persevere until the sponge reforms as a three dimensional image in your mind. Along with the image itself you also sense the exact distance between you and the sponge, its size, density and, most exciting of all, its internal structure of fine glass-like fibres arranged in an exquisitely beautiful lattice pattern.

In the following days and weeks you learn how to probe the sand in search of fish trying to hide from your sonic waves; you discover which frequency modulations work best for different substrates, as well as the best body positions for searching, locating then homing-in on your prey. You also learn how to send out multi-frequency beams at the same time. As your skill and proficiency increases you start to experiment, sharing sound images with your siblings and you're surprised and delighted by the amount of information and depth of meaning that can be conveyed through these moving pictures.

Your final lessons are in the art of internal scanning. For this you need to modulate your click-trains to their highest frequencies so they can more easily penetrate skin and blubber. This is by far the most difficult skill to master as the returning echo streams are so densely filled with information that deciphering them requires both analytical and intuitive skills. Your first attempts at scanning your mother are disappointing, but slowly these murky images resolve into solid form and you can discern the hard skeleton and eventually even some of her organs. The one that fascinates you the most is her beating heart. It seems you can 'see' feelings and emotions pulsing through the image and before you've even formulated the question your mother answers. 'The heart is the centre of our emotions and projects a very powerful energy field, even beyond the body. Your sound pulses reflect that energy field back to you, and in this way we can always be aware of how our loved ones are feeling.'

Of course we can only really speculate as to what a dolphin 'sees' with her bio-sonar. Likewise we can only imagine the acute electromagnetic world of the shark, or the vibrant polarized world of the cuttlefish. But one thing seems abundantly clear: to live within the Ocean's body is to live in a richly sensual world, in which every being is acutely aware of their surroundings and of everyone else within their sensory range.

We know from our own experience that our senses never work in isolation. We may focus our attention visually, but all our other senses are tuned-in, working behind the scenes, contributing information and depth to the subject of our attention. Much of the time we're not even conscious of this sensory teamwork: it's our body consciousness that's orchestrating this symphony of sensations, employing all the tools at its disposal, including our brain, to analyze, recognise and categorize our sensory experience. Our emotional response to this felt experience is what triggers conscious choice making, and the key to appropriate choice making is the ability to feel, and be aware of our emotional response. With this awareness let's now dive into an exploration of the emotional lives of some of our Ocean friends.

8

I Feel Therefore I Am

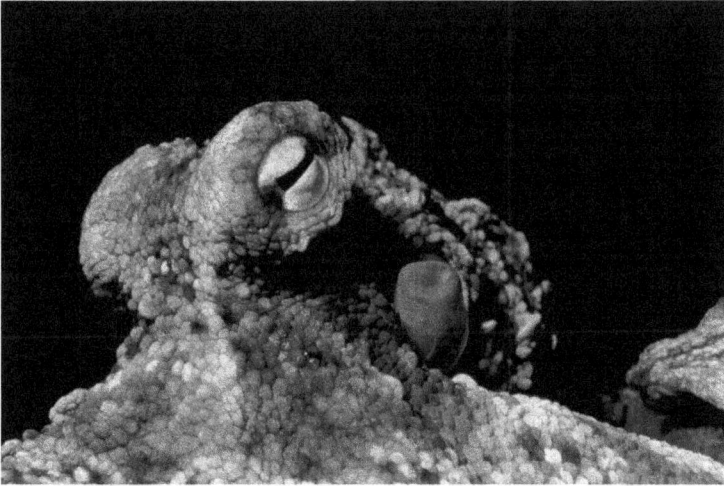

Eighteen metres below the surface, just inside Riko Riko, the world's biggest sea cave, sits a truck-sized rock, fallen from the roof an age ago and now extravagantly festooned with a patchwork of encrusting sponges, corals and anemones.[1] Camera in hand, I was exploring its nooks and crannies in search of new species of nudibranchs to add to my photo library. Working my way along a rock face my gaze passed over a narrow recess near its base. A moment or two later I stopped and turned back towards the recess. Did I see something, a movement perhaps? I wasn't sure. I just had a sense, a feeling something was there. At first I didn't notice anything unusual, but then, clear as day I saw it; an eye staring straight back at me. Once I had it as a point of reference, the owner of the eye materialised in the form of a small octopus.

Apart from his eye the perfection of his camouflage was complete, but as soon as he sensed I'd blown his cover he morphed into a dark, spiky and very menacing 'monster', nearly twice the size he'd been just a moment ago. Well, at least I think menacing monster was the effect he was hoping for. The only result though, was my mask filling with water as my face creased into laughter – probably not the response he was hoping for. Intrigued, and forgetting all about nudibranchs, I settled on a nearby patch of sand near enough to get some close up photos of his head and eyes.

While I was focusing my camera and positioning my underwater strobes the octopus reverted to his former camouflage. As I started taking photos I noticed that every time the strobes fired the poor wee fellow flinched, just as we inadvertently blink when someone snaps a shot of us with the camera's flash on. But more than that, his distress was obvious in the rapid colour and pattern changes pulsing across his body. Feeling guilty, I laid my camera on a nearby rock and pondered how I might 'apologise' for my rudeness. For lack of any better idea, and to satisfy my own curiosity, I defaulted to the very human response of extending the 'hand of friendship'.

For quite some minutes we sat there eyeing each other up, me with my bare hand extended palm up, while the octopus kept all eight of his arms tightly coiled under his now uniformly pale body. I became quite mesmerised by the rhythmic exhalation of water through his *siphon* as he breathed. He could have used his siphon to jet propel himself away at great speed, but he seemed happy to keep observing me through those strange, rectangular pupils. Maybe he was just as mesmerised by my regular exhalation of bubbles.

Eventually curiosity got the better of him and he slowly unwound one of his arms and inched it towards my outstretched hand. The fine tip of his arm made contact with the tip of my index finger, hesitated momentarily, then continued forward until it was about halfway up my palm. The sticky sensation of his suction cups moving across my bare skin was unlike anything I'd experienced before. Each cup seemed to be acting independently, holding my hand in place with a muscular grip and yet exploring the folds and creases of my skin with supple dexterity. Each cup is equipped with chemoreceptors, so besides feeling my hand, he was also 'tasting' it. All this time his skin was pulsing pale shades of green and off-white in faint patterns, while the texture lost its spikiness and became uniformly smooth.

He continued exploring my hand, extending his already impressively stretched arm even further until it reached my wrist and the neoprene cuff of my drysuit. The rubbery feel of the drysuit must have surprised him because he suddenly recoiled, just as we would on touching something unexpected. His surprise was immediately written across his body, which now pulsated a cryptic pattern of dark splotches. Undaunted though, he tentatively stretched out his arm again to investigate this strange new sensation. After a moment's consideration he obviously decided that my wrist seal posed no threat, because his pulsating flush relaxed back to cool greens and whites. With 'first contact' now firmly established it was time to study the strange, alien creature in more detail. So, with slow, deliberate movements the octopus started disentangling his seven other arms in preparation for a closer look at this odd, bubble-blowing giant that seemed to have most of its body covered in dead skin.

The way an octopus moves defies description. There appears to be no coordinated rhythm or pattern to the way his arms move in relation to each other, as if each has a mind of its own, a concept that recent research supports.[2] And yet, somehow out of this chaotic choreography, the octopus 'shape shifts' from place to place with sublimely fluid movements.

Thus, I now found my new friend materialised on my hand, with various arms wandering up my drysuit sleeve, exploring the dive computer on my wrist and reaching across to bring my other hand closer. And there we stayed, with me lying prone, elbows resting on the sand, forearms outstretched and hands cupped like some kind of organic 'easy chair', while the octopus rearranged his arms into a tightly coiled pillow to rest on. For the next twenty minutes we contemplated each other, our eyes locked at half an arm's length, the only movement our respective breathing.

What his exact experience of our interaction was I can't say, but that his attention was focused I was certain of by the intensity of his gaze. Likewise, the subtle colour changes pulsing across his body were clear signs that he was responding emotionally to the experience. More than that, I could feel a range and quality to his emotions that I could empathically identify with; they were familiar. Less clear is what was going through his mind, what was he thinking? For my part, I experienced a huge range of emotions; not least of which was a great sense of awe and wonderment to interact on equal terms with a being that represents such 'otherness'. I had extended an invitation, which he accepted and then took the lead in establishing the connection between us. What followed was a mutual exploration, more than just physical, that evoked emotional experiences to which we both responded. We were exploring each other's perspective.

The Problem of Perspective

Perhaps my encounter with the octopus isn't too much of a surprise. After all, they're well known for their intelligence, curiosity and dexterity. The internet is awash with videos of octopus opening jars, solving puzzles, negotiating mazes and performing escape routines that even Houdini would envy. But all of these are *signs of intelligence* from our perspective, designed to titillate with their implied comparison to our own intelligence. Observing octopuses in their Ocean home is more useful as it provides the proper context to contemplate how they relate to their world. And it's not just the big-brained octopus – observing other inhabitants of this deeply contextual world reveals that complex, emotional and social lives are the norm rather than the exception. But how do we recognise that which is so different from our own experience?

Naturalists have long studied the emotional and social lives of animals. Charles Darwin was an early pioneer. His 1872 treatise *The Expression of the Emotions in Man and Animals* is considered the first serious treatment of the subject. Today the scientific study of animal behaviour is multidisciplinary, but the general study of the social lives of animals is known as *ethology*, while *cognitive ethology* is the specific study of animal minds from a comparative, evolutionary and ecological perspective. Cognitive ethologists are interested in what animals think and feel; their emotions, reasoning, beliefs, consciousness and self-awareness.

In recent years this interest has extended beyond the study of the so-called higher life forms, such as mammals, to include other vertebrates, and even some invertebrates like our friend the octopus. We know what it feels like to be conscious and self-aware, and with our ability to empathize we can imagine what it might be like to be someone else. But the further removed we get from our own kind, the harder it is to imagine 'what it is like to be' and our ability to empathise with their emotional experience becomes suspect. And you can't get much more removed from human experience than fish, octopuses or lobsters.

It's not too surprising then, that after 400 years of denying the existence of consciousness and self-awareness in non-human animals, science is treading carefully in its exploration of 'otherness'. After all, despite the fact that we experience it in every waking moment, we barely understand how consciousness arises within ourselves, let alone trying to explain it in others. While much research has centred on the brain and neurological function, in an attempt to identify the physiological factors involved in consciousness, cognitive ethologists concentrate on studying behavioural clues that point towards conscious awareness. One of the clues they're looking for is behavioural flexibility when faced with new or complex situations requiring more than just instinctual responses. Behavioural flexibility shows an ability to learn from experience, retain memories of past experiences and modify, or even develop completely new, behaviour patterns based on the contextual subtleties of the situation.

One of the world's foremost authorities on animal emotions and cognition, Professor Marc Bekoff, puts it this way:

> Flexibility in behaviour is one of the litmus tests for consciousness, for mind at work. Consciousness evolved because it allowed individuals to make choices when confronted with varying and unpredictable situations.

And in a clear indication that just beneath the surface of the supposedly detached and objective scientist lies the heart of a true naturalist, he goes on to say:

> However, once we've established that other animals have conscious minds, then we get to the really interesting questions. What are they thinking? What do they feel? What do they know? The excitement to answer these questions is what drives cognitive ethologists. It's what gets us out of bed in the wee hours of the morning.[3]

To answer these questions we need to go back to our naturalist roots, dedicating long hours to detailed and open-minded observation in the field, or in our case, the Ocean. We need to use all our empathic powers to 'get inside their skin' and see their world from their perspective; to ask, 'what is it like to be'? In doing this though we need to be very careful that we aren't just projecting our own experience onto them, but instead, we need to 'think like a fish lives'.[4] This is where the practice of *phenomenology* comes into play. In phenomenology we give full attention to the actual experience of our interaction with our subject, rather than attempting objectivity by imagining ourselves as completely detached observers and pretending that we aren't part of the experience. In other words, by being fully present to our own experience we can notice what isn't us, but is instead, coming from the other.[5]

Before we dive into this rich emotional and social world, I'd like to address a particular aspect of recent scientific research that's not only controversial, but is occupying a surprisingly large amount of the animal consciousness research effort, not to mention an inordinate amount of media attention. It's controversial because the implications of this research are far-reaching and potentially very costly, as it calls into question our moral and ethical treatment of Ocean beings.

Do Fish Feel Pain?

The question is not can they reason, nor can they talk, but can they suffer?
– Jeremy Bentham *(1789) The Principals of Morals and Legislation.*

In 2003 a groundbreaking study was published in *Proceedings of the Royal Society* showing that fish have the same pain receptors as other vertebrates. *Nociceptors*, as they're known, are the body's way of detecting damage or potential injury. When they're triggered, ultra-fast electrical impulses start firing inside special nerve fibres dedicated to transmitting information about tissue damage, which in turn causes a reflex response that will, hopefully, avoid further damage. But this study revealed something even more surprising. The researchers observed that the trout used in the study showed clear signs of being consciously aware of the pain they were experiencing and took active steps to avoid a repeat situation.[6]

Since then there have been numerous studies corroborating those initial findings. In fact, the evidence shows that fish feel pain in much the same way as other vertebrates, including us, and in some cases may be even more sensitive to pain. In her book, *Do Fish Feel Pain?* Victoria Braithwaite (one of the authors of the original study) provides a balanced, comprehensive and comprehensible overview of the research to date, including research arguing against the ability of fish to feel pain.

The argument against fish awareness of pain is based on a comparison of brain structure between fish and other vertebrates, such as us. The part of our brain that affects our emotional behaviour, and becomes active when we feel pain, is the *limbic system*, located in our *neocortex*. The argument goes that because fish don't have a neocortex, they're incapable of processing feelings and emotions, therefore can't consciously experience the feeling of pain. It turns out though, that fish do have a kind of limbic system, which functions in much the same way; it's just in a different part of the brain.[7] We were simply looking in the wrong place.

The overwhelming evidence points to the fact that fish do indeed feel pain and they do have an emotional response to the pain sensation. Victoria Braithwaite sums up where she believes fish sit along the pain perception continuum:

> I have argued that there is as much evidence that fish feel pain and suffer as there is for birds and mammals — and more than there is for human neonates and preterm babies.[8]

So, the controversy is no longer whether or not fish feel pain, but rather, what we do about it in terms of our moral and ethical relationship to them. In a recent review paper in the journal *Animal Cognition* entitled *Fish Intelligence, Sentience and Ethics*, Associate Professor Culum Brown, of Macquarie University in Sydney, highlighted the fact that fish are amongst the most exploited animals by humans, but are seldom accorded any level of welfare or protection against undue cruelty. While he acknowledges the potential legal minefield and the serious impact that it could have on the global fishing industry, he also makes it abundantly clear that from a moral and ethical perspective there is no justification for 'business as usual':

> A review of the evidence for pain perception strongly suggests that fish experience pain in a manner similar to the rest of the vertebrates. Although scientists cannot provide a definitive answer on the level of consciousness for any non-human vertebrate, the extensive evidence of fish behavioural and cognitive sophistication and pain perception suggests that best practice would be to lend fish the same level of protection as any other vertebrate.[9]

Research into pain reception in the Ocean isn't just limited to fish. In recent years researchers have been asking the same questions about a wide range of invertebrates: from octopus and squid to lobsters, crayfish, shrimps and crabs. In every case, some form of pain perception ability has been found. These invertebrates have very different physiologies to fish, so most researchers have been reluctant to speculate too much on the emotional consciousness of lobsters, crabs and others. However, a recent study showed that crayfish display emotional signs of stress after receiving mild electric shocks, which can be alleviated by the same anti-depressant drugs used for human stress.[10]

Short of developing the communication skills to ask the crayfish themselves, we'll never know for sure how they experience stress or pain. And because we haven't thought to look, we'll remain largely ignorant about their experience of other emotions as well. But I am reminded of the words of the enigmatic 20th century astronomer and philosopher, Carl Sagan when he wrote, 'Absence of evidence is not evidence of absence.' As the mounting evidence points towards some form of conscious awareness, surely we must ask ourselves – at what point do we give them, and all Ocean beings, the benefit of the doubt and treat them with the level of care and respect we supposedly afford to land animals?

Perhaps, in moments of reflection, we might also ponder why it is that we humans have focused so much on pain and suffering when it comes to our ethical treatment of other beings, when there is so much more we can learn with a little thoughtful observation. As we do, it becomes abundantly clear that the Ocean is full of meaning, expressed through the intelligent, social and emotional lives of those who dwell within her fluid body. So let's return to that richer world with a few examples that show there is a lot more to life in the Ocean than just pain and suffering.

You Scratch My Back and I'll Scratch Yours

Coral reefs are amongst the most diverse, complex and cosmopolitan ecosystems on the planet. To survive and thrive here you need more than instinct and blind luck. You need a well-developed set of social skills to cope with the dynamic and ever-changing social landscape. In various situations and to varying degrees, you might need to be an entrepreneur, salesman, politician, counsellor or security guard. In every case you'll need to keep your wits about you and know exactly when it's time to cooperate, dominate, placate or vacate. Along with this social intelligence you'll probably also need an outstanding long-term memory for faces, places and happenings. Such are the sophisticated skill-sets researchers have observed on the reef by being there and being 'present'.

In an exquisite example of entrepreneurial salesmanship and cooperation, researchers have discovered that some grouper enlist the services of moray eels to help them hunt. This unlikely alliance appears to happen when the grouper's meal manages to evade his lunging jaws, escaping to the safety of cracks and crevices amongst the coral. Undeterred, the grouper makes a beeline straight for the nearest cooperative moray, where he shakes his head from side to side in invitation. If the eel's feeling so inclined he'll leave his sleeping hole and follow the grouper back to the hiding fish. The long sinuous body of the eel then disappears into the crevice to flush out the hapless fish while the grouper waits, jaws at the ready, to grab him as he flees the needle sharp fangs of the moray. It appears that both grouper and eel get a bite of the 'fish pie'.[11]

There are several very tantalizing aspects of this remarkable alliance for us to ponder. The first is that at some point in the past, this behaviour was learned: perhaps by a grouper observing the hunting techniques of a moray eel, comparing them to his own and deducing the hunting advantages in employing the eel's services. The second is that the grouper then worked out a way to communicate his 'job offer' to the eel. For the eel's part, not only must he have possessed the social intelligence to understand what the grouper was proposing, but he would also have gone through a process of deciding if the offer was worthwhile getting out of bed for. After all, moray eels are nocturnal hunters and usually spend their days safely tucked up in their cosy crevice.

Even more interesting, is that individual grouper can remember which morays in their territory are more likely to participate so they approach them first. It could be that the eels also recognize groupers who have shared the meal fairly in the past, and are more likely to put themselves out for fair-minded fish over selfish ones.[12] In a wonderful example of how far this kind of friendship can extend, dive guides on the Caribbean island of Cozumel witnessed a long-term relationship between two individuals. Divemaster Rob Groth describes the friendship:

> For many years we had an older eel and grouper team who not only hunted together but lived together in an over hang on the top of Punta Tunish wall. It was a favorite photo site for our dive groups. The Green Moray had a head bigger than a basketball and was about three meters long. Towards the end of her life she had lost all of her teeth and we witnessed the grouper bringing her food. This went on for a couple of years until the grouper disappeared. We fig-

ured that she (the grouper) finally ended up someone's meal. After that we (the dive masters on the island) brought food daily to the eel. This only lasted for a few months until the eel also disappeared.[13]

Grouper/moray eel partnerships have been observed in many parts of the Ocean, raising a number of tantalizing possibilities as to the nature and sophistication of communication and cultural learning in the Ocean

This story not only demonstrates the cooperative nature of the relationship, but also clearly shows the altruistic actions of the grouper. This is exactly the behaviour we would expect from the strong emotional bonds of a true friendship. While not every grouper or eel participate in this cooperative behaviour, it is widespread enough that some kind of cultural learning must be at play. We'll delve into this further in the next chapter.

Another example of 'back scratching' literally is, back scratching, and it comes about as part of the complex social interactions between multiple species at the reef's cleaning stations. Cleaner fish often set up shop around prominent features, such as rocky outcrops, where there is a good 'passing trade' of other fish who need the services of a talented parasite picker to remove unwanted hitch-hikers, dead skin and sometimes even provide a dental cleaning service.

These cleaning sessions are often very delicate affairs, requiring a high degree of trust between cleaner and client. After all, it's no small thing to swim straight into the gaping mouth of a fish or shark many times your size, sporting rows of razor sharp teeth that could rip your tiny body to shreds in seconds. To get her customers 'in the mood', a cleaner will often give them a gentle back massage by rubbing her pelvic and pectoral fins along their dorsal fin and back. This caress seems to put the fish into a kind of relaxed trance, and it drifts motionless while the cleaner gets to work – a bit like hairdressers who give their customers a gentle head massage before they get to work with the scissors.

It also appears that the back rub can be used to appease disgruntled clients. Cleaners can sometimes get a bit carried away with their parasite picking and succumb to the temptation of taking a little bite of their customer's nutritious body mucus. This obviously hurts the unsuspecting fish, who will give a little 'jolt' and swim off, unless the cleaner can persuade them to stay with an appeasing caress. There's good reason for the cleaner to keep her client happy. Just like the beauty salon or barbershop; there are other customers waiting and watching. Researchers have observed that the waiting fish are much less likely to solicit the cleaner's services if they see a cleaning session end in conflict. More than this, it seems that fish remember these painful encounters and will avoid that cleaner in favour of others who have an untarnished reputation.[14] If you get a bad haircut you're much more likely to try somewhere else next time.

A good reputation goes a long way in the cleaner fish world and it seems 'husband and wife' teams are highly regarded by discerning cliental. Some species of cleaner wrasse work in male/female pairs; not only providing a 'two for one' cleaning deal, but also it seems, keeping each other on the straight and narrow when it comes to those tempting mucus treats. The result is a steady stream of satisfied customers.[15]

These two examples give us a glimpse of the complex world of the reef, where social intelligence, cooperation, communication and self-awareness are the keys to a successful, happy life. Careful observation by disciplined, yet open-minded, researchers has provided us with these powerful insights. The researchers' presence most certainly won't have gone unnoticed by the reef inhabitants, but their unobtrusive observations didn't require them to participate in reef life to gain their insights; they could literally 'observe from a distance'. Sometimes though, the only way to get an idea of 'what it is like to be' is to interact and be accepted by the other.

Shark Culture

Interacting is exactly what shark ethologist Ila France Porcher had in mind back in 1995, when she saw her first black-fin reef shark while snorkeling in the shallow lagoons of French Polynesia. Sharks are famously cautious and difficult to approach in the wild, which is why the little that was known about their lives up to that time came primarily from observing them in captivity, or from occasional glimpses of wild sharks afforded to lucky divers.

To get the kind of insights into their private lives she was hoping for, Ila knew she would have to convince them that she was worth spending time with. The only way to do this was to bring an offering, in the form of leftover fish scraps and tuna heads from the local fish market. While obviously creating an unnatural situation, it nevertheless provided her with the essential ingredient for in-depth study: prolonged periods of uninterrupted observation. And because the focus of her research was their social behaviour and cognitive ability, the introduction of a novel situation actually provided additional opportunities to observe their behavioural flexibility.

Over a seven-year period of intensive interaction, primarily with black-fin reef sharks, but also white-tip, grey-reef, lemon and nurse sharks, Ila discovered a complex shark culture hitherto undreamed of. Once the sharks had become comfortable with her calm presence and accepted her into their community, she was witness to a huge range of behaviours and social interactions that left her in no doubt as to the deeply emotional lives of these most maligned and misunderstood Ocean beings. In her beautifully illustrated book *The Shark Sessions* Ila chronicles the many hundreds of hours of dedicated observation and insights gained from her time spent in the company of sharks.[16] Key to her work was being able to identify individuals. By making detailed sketches of unique features such as dorsal fin markings, she was able to identify 600 black-fin sharks alone and keep track of their comings and goings, building up a picture of their lives.

She discovered that individuals had unique patterns of roaming, with some almost always present in their home range, while others might be absent for months at a time. She also observed that many of them had preferred travelling companions, usually of the same gender and similar age, and would nearly always stick with their 'special friend' when they traveled outside their home range, while others swapped companions quite frequently.

Sometimes residents of the areas they were passing through joined the travelling companions, and it was clear that the residents recognized their visitors. These meetings appeared to be very social times, with long periods of 'side-by-side' swimming, and frequent friendly touching. Ila noticed that the sharks' roaming behaviour was influenced by the lunar phase, and on many occasions she witnessed large social gatherings as the full moon rose. At these times, visitors and residents alike became very excited, with stunning displays of speed and acceleration as they soared in unison through the water. Her observations clearly showed that these sharks knew each other as individuals: a prerequisite for their ability to maintain complex social lives. But more than that, it also pointed towards strong emotional bonds between individuals.

Ila's long term interactions with the reef sharks of French Polynesia yielded many other fascinating insights into their lives, including clear evidence of self-awareness, contextual decision making, social learning, long-term memory, forward planning and an innate curiosity about their world.[17] But perhaps the most valuable lesson we can learn from her work is how careful we must be not to neglect, or even exclude, the importance of the emotional and social lives of Ocean beings, especially when our assumptions are based on very limited 'snapshots' from the surface.

Sometimes the scientific fear of subjectivity and obsession with objectivity can cloud our appreciation of 'what it is like to be', and instead replace it with a one-dimensional representation of life, devoid of emotional depth. We become so focused on counting, measuring and categorizing that we completely miss this 'hidden' dimension. My own experiences with humpback whales have highlighted to me the limitations of a purely objective approach.

Hidden Lives

Humpback whales are probably the most studied of all the great whales. Their gregarious nature, hauntingly complex songs and penchant for acrobatic surface displays make them a favourite with researchers and whale watchers alike. Every year these whales migrate from summer feeding grounds in the polar regions to their winter breeding areas in the tropical zones of both hemispheres, providing relatively easy and reliable access for researchers. And yet, so much of their lives remains hidden to us, veiled not only by the liquid boundary between our worlds, but also by our preoccupation with testing our own theories.

A good example of these twin barriers to understanding is the body of research into social groupings in the breeding areas. Generally, researchers consider humpbacks to be loners, who don't form long-term bonds, and only come together temporarily in response to biological imperatives.

There are a number of different social groupings during the breeding season, but a reasonably common one is that of mother, calf and a male escort. This relationship has been the subject of numerous studies in recent years, with much of the focus on the role of the escort. The general consensus is that the relationship is opportunistic on the part of the escort and that it's related to mating. A range of hypotheses have been put forward as to whether the escort provides any benefit to the mother and her calf, or whether it is purely associated with a mating advantage for the male, or perhaps even that the attentions of an escort may be detrimental to their wellbeing.[18]

There's no doubt that males compete with each other for mating rights and this can become very physical indeed when several males are vying for the attentions of the same female; with violent head butting, body slams and tail slaps. Sometimes several males will challenge an escort, who defends his position with the mother and calf, driving off the challengers. Females have a twelve month gestation period and there's usually a gap of one or two years between calves, so researchers have puzzled over why males pay so much attention to mothers with calves, when their chances of mating are better with females without calves.

During my six years of observing and interacting with humpback whales in Tonga, I had no hypothesis to test or theory to prove. I was just interested in getting to know them, as much as they would allow, without unduly intruding on their privacy. My goal was to observe as much of their daily lives as possible, without a particular focus on any one aspect, but with an open-minded curiosity. I tried to suspend my assumptions and preconceptions in the hope that at least a little of their life story might emerge over time. One thing became abundantly clear: if I wanted to gain any useful insights into their lives, I would have to spend as much time as possible in the water with them. After all, they spend 90 percent of their time underwater.

In the many encounters I had with mothers, calves and escorts I tried to focus on the dynamics of the relationship itself. I paid particular attention to how the whales interacted with each other in various circumstances, for example: during nursing, resting, sedate travelling or active surface play. I didn't measure anything, but rather, focused on the quality of the interactions between them. I especially noted any physical contact between the mother and her escort and tried to get a sense of the emotional quality, or intention behind it. But most importantly, I endeavoured to engage empathically with them: to identify, and identify *with*, their emotional lives.

Many of my in-water encounters involved resting whales – something they spend quite a lot of time doing – either at the surface, or sometimes a few metres below. I noticed that when a mother and her calf were resting at the surface, the escort was usually more alert, as if keeping guard. Sometimes he'd stay below the surface, just out of visual range, only coming up for a breath every ten minutes or so; far enough away not to disturb the sleeping mother, but close enough to remind me he was watching. If I got too close to the mother for his liking, he would surface right beside her and then all three of them would turn away from me and swim off a short distance.

When resting underwater the mother and escort were often much closer together, sometimes even physically touching. They might have their long pectoral fins draped across each other, or occasionally, even stroking each other with gentle caresses. On a number of occasions I also witnessed the mother and escort spending prolonged periods with their heads together, sometimes with one resting their head on the other's flank. Spending time with the whales during these interactions I was struck by the level of affection often shown by both mother and escort, indicating strong emotional bonds between them. It seemed clear to me, that whatever else it may provide, this relationship is often a loving one where the mother is supported, rather than hindered, in her efforts to care for her calf.

For me, this calls into question the notion that these relationships are purely opportunistic, as well as the idea that humpbacks don't form long-term bonds with each other. We simply don't know what these relationships mean to the whales themselves, but it's certain that when we exclude the emotional content from our measurements, our theories will always be lacking contextual meaning. An essential part of that context is our own participation in the process of observation. We are being observed, as much as observing. We pretend otherwise through arrogance or ignorance, but either way, our pretence of objectivity ultimately damages our chances of gaining insight into 'what it is like to be'. We are a part of this world, not *apart from* it and we can only delve into the depths of meaning when we acknowledge and embrace our participation: when observation becomes interaction.

Rarely have I experienced the importance of embracing my own participation more than when interacting with mothers, calves and escorts. During these encounters I started noticing another dimension to this three-way relationship: both mother and calf often seemed much more at ease when there was an escort present. Calves were often more playful than usual, and mothers seemed more willing to let them explore further afield. Indeed, sometimes it seemed that the mother was actively encouraging her calf to interact with us.[19]

On one occasion we spotted a mother, calf and escort travelling more or less parallel to us. Unexpectedly, they altered course to intercept us, so we lowered the sails and prepared the swim platform incase there was an opportunity to get in the water with them. As soon as they approached the boat it was clear they were interested, so we donned masks and fins, and slipped into the water. Almost immediately the mother approached us with her calf. The escort dived down and watched from below, but the mother seemed intent on educating her calf about these strange visitors from the world above.

At first the calf was a bit nervous, keeping his mother's enormous bulk between us, but slowly he warmed to the game, so that by the third or fourth pass he was showing off by lying upside down across her head, splashing the surface with his inverted tail. With each pass the mother carried her calf closer, until they were so close that she had to lift her pectoral fin over me as I floated on the surface and I felt it gently caress my back as it passed. This level of intimacy was definitely out of the ordinary, and I couldn't help but feel profoundly privileged to be interacting freely, equally and on her terms, in her realm.

When we are present to our own experience, fully immersed in our interaction with another, we feel a deep sense of connection. Our bodily senses are alive to the other, tuned into sensory communication channels that feed our body consciousness with streams of reciprocal information, which we become aware of and identify with empathically: we have communicated and have knowledge of each other. Mind is awakened in the act of deciphering and making coherent sense of this knowledge. But what if mind and knowledge are one and the same thing? What if this so-called mind is the individual and collective manifestation of a knowledge process, brought into existence through our participation in the world? Where then does mind reside? Can it be confined to our bodily experience alone, or is it inherent to a living *knowledge process*, in which we are both contributor and recipient?

It's clear from the last three chapters that the Ocean is a sensual world, inhabited by deeply sentient beings who experience richly contextual lives. In the final chapter of our living Ocean journey we'll explore Ocean Mind, brought into existence by a knowledge process nearly four billion years in the making, and expressed through all her myriad children. To get us in the mood, let's imagine what it might be like to experience Ocean Mind through the eyes of a humpback whale.

* * *

Becoming Whale

Close your eyes and focus on your breathing. As you breathe in feel your connection with all other life that breathes the same air and imagine your body transforming into a magnificent humpback whale.

As your whole body expands you feel your arms lengthening into the longest, most elegant pectoral fins in the cetacean world. Tracing a perfect arc through the water, you notice how even the slightest movement gives you absolute control over your balance and manoeuvrability.

Feel your legs fusing together; the strong thigh and calf muscles combining with ligaments to form the caudal muscles that drive your mighty tail flukes. Sense how flexible your newly lengthened spinal column has become to accommodate the powerful thrusts of your tail flukes. Giving them a gentle flex you are amazed at how easily they propel your enormous bulk through the water.

Gradually you feel your head elongating, your nostrils becoming blowholes and your now cavernous mouth filling with bristling baleen plates. Run your giant tongue around the inside of your baleen and imagine licking it clean of delicious krill clinging to the fine bristles.

Opening your twin blowholes you take your first breath as a humpback whale. Your rib cage expandes and becomes much more flexible to accommodate your enormous heart and lungs. As your lungs fill you can sense their efficiency as they exchange spent air for a fresh supply of lifegiving oxygen. Your heart is pumping vast quantities of oxygen-rich blood through your body and after several breaths your muscles are tingling in anticipation of your first dive.

With back arched and tail flukes held high you incline your head and slowly sink below the surface. Your first sensation is one of absolute weightlessness; your 30 ton bulk completely supported in liquid space. As your other senses awaken, feel the Ocean caressing every part of your highly sensitive skin as you glide downwards. Marvel at how easily you move air around your skull to equalise the pressure in your nasal passages. Your perfectly adapted eyes provide you with a crystal clear view of your blue universe. Gliding past a shallow reef you see myriad fishes and other creatures going about their daily lives.

You now become aware of an even greater sensation. Your underwater world is full of sound and your acute hearing picks out astonishing detail from the cacophony coming from the reef: the crackling of shrimps as they dance above the coral, the grunts of snapper as they jostle in their schools and the thud of parrot fish devouring the very coral itself.

Opening your mouth slightly, you take in a few litres of water and swirl it around your tongue. You can taste the chemical makeup of the water, its pH level, salinity, oxygen content and temperature. You can also taste the reef – every fish, every invertebrate, even the coral gives off its own chemical signature, sharing information about itself.

Diving deeper the sounds of the reef are left behind and you become aware of other familiar sounds. Concentrating your senses downwards, you can hear and feel the booming sonar of a mighty sperm whale as he echolocates his prey in the pitch black depths 1000m below.

Bringing your attention back to your own surroundings, you focus on another humpback nearby. He is a singing male and his complex song saturates your senses and fills your whole being as intimately as a lover's embrace. You are totally aware of his physical presence, who he is, what he has experienced, where he has travelled and who he has met along the way. His voice vibrates with emotion: his joys, sorrows, fears and aspirations.

Finding your own voice deep within, you respond. Your song resonates in waves and others join in, filling the Ocean with the life-force of your kin. Your sense of belonging and wellbeing overflows.

Gradually, the urge to breathe creeps into your awareness and rising slowly towards the surface, you remember that you are a creature of both worlds: at home and free in the womb of the Ocean planet and yet also bound to the world of light and air. Nearing the surface this sense of connection with both worlds fills you with exuberance. Giving a mighty thrust of your powerful tail you explode through the surface and into the air! In that moment of stillness – before arching your back and crashing back into the Ocean in a thunderous cascade of water – you exhale your spent breath in a mighty blow and breathe in fresh air once more.

9

Ocean Mind

Hovering just below the surface at the Poor Knights Marine Reserve I can see, and hear, a wall of mouths moving towards me. It's the *feeding edge* of a mixed school of trevally and blue maomao feasting on a swarm of tiny *mysid* shrimps. These two species of plankton-feeding fish have different feeding styles, but come together in coordinated schools of hundreds, sometimes thousands of individuals, to take advantage of this seasonal shrimp bonanza.

Above the surface all that's visible are the arched backs and gulping mouths of fish, churning the water into the frenzied, bubbling foam that fishermen call a 'boil up'. It seems, at first glance, completely chaotic and it's hard to imagine how the fish behind the feeding edge get any shrimps at all. But careful observation from just below the surface reveals the breathtaking level of spontaneous cooperation, which keeps the feeding edge in a constant state of dynamic movement, ensuring the whole school gets a share of the banquet.

As the feeding edge approaches, the water in front of it turns hazy with uncountable hordes of shrimps swimming for their lives. From below, a contingent of fish overtakes the feeding edge, cutting off any escape into the depths and forcing the shrimps to the surface. Lifting my head I can see shrimp jumping clear of the water in a vain attempt to flee the onslaught of hungry mouths. Sometimes the shrimp swarm veers sharply away to the left or right, and as the school turns to follow, fish that were behind the feeding edge now find themselves in the front line. The fish that had come from below fall in behind the new feeding edge so that they'll be next in line when the shrimps veer off again.

Another strategy involves the school slowly wheeling in a circular motion, with the feeding edge herding the shrimp in a wide arc. At some point fish in the back section of the school, responding to some hidden signal – perhaps the minute vibrational changes caused by the turning shrimp – break off to intercept the feeding edge as it wheels. Occasionally two separate feeding edges drive shrimp swarms towards each other from opposite directions, merging together in a 'super-school' to gorge on the dense shrimp soup. When too few shrimp remain to sustain a feeding edge the whole school descends and moves off in search of another swarm, and once located the process starts again.

Collective Mind at Work

My description above really doesn't do justice to the experience of being in the middle of these feeding schools. The surface boils with the thrashing of hundreds of dorsal fins and tails and you can hear the gurgling roar of all those gaping mouths 'vacuuming' shrimp after shrimp into waiting gill-rakers. You can literally feel the shrimps' panic as they attempt to flee the onslaught; the water feels heavy with the scent of their fear and you find yourself empathising with their plight. At the same time you can't help feeling infected by the thrumming excitement and intensity of the feast. Your whole body tingles with it, as if you're a part of the school yourself obeying some kind of primal instinct, as if your senses have connected you to the living intelligence of the school.

Now more than likely, your rational mind – uncomfortable with these unruly sensations – will take over and remind you that they're 'just a bunch of fish, eating some shrimps'. But the truth is that you have connected with something real: the collective mind of the school. This collective mind is responsible for the school's ability to function – for its purposefulness: bringing together enough individuals to make the herding of shrimp possible; for its intelligence: enabling it to devise the strategies for successful herding; and for its adaptability: maintaining the creative flexibility that allows for spontaneous response to the ever-changing dynamics between the school and its dinner.

The school has no leader or organising committee; there's no training camp for young trevally and blue maomao to practice the techniques, no 'school' to learn how to school. Individual fish just know how to participate in a way that creates a feeding opportunity, which simply couldn't exist any other way. We dismiss this knowing as instinctual behaviour, as if there's nothing special to it: 'it's just what fish do'. But the 'instinct' label blinds us to the creative intelligence of the school, the 'mind at work' that can adapt instantly to the ever-changing conditions, responding with a sublime coordination that's impossible to pre-plan.

Certainly there's instinct involved: each individual within the school is following a path, a pattern of behaviour laid down by uncountable numbers of fish that have gone before. They are drawn to come together to form the school, as if performing an ancient ritual, the origins of which have long been forgotten. But the meaning behind it is as strong as ever and further strengthened with every performance. These fish are participating in an ongoing *knowledge process*, and in this case the knowledge is 'how to eat shrimp'. The instinct then is to participate, and in doing so we might say that each fish becomes *knowledged* by the collective mind that emerges to orchestrate that knowledge, and indeed, contribute to its continued evolution.

The collective mind of the school is awakened by the participation of a critical mass of individual fish and yet, it's far more than just the sum total of all those separate minds coming together. Participation in the knowledge process not only connects individual fish to each other, but also connects the collective mind of the school to all the schools that have gone before, to a pattern of behaviour that's been honed over millennia into a *behavioural habit* inherent to this particular activity. In this way the behavioural habit, this 'way of knowing', is the school's cultural inheritance.

However, there's an important distinction between this behavioural habit and the concept of instinctual behaviour. Instinct implies a rigidity of mind, even mindlessness that's devoid of choice, or at least limited to a narrow and immutable set of choices such as 'fight or flight', whereas habits are adaptable and can change over time. They allow for the behavioural flexibility the school needs in order to creatively respond to the ever-changing dynamics of each incarnation of the behaviour.

Rupert Sheldrake, the English biologist, explains these flexible 'habits of nature' with his concepts of *morphic fields* and *morphic resonance*. Sheldrake's hypothesis of *formative causation* suggests that all self-organising systems (our fish school for example) come into being and function through the 'characteristic organising field' of that system: its morphic field.[1] An example of morphic fields according to Sheldrake, is the fields of influence involved in the *morphogenisis* – the coming into being of form – of biological organisms.

Biologists believe that these *morphogenetic* fields shape the organism as it develops from embryo through to its adult form.[2] The morphogenetic fields, rather than genetic coding, are responsible for how the cells of an organism, which share the same genetic programme, can differentiate into various body parts such as arms and legs, or pectoral and tail fins. With each repetition the field becomes stronger, increasing the probability of the pattern happening again, so as the field evolves over time it builds a cumulative memory that becomes increasingly habitual. This cumulative memory creates a morphic resonance, through space and time that influences subsequent similar patterns. Sheldrake explains:

> Morphic resonance is the basis of the inherent memory in fields at all levels of complexity. Any given morphic system, say a giraffe embryo, 'tunes in' to previous similar systems, in this case previous developing giraffes. Through this process each individual giraffe draws upon, and in turn contributes to, a collective or pooled memory of its species. In the human realm, this kind of collective memory is closely related to what the psychologist C.G.Jung called the 'collective unconscious'.[3]

Just as there are morphic fields associated with morphogenesis, there are also fields of influence involved in the organisation of perception and behaviour, as well as cultural and social fields. Sheldrake describes these fields in terms of 'wholes within wholes' that form 'nested hierarchies' or *holarchies*, comprising successive levels of organisation. He suggests that: 'At each level, the morphic field gives each whole its characteristic properties, and makes it more than the sum of its parts.'[4] In the case of our feeding schools of trevally and blue maomao, the nested holarchy of influence would include morphogenetic, perceptual, behavioural, social and mental fields.

From this perspective we can view the knowledge process of the school as a continuum, influenced by the resonance of a collective inherited memory, and evolving through a collective mind at work. But our feeding school example takes us even further into Ocean Mind when we consider the other players in this dance of life: the shrimps. They too have their nested holarchy of morphic fields, resonating with their own knowledge process, and orchestrated by their collective mind. Both fish and shrimp holarchies are wholes within a greater whole: the fish/shrimp – shrimp/fish holarchy. Within this larger field there is shrimp knowledge, trevally knowledge and blue maomao knowledge, but the overall knowledge process that emerges is more than just the sum of those individual parts.

The Ocean abounds with examples of these 'meeting of minds', but amongst the most extravagant is the famous sardine run that happens each year in the rich upwelling waters off the coast of southern Africa. Sardines gather here in their billions to feast on the rich plankton soup and participate in a mass spawning without equal. The collective mind at work here is truly impressive, but takes on even greater proportions with the vast number of predators that are attracted to the event. Tens of thousands of dolphins, whales, seals, sharks, sailfish, marlin, tuna, mackerel, and seabirds converge from near and far to participate in this sardine bonanza. The collective mind at work in these coordinated feeding frenzies transcends the species, cultural and social boundaries that would normally keep these diverse diners apart.

The first act is to herd the sardines into tightly bunched 'bait balls' of a manageable size, usually no bigger than ten to twenty metres in diameter and ten metres deep. It's often the dolphins who take the lead in this, but they are helped by the sardines themselves whose collective response to danger is to mass together in an attempt to confuse the predator. This strategy works extremely well when there are only a few predators, as regardless of the speed of attack, the school can instantly respond with coordinated moves that leave the predators completely bamboozled and literally swimming in circles in the gaping hole where the school was, just a fraction of a second before. The speed of the sardines' evasive manoeuvres is simply impossible to explain by means of individual fish responding to the movement of their neighbours.[5] Rather, it's a single, instantaneous movement of the whole school at once, coordinated through the morphic field of the school's collective mind.

The problem for the sardines comes when there are too many predators working cooperatively to overwhelm their defensive strategies. If they scatter, waiting mouths are ready to pick off confused and bewildered individuals. If the school is forced to stay huddled together by circling predators, it becomes easy for other predators to simply swim, mouths wide open, through the middle of them. The level of coordination and lack of conflict between the various predators suggests that there's more going on here than just a wild free-for-all. Rather, there is a collective intelligence, crossing species boundaries and encompassing all the various knowledge processes of dolphins, sharks, tuna and other predators – as well as the sardines themselves – so that what emerges is a truly majestic manifestation of Ocean Mind.

Mind on the Move

In Chapter 7 we touched on the impressive navigational feats various Ocean beings achieve using their finely tuned sensing abilities. We are still only vaguely aware of how these extraordinary sensing abilities work, but even if we do decipher their secrets, we'll really be no closer to understanding how these beings know where to go. We will have worked out how their internal compass works but not how they know which course to follow. Perhaps we can explain the pinpoint navigation of turtles returning to the very same beach from which they hatched, or salmon returning to their natal stream, in terms of imprinting at birth. We could also ascribe a cultural learning process to migrating whales, with calves accompanying their mothers on the long migrations from winter breeding grounds in the tropics, to their summer feeding grounds in polar seas.

But what about the many beings who find their way to important places at exactly the right time with neither mother nor birthplace to guide them? How is it that hammerhead sharks and manta rays navigate across thousands of kilometres of Ocean to join in mass gatherings, when they've never been there before and there's no one to follow? What inbuilt instinct directs schools of juvenile tuna hundreds of kilometres to specific feeding grounds for the first time? What deep wisdom drives great whites and tiger sharks on their circuitous, marathon journeys to specific hunting grounds? How do we explain the long migration 'walks' of lobsters from their home reefs into the Ocean depths?

A convenient answer to these migration riddles is to once again invoke instinctual behaviour as the mechanism, but what's much more likely is that this 'wander-lust' is the result of cultural inheritance, passed on via the morphic resonance of past generations.[6] While cultural inheritance very likely plays a large part in providing the 'map', it still doesn't explain how individuals, or even schools, enact that inheritance; how they 'read' the map, interpret its meaning and connect it to the real world territory in which they are travelling. To achieve that would seem to require a mind that is conscious of its own participation, and capable of recognizing opportunities and obstacles along the way that may require a temporary deviation from the ancestral path. This would be a mind that has the behavioural flexibility to incorporate new information without losing the old and to choose, or sometimes create, a knowledge path best suited to the circumstances.

Perhaps Ocean navigation has its own morphic field, resonating with the collective memory of countless past Ocean journeys, providing access to navigational knowledge built up over millions of years. Within this holarchy of knowledge, different species develop their own unique navigational practice, their own knowledge process appropriate to their needs. From this perspective it comes as no surprise that long-range navigation shows remarkable similarities across species, with each finding their way through different mediums such as magnetic fields, Ocean currents, moon phases, sound, and chemical signals, as well as physical sign-posts, like underwater mountain ranges and deep Ocean trenches. Enfolded within the navigational knowledge of their kind, individuals and schools roam the Ocean without fear of losing their way. Using their own creative intelligence they tap in to Ocean Mind.

Cultural Learning at a Distance

Reefs are the cities of the Ocean: crowded, bustling and noisy, yet colourful, cosmopolitan and full of cultural interaction between their diverse citizenry. Just as with human cities, the culture of the reef isn't static, but is in a constant state of evolution. The collective mind of the reef emerges from the nested holarchy of morphic fields encompassing the reef city's dynamic social vibe. Within the overall vibe there are individual and collective stories that make up the fabric of the reef's cultural flavour. As these stories unfold over time, new cultural traits and behaviours emerge, manifestations of the myriad, ongoing knowledge processes, mingling and merging in a creative flow. Individuals and groups learn from each other, copying or adapting behaviours and sometimes creating completely new ones.

Our story of the cooperative friendships between grouper and moray eels from the last chapter is a great example of a novel behavioural adaptation that spreads through cultural learning, sometimes referred to as *cultural transmission*.[7] This strikingly mutual relationship will have most likely started from a single interaction between an ancestral grouper and moray, on a reef somewhere, sometime in the Ocean's past. That first tentative collaboration may have been hundreds, thousands or even millions of years ago, or it may have been as recent as our own first forays beneath the waves with scuba equipment, little more than six decades ago, when it was first observed by divers. We have no way of knowing. But we can see that its success has resonated far and wide throughout the Ocean.

Wherever that first collaborative experiment took place, it didn't happen in secret, it was noticed. Perhaps other grouper watched from a distance, observing, taking mental notes for future reference. Once the success of this new relationship was verified those observers would become participants. We can imagine the first eel pioneer being inundated with grouper eager to test this new hunting technique. It wouldn't take long for these grouper to realize that they'd be better off finding their own eel collaborator, and so new grouper/eel partnerships would form. Before long the whole neighbourhood would be buzzing with the excitement of this latest cultural trend - although one could imagine the victims of these dynamic duos being less than thrilled with its development!

But where next? Neither grouper nor morays travel very far, preferring to stay within their home range. How did the cultural transmission of this behaviour move beyond that first reef and spread, not only to nearby reefs, but across entire Ocean basins? Remember, we're not talking about natural selection by way of random mutation that slowly spreads through the generations, like fertilized eggs floating far on the Ocean currents. This is learned behaviour, enacted, copied and remembered by 'minds at work'.

How can we account for the long distance migration of such a unique and unlikely partnership?

A plausible explanation is that the long distance cultural transmission of the grouper/eel relationship is the result of a morphic resonance, set in motion by those first pioneers and strengthened with every subsequent discovery. The more often it happens the more likely it is to happen again. Thanks to the resonance of the collective memory of past discoveries, it would only take one grouper and eel partnership to form on a reef, for local cultural transmission to take care of the rest. In his book *The Presence of the Past*, Rupert Sheldrake provides several examples of how new patterns of behaviour have appeared in different populations of the same species, even when widely separated in both space and time.[8] If this is the case for our grouper/eel alliances, it points us in the direction of a continuing knowledge process, passed down through generations and spread across the Ocean by the resonance of a mind at work.

There is another tantalizing aspect to this relationship for us to ponder. How is it that the grouper is able to present this remarkable idea of joining forces to the eel in the first place? It's clear from observations that once the relationship is established, the grouper uses a slight shake of the head to signal to the eel that his services are required. Likewise he uses a head-down, pointing posture to indicate to the eel where the fish is hiding. But how did he convey the meaning of those gestures in the first place? What is the nature of this communication of meaning? Indeed, how does one mind communicate meaning to another without the use of language as we understand it?

Mind and Manta

The Poor Knights Marine Reserve in New Zealand plays occasional host to visiting manta rays during the summer months. They travel with the warm currents flowing south from the tropics and linger to enjoy a southern feast of shrimps and other plankton in the rich waters of the reserve. At this time of the year it's always worth spending a bit of time in the blue water, away from the reef walls, just in case you're lucky enough to see one.

Hovering ten metres below the surface, just outside Northern Arch, I was peering out towards the edge of visibility when out of the blue a massive shape emerged and headed straight for me. 'This is my lucky day', I thought as the manta ray slowly approached. He was a young male with a wingspan of about 3.5m, small by manta standards, but still much larger than their barbed cousins the stingrays, who gather at the Poor Knights to breed. The manta glided to a stop barely two metres from me and paused for a few moments, as if contemplating his next move. Then, with an almost imperceptible flicker of movement along his wings, he moved off. 'Well, that was nice while it lasted', I thought, expecting the young manta to swim off into the distance. Instead, he banked around gracefully and glided back to his position just a couple of metres in front of me, where to my amazement, he started manipulating his distinctive 'horns', first folding and un-folding, then rolling them into long 'cigars' in an impressive display of dexterity. These horns are known as *cephalic lobes*, and are normally used to funnel plankton-rich water into his cavernous mouth, but can be rolled up to reduce drag when not feeding.

In this case I felt sure that these gestures were directed towards me, and I found myself responding by imitating his movements with my hands and arms. To my delight he moved even closer until were within touching distance. Slowly he turned to one side, so that I was gazing straight into his right eye. At this point one of his attendant remora fish moved from its position near his gills on the underside of his body and attached itself directly over his eye. It appeared that the remora was actually cleaning the manta's eye. After about fifteen seconds it slid from his eye and returned to its original position. I was stunned!

Had the remora really been cleaning the manta's eye? And if so, had the manta somehow signalled his requirements to the remora? I certainly hadn't noticed any physical signs from the manta, but I had the distinct impression that he was somehow 'eyeing' me with greater clarity after the remora's ministrations. I'm not sure how long we floated there contemplating each other, but eventually he broke the spell with another slight flick of his wings. Rather than moving off though, he led me through a series of acrobatic barrel rolls and loops that I did my clumsy best to emulate. For ten minutes we played together and I managed to remember the camera in my hand and snap off a few shots before he finally approached me for the last time, gesturing once again with his horns, then turned and glided gracefully off into the blue. I was left floating and wondering about what had passed between us: an interspecies communication, but how much had I missed?

Upon reflection I have no doubt that the remora was indeed responding to the manta's request to have his eye cleaned. The question is: how did the manta ask for his eye to be cleaned? What signal passed between them? If it was physical then it was subtle in the extreme, but even if it was physical, the question would still remain as to how the meaning of his request was conveyed. Just as with the grouper and eel, the physical gesture can only convey meaning once that meaning has been agreed upon. Whereas the grouper's headshake carries a simple 'follow me' meaning that could be explained by means of trial and error, or repetition, the manta's request was far more complex. What kind of subtle movement would be required to distinguish between 'please clean my right eye', as opposed to 'my left eye needs cleaning', or 'I have an itch halfway along the leading edge of my right wing'? And then of course, there would need to be another signal to let the remora know when to stop.

After pondering this for many years, especially after my communion with the humpback mother, I've come to the conclusion that a much more likely explanation is that there was some kind of conscious communication involved: two minds exchanging meaning directly, without the clumsiness of symbolic gesturing. We call this kind of mental communication *telepathy*, which in our modern scientific reality is viewed as little more than a lingering fantasy from ages past, when we were still burdened by a belief in the supernatural. This direct communication of meaning may have been dismissed by mainstream science, but it is far from being disproved.[9] In fact, the now sizeable body of research that has been conducted suggests that rather than being supernatural, it is in fact, *super-natural*.[10]

When Minds Come Together

If we once grant the simple proposition that thought is a force, that it moves inevitably from its source to its object, the conclusion is inevitable that any thinking mind should be able to send its silent message to any other mind in the universe. There is nothing in the nature of either mind or matter to preclude such a possibility; only our present habit of speech, of too much speech, prevents us from viewing it frankly.
– William Long (1919) *How Animals Talk* [11]

The word telepathy literally means 'distance feeling' and refers to the ability to sense something beyond the limits of the physical senses. It's a word that almost never fails to illicit passionate debate between believers and non-believers, and yet these debates seldom make much head way: partly because the non-believers may feel threatened by any challenge to the current status quo of scientific 'wisdom', and partly because the believers can't provide any mechanism to explain these so-called supernatural – or paranormal – phenomena. If we first accept that in science, as with any knowledge process that 'we don't know what we don't know', then perhaps we can move beyond the prejudice of our ignorance, and acknowledge that there is some form of communication going on that we can't yet explain, but is nevertheless experienced by many.

This isn't the place for an in-depth review of the research into telepathy, but suffice to say, there is now clear, experimentally replicated and peer-reviewed evidence for direct mind to mind communication.[12] The search for a workable theory as to how telepathy and other paranormal aspects of the mind function, is leading researchers into the quantum world of particle/wave forms, non-locality and zero-point field theory.[13] Considering how little we understand about the so-called normal functioning of the mind, it seems counter-productive, even contradictory, to treat direct mind to mind communication as some kind of paranormal pariah from the wilderness of the unknown. Within this strange Universe of quantum entanglement it seems more sensible to remain open-minded and dispense with the *super* and *para* prefixes altogether. Then we're simply dealing with something *natural* and *normal* that we have yet to fully comprehend.

From this *normative* perspective, telepathy makes sound evolutionary sense. From the very beginning of life in the Ocean there was a need for organisms to clearly and precisely communicate meaning to each other. As life became ever more complex, the risk of ambiguity of meaning led to the development of increasingly sophisticated communication channels. Natural selection would have favoured forms of communication that provided the most direct and accurate transfer of meaning between organisms for the least energy expended. At a distance, some form of thought transfer would be the most efficient, especially if the two minds involved shared a common field of experience. Indeed, the concept of morphic fields and morphic resonance that we've already explored, would suggest that the closer the social bond is between organisms, the stronger their telepathic link is likely to be; our manta and his remora travelling companions for example.

It could be that this type of telepathic connection underlies all of our other sensory communication channels, working behind the scenes and only coming to the fore when needed or intentionally called upon – an evolutionary tool that we've all but forgotten. Perhaps this 'behind the scenes' activity may be what we experience as gut feelings and intuition, neither of which interfere with our physical senses, but seem to inform them nonetheless. Occasionally though, we appear to become more aware or open to this direct communication, perhaps through our own attention to it, or sometimes through the determined efforts of another's mind. But as William Long observed nearly 100 years ago, our habit of '… too much speech prevents us from viewing it frankly.'

Can our connection with Ocean Mind help us 'hear' other voices beyond our own? Our close sense of connection with dolphins may be a good place to start. Here are three examples to help us on our way.

Pictures in the Dolphin Mind

Frank Robson grew up surrounded by animals in rural Hawke Bay in New Zealand. From an early age he was aware of his ability to send mental images to the animals in his care, but never questioned it. It was only when he took up commercial fishing and got to know wild dolphins that he started to explore this gift.

> Out on the boat I could mentally leave my world…I could experience calmness and tranquility and give the dolphins my undivided attention… It was quite clear that the dolphins were able to read my thoughts and were well on the way to responding to them before I had time to utter a word…They appeared to be short-circuiting my thought processes and taking the word directly from my mind. This was the great breakthrough in my understanding of mental communication.

Frank Robson believed that the dolphins were responding to mental images forming in his mind, as projections of his thoughts. He practiced forming these 'thought images' and sending them outwards to the dolphins. He was able to demonstrate this skill to others with the help of Horace, a lone bottlenose dolphin, who had made himself at home in Hawke Bay. Over a nine-month period he and Horace formed a close bond, in which Frank was able to 'ask' Horace to perform various maneouvres, to the delight of onlookers. But for Frank this was more than mere party tricks to entertain the crowds. Rather, it was a step in a life-long journey of discovery that would take him around the world to meet dolphins and 'dolphin people', in an attempt to understand the 'pictures in a dolphin mind'.

> The great unanswered question is – what triggers off the picture transfer? What takes the image from my mind directly to that of the dolphin so that it immediately performs the action I have pictured? ...I don't know what activates it, but determination, compassion and concern seem to be involved. ...I ask myself – when an image passes from a human to a dolphin, how much is it the result of the human's effort, and how much is the dolphin picking up the image in the same way as it reads the layout of the sea and coastline around it? What is the dolphin ability? Can we protect the dolphins and whales from our destructiveness long enough to learn it from them?[14]

Project Interlock

In the 1970s pioneer diving couple, Wade and Jan Doak, started Project Interlock in a '... quest to discover the capacities of mind in the sea.' In their Polynesian-style Wharram catamaran, they sailed the northeast coast of New Zealand exploring the possibilities for interspecies communication with dolphins. With each interaction they extended their understanding of dolphin society, but they also noticed that the dolphins were responding to their 'invitations'. As Project Interlock progressed, Wade and Jan became convinced that the dolphins were able to link directly with their thoughts or intentions, and this was confirmed for them when they were late for a 'pre-arranged' meeting.

> We were heading south along the coast towards the Hen and Chicks Islands when I thought I saw a dolphin leap. ...It was during a hard gust and the catamaran was screaming along. ...Jan yelled to them, 'We can't get in the water and play with you out here. It's too rough. We'll see you in on the coast in the shelter of the land.' ...As we entered the lee, out of rough water, we suddenly saw the dolphins pop up just ahead. This was wonderful. They swam on the bow for quite some time [but] ... the conditions were still not good enough for us to leave the boat so Jan said, 'We'll see you up at Goat island'. There we knew it would be flat calm in the sheltered little cove. The dolphins vanished and we continued on our way.

Instead of sailing straight to Goat Island they decided to stop and dive on a reef first. Taking their time they finally anchored at Goat Island, only to learn that the dolphins had come into the bay about an hour earlier, jumping and playing in the shallows to the delight of onlookers, but had left soon afterwards.

> That was a great 'rap on the knuckles' for us. If we had not stopped; if we had just kept going without worrying about lunch and taking our time, as we intended, we would have been there with the dolphins. We had let them down! …Thinking it over I realized that we really expected the dolphins to stay with us, if they understood Jan's words. But from the dolphins' point of view that would be absurd – it would only mean they had followed us. With their speed what better response than to head off and wait our arrival?[15]

Of course we could just dismiss this episode as coincidence. Perhaps the dolphins were simply swimming along the coast and happened to stop in at Goat Island Bay, just as they had appeared again in the lee of the mainland after Jan's first message. But it's also possible that they were picking up on the mental images in Jan's mind, as she spoke her request to them; taking the meaning, not from her words, but from her thoughts, or possibly even her mental images of both places. If so, the fact that Wade and Jan altered their plans after the communication and then didn't inform the dolphins of their delay, would explain why the dolphins had already left by the time they arrived. After all, why wouldn't the dolphins expect them to keep their word?

The Long Way

In 1968 Bernard Moitessier, a French sailor competing in the first non-stop solo round the world yacht race, was approaching Stewart Island, New Zealand, in his boat Joshua. After months at sea and with thousands of nautical miles sailed, he was completely in-tune with the rhythms of the Ocean. With sails set and a course laid to clear a dangerous reef, he went below to cook some food and rest. Roused by a familiar whistling, he went on deck to discover at least 100 dolphins keeping pace with his boat.

> A tight line of 25 'porpoises' [dolphins] swimming abreast goes from stern to stem on the starboard side, in three breaths, then the whole group veers right and rushes off at right angles."… I watch wonder-

struck. More than ten times they repeat the same thing. ...I have never seen such a perfect ballet. And each time it is to the right that they rush off, ...They are obeying a precise command, that is for sure. ...They seem nervous; I don't understand. ...Something pulls me, something pushes me. I look at the compass. Joshua is running downwind at 7 knots straight for Stewart Island [and the dangerous reef] The steady west wind had shifted around to the south without me realizing it.

After correcting his course to steer Joshua out of danger, Moitessier went below to get dry, roll a cigarette and wonder about how long he had been off-course. When he went back on deck the dolphins were still there, but now they were behaving normally: bow riding and frolicking.

And then something wonderful happens: a big black and white porpoise jumps ten or twelve feet in the air, in a fantastic somersault, with two complete rolls. ...Three times he does his double roll, bursting with a tremendous joy, as if he were shouting to me and all the other porpoises: 'The man understood that they were trying to tell him to sail to the right...you understood...you understood...keep on like that, it's all clear ahead!'

After two hours all but two of the dolphins left Moitessier. The two that stayed behind took up positions on each side of Joshua's bow.

For three hours longer they swim like that, each isolated on his own side, without playing, setting their speed by Joshua's...I have never seen anything like it. Porpoises have never kept me company this long before. I am sure they were given the order to stay with me until Joshua was absolutely out of danger. ...I will round the Horn thanks to porpoises.[16]

A familiar theme runs through these three stories: in each case it seems that the dolphins are 'reaching into the minds' of the humans, accessing the meaning of words or images directly, perhaps even before the humans are aware of them themselves. In the case of Moitessier, he seems convinced that the dolphins somehow knew that he was completely unaware of the impending danger he was in. Perhaps they searched his mind for any signs that he was planning to alter course and, finding no such thoughts decided to act, even though the reef was still miles away.

We 'See' the World as we Believe it to be

There's another theme running through these stories: they are all lived experiences, mediated through the senses and working in unison with minds, alive to their own participation with the living Ocean. Unlike the scientific testing of telepathy, proved or disproved through experimental replication, the lived experience stands or falls solely on our ability to be present to it. Whether we embrace our experience or push it aside will largely depend on how well it fits within our wider belief systems – unless the experience is so powerful that it overrides our beliefs. The degree to which we resonate with others' experiences is also influenced by our beliefs and the strength of our own experiences.

Our beliefs are shaped by a combination of cultural inheritance, social norms and lived experience. The balance of these component parts determines the strength, and sometimes rigidity, of our beliefs. In our dominant Western culture, prevailing social norms and a scientific model, which on the whole still favours the materialist view of life as essentially physical and mechanistic, often overwhelm our lived experience. We've become conditioned to override our lived experience in favour of a scientific explanation of the facts that, by their very nature, are limited by the experiments designed to test them. Any experience that falls outside the facts of the accepted theory is either ignored or denied, particularly if that theory is considered a cornerstone of current scientific thought.

This has certainly been the case with telepathy, but as the supporting body of experimental evidence grows, we may see a re-balancing of our beliefs about direct mind-to-mind communication, in which we give equal value to our lived experience. With this more balanced approach, not only will we be more likely to acknowledge our own and others' experiences, but also, with solid scientific validation, we may find ourselves more inclined towards actively developing our own telepathic skills. From my own experience with the humpback mother, and from the dolphin examples above, it appears that in our warm-blooded Ocean cousins, we have willing and capable teachers. Indeed it may be that they've been our teachers for quite some time.

On Mornington Island, in the Gulf of Carpenteria in Northern Australia, lives a tribe of Aboriginies known as the Dolphin People. This tribe has been reported to be in direct communication with the wild bottlenose dolphins who reside just off the coast, and for many thousands of years as well. Their Shamans remain heir to a complex series of whistles that signal the dolphins to venture close to shore. Then the whistling first becomes more animated, and then stops altogether. The Shamans explain that, at that point, they begin to speak to the dolphins mind to mind. – Jim Nollman in Heathcote Williams (1985) *Whale Nation*[17]

The Ocean Really is Alive

Our living Ocean story has taken us into the depths of time – from the Ocean's physical formation to life's first beginnings and her coming into being as a living force. We've followed her slow and sometimes tumultuous journey towards the diverse and complex living system we are familiar with today. Along the way we've deepened our understanding of her physiological processes – respiration, circulation and metabolism – which we can now appreciate as the bodily functions of a living being, so vast that she influences every aspect of this beautiful Gaian system we call Planet Earth. We are, all of us, utterly dependent on her continued, healthy functioning.

But our journey has taken us much deeper than a purely physical exploration of her bodily functions. We've taken an emotionally charged ride into the richly sensual world of those who dwell within her liquid embrace. We've discovered an interconnected world, full of intelligence, sentience and awareness; a world where the growing complexity of the lived experience brought forth the art of communication and nourished its evolution as the very foundation of social living.

We've used a mixture of science, intuition and visualisation to delve into 'what it is like to be' and through some interactive living examples we've explored the emotional and social lives of just a few of the Ocean's myriad beings. The story that's emerged is one of contextual richness, emotional depth and interdependence. It's also the story of an emergent Ocean Mind capable of self-awareness, perhaps even self-reflection, out of which a deep sense of interbeing unfolds. Such is the richness of the Ocean, alive to herself and alive to us also if we are willing to take the plunge.

And so our living Ocean story comes to a close. But 'sadly' it's not the end of our journey. We can no longer stand upon her boundless shores and contemplate life, wild and limitless. Almost on a daily basis we are discovering that the Ocean does have limits. We are coming to realise that there's a price to pay for the centuries of wonton abuse we have inflicted upon her, and the disregard and contempt we have shown for her living nature. We are slowly waking up to the consequences of our actions as we ponder an ever-growing list of mortal threats to the Ocean's survival and therefore, our own!

Part Two

Re-visioning our Relationship

with the Living Ocean

10

Is the Ocean Really Dying?

It is a curious situation that the sea, from which life first arose, should now be threatened by the activities of one form of that life. But the sea, though changed in a sinister way, will continue to exist: the threat is rather to life itself.

– Rachel Carson

Coral bleaching – acidification – habitat loss – dead zones – toxic algal blooms – overfishing – species extinctions – biodiversity loss – destructive fishing technologies – oil spills – deep sea mining – heavy metal pollutants – plastic islands – micro-plastics – increased shipping – noise pollution – sea-level rise – sedimentation – agricultural runoff – melting ice shelves – Ocean warming – severe weather events. The list of threats facing the Ocean today is daunting to say the least.

Any one of them on their own is cause for concern and warrants immediate action, but taken together they represent an unprecedented threat to the very fabric of the Ocean as a living system, perhaps even to her very survival. Indeed, over the past two decades or so, the rhetoric from scientists, conservationists and even mainstream media has shifted from cautionary murmurings about overfishing, coral bleaching and pollution, to dire warnings of imminent collapse. A recent feature story in the prominent current affairs magazine *Newsweek*, was titled 'The Death of the Oceans'[1], while *Rolling Stone* magazine is warning of 'The Point of No Return'.[2] We are already witnessing the death of entire ecosystems, from coral reefs to deep sea 'cities', that we have barely discovered, let alone explored. But is the whole Ocean really in danger of dying?

To answer this question we first need to be clear about what we mean by dying and indeed, what we understand to be the living state. If we take a strictly biological approach and ask: is it possible that all biological life in the Ocean will be extinguished, then the answer is an – almost – emphatic 'No'. It's beyond imagining that the Ocean will become biologically dead any time in the foreseeable future. Life in the Ocean has survived, and mostly thrived, for around four billion years despite the occasional tumultuous upheaval. From this perspective, and given the long list of calamities above, a more relevant question would be: what kind of life might we expect to see in the Ocean of the future, and how well will she be able to fulfill her role as primary contributor to Gaia, the living planet?

I think there's a deeper question here, and it concerns much of what we've been exploring in the previous four chapters: the Ocean's living essence, her sentience, intelligence and the interconnectedness that emerges as Ocean Mind. What becomes of this living state of interconnectedness, this *Ocean Spirit*, when all the dolphins and whales are silenced; when the sharks, mantas, tuna and turtles no longer roam far and wide; when the collective minds of the great sardine schools fade into memory; when the reef cities become ghost towns, their remaining inhabitants dwelling within the crumbling skeletons of once vibrant, coral castles? How can the living *Soul* of the Ocean survive such loss, becoming little more than an empty shell, bereft of all but the shadow of her once vibrant spirit? For surely this is the *death* we risk if we continue with 'business as usual'.

Time for an Ocean 'Check-up'

There's no doubt that the deterioration of the Ocean's wellbeing is a direct result of our actions, but what state is she actually in? It's important to acknowledge and take responsibility for the damage we've wrought, but before we can turn responsibility into *response-ability* we need a clear understanding of the effects of our actions. When we're faced with such a long list of overlapping maladies it becomes difficult to isolate specific cause and effect relationships, so rather than trying to deal with each symptom in isolation, we'll take a more holistic approach and aim for an insightful overview of the Ocean's current state of health.

We'll frame our holistic Ocean Check-up by looking at how her physiology is being affected by the various man-made influences she is subjected to. To help us gain an overall picture we can group these anthropogenic (human-induced) influences into three broad categories:

Climate change: including greenhouse gas emissions, Ocean warming and sea-level rise.

Pollution: including plastic pollution, heavy metals and persistent organic pollutants, land-based runoff as well as noise pollution.

Industrial scale fishing: including overfishing, destructive fishing technologies, habitat loss, aquaculture and loss of biodiversity.

This approach will help us identify how these various causes inter-connect to undermine her overall wellbeing.

Before we get started though, we need to be clear about our motives. A big part of the reason we are facing such a dramatic and potentially catastrophic ecological collapse, is our self-inflicted 'separation' from the rest of life, and our predominantly selfish perspective of 'what's in it for us?' In other words, if we are only motivated with how we as a species will be affected by the demise of the Ocean, rather than from concern for the Ocean herself, we run the risk of remaining preoccupied with quick fix solutions – such as *geo-engineering* – that may suit us in the short term, but will do little to change the underlying causes. It's important that we leave behind our somewhat arrogant belief that we have the right to save or destroy. Rather, we need to show a little more humility by accepting that we simply aren't qualified to hold that power and instead, embrace the understanding that the only thing that is truly within our power to change is our own behaviour.

The Ocean will heal herself if we give her the chance.

Anthropogenic Climate Change

As we've come to understand, Gaia's climate is an intimate dance between the life process and the planet's geophysical forces, and like any good dance, there's a dynamic fluidity to the movement, which allows for creative expression, but nevertheless keeps to an overall rhythm. The beat of Gaia's climate dance has seen dramatic pauses in the past, including the five mass extinction episodes. Each of these rhythmic changes has been preceded by a prolonged build-up over thousands, or even tens of thousands of years, before reaching their dramatic crescendo. This allowed time for some species to adapt to the changing tempo and ensured that enough of life's dancers were left to pick up the beat and carry on the dance.

A key trigger for change in all these events was a dramatic rise in the level of 'greenhouse gases', primarily carbon dioxide and methane. The causes behind the build-up of these gases have varied, but the lesson for us is that it's the *speed* of change, rather than the total amount, that seems to have the biggest impact on the ability of individual species, as well as whole ecosystems to adapt, and therefore survive.[3] During the five mass extinction episodes it was the Ocean that bore the brunt of the extinctions, but it was also the Ocean that Gaia largely relied upon to bounce back, pick up the beat and inject life's movement back into the climate dance.

Anthropogenic climate change is causing greenhouse gases to rise at an unprecedented rate. At just over 400ppm (parts per million) they are already 40 percent above pre-industrial levels, and higher than they have been for at least the last 800,000 years.[4] Even if we manage to stabilize the rate of our current emissions, it's predicted that we will more than double pre-industrial levels by the end of this century.[4] Just to put this rate of increase into context, we can compare it with the largest mass extinction of all – the late Permian extinction 250 million years ago – when 95 percent of Ocean species became extinct. Leading up to the Permian extinction there was intense volcanic activity that spewed out an estimated 100,000 billion tons of carbon dioxide over a period of 18,800 years, amounting to somewhere around five billion tons per year. In contrast we are currently emitting 32.3 billion tons per year. In other words we are emitting carbon dioxide into the atmosphere at a dramatically faster rate than that associated with the largest mass extinction of life the Ocean has ever experienced.[5]

So, lets examine how this rapid change is affecting Ocean physiology.

Acid Stomach

The Ocean's pH (acidity-alkalinity balance) is critical to the healthy functioning of her physiology, but she must walk a delicate chemical 'tightrope' in which this balance is strongly influenced by the equilibrium-seeking dynamics of gas exchange with the atmosphere. As more carbon dioxide is emitted into the atmosphere the Ocean is compelled to absorb as much as is required to maintain equilibrium - she has absorbed around a third of the carbon dioxide we have emitted since the industrial revolution. When carbon dioxide dissolves in the Ocean it produces carbonic acid, which in turn releases hydrogen ions, and the more hydrogen ions there are, the more acidic the water becomes. Acidity has already increased by 30 percent since the latter half of last century, and at current carbon dioxide emission levels it's predicted to rise to 150 percent by the middle of this century, faster than at any other time in the last 65 million years.[6]

The implications for the Ocean's physiology are far-reaching. The acidity of the water affects the ability of calcifying organisms, such as oysters, shrimps and corals, to secrete their hard shells and skeletons. Most of them have evolved to thrive in a slightly alkaline Ocean in which the chemical balance of dissolved inorganic carbons enables them to build their calcium carbonate shells, stony skeletons and elaborate internal structures. But as the Ocean becomes more acidic many of them will find it increasingly difficult to build new structures, or even maintain existing ones.

Already the Ocean's coral reef cities are being affected. Researchers are finding that coral skeletons on some reefs now contain less carbonate by volume than they used to, which not only slows their growth, but also weakens their structural integrity, making them more susceptible to damage from increasingly intense storm events.[7] It may be only a matter of decades before some parts of the Ocean become so acidic that corals will no longer be able to construct new skeletons at all, and existing skeletons will corrode and crumble. But it's not only corals that are affected. Coral reefs rely on a type of encrusting *coralline* algae that literally cements the reef together. The type of calcium carbonate that the algae secrete is particularly susceptible to corrosion. If we continue as we are, the reef cities could become little more than a memory by the end of this century.[8]

An even bigger cause for concern is the effect acidification is having on the very small calcifiers: the many and varied species who live in the rich plankton layer at the Ocean's surface, as well as on the Ocean floor. The surface layer is bearing the brunt of acidification, especially in polar regions, where the colder water holds more CO_2 than warmer climes. Some parts of the Arctic have already become too corrosive for the tiny, but plentiful pteropod: a free-swimming, planktonic snail that is the keystone species in the entire Arctic food web. They build their beautiful transparent shells from the carbonate-saturated waters, but as acidity increases carbonate saturation decreases, and their shells literally dissolve into nothing. Without pteropods the Arctic food web will collapse, meaning death by starvation for those that feed directly on them, leading to a cascading decline in all other species. This could become a reality in as little as 50 years if acidification continues on its current trajectory.[9]

Polar acidification is further increased by melting ice shelves, and it's now apparent that Antarctic waters are on the same corrosive trajectory as is already being experienced by the pteropods in parts of the Arctic. What effect this may have on Antarctic krill is still unclear but the signs aren't promising. Studies so far suggest that acidification levels predicted for the end of the century will interrupt their embryonic development, preventing normal growth into adulthood.[10]

The Ocean's metabolism will undoubtedly be severely affected by acidification, but the ramifications don't end there – her respiration is also under threat as the corrosive effects of our carbon emissions begin to eat their way into the delicate chalky bodies of coccolithophores and other calcifying phytoplankton. It's uncertain yet how well coccolithophores and their photosynthesizing comrades will fare in more corrosive seas, but apart from the potential risk to their chalky bodies, acid waters will reduce the availability of iron, essential for their growth.[11] Given their major role as the 'lungs' of the Ocean, as well as the fundamental part they play in her metabolism, not forgetting their contribution to the sulphur cycle, we'd better hope that they find a way to cope with our acid 'breath'.

Ocean Fever

The Ocean has a burning 'fever' and it's a direct result of human-induced climate change. She has absorbed at least 90 percent of the extra heat caused by our greenhouse gas emissions since the start of the industrial revolution. Even so, her average surface temperature has only risen by a modest 0.7°C, but because of her enormous size and the complexity of her circulatory system, we didn't really notice the severity of her growing fever until recently. With the development of more sophisticated measuring equipment, scientists have discovered that over the past few decades her temperature has been rising up to 55 percent faster than previously thought. Most of the extra warmth has been accumulating in shallow waters above 700 metres, but more recently measurements are revealing that the deep Ocean has started to warm as well.[12]

Adding to the complexity of the picture is the fact that warming varies widely for different parts of the Ocean. In particular, polar regions have warmed much more than the global average, as have parts of the north Atlantic, such as Europe's North and Baltic Seas. But once again, it's the rate of warming that's causing climate scientists so much concern. Even the remote vastness of the Pacific has warmed faster in the last six decades than it has in the previous 10,000 years. In addition, there are complex decadal oscillations in both the Atlantic and Pacific which influence how much, and how fast, extra heat caused by our emissions gets absorbed.[13] These and many other factors render predictive modelling of Ocean warming more of an art form than a reliable science. Even so, the implications of this rapid warming for the Ocean's physiology are very disturbing indeed.

One of the first effects to be noticed was the phenomenon of coral bleaching. This happens when coral colonies become stressed by periods of excessively high water temperatures. Their stress response is to expel the symbiotic algae that live within their fleshy polyps. In return for safe lodgings the photosynthesizing algae not only supply the bulk of the corals' food, but also give them their kaleidoscopic colours. Without them, corals face a slow death by starvation and within a few weeks all that remains of the colony is their deathly white skeleton. Mass coral bleaching events, affecting entire reef systems, have been on the rise in the last two decades and are predicted to become yearly events by the middle of this century.[14] Even as I write, Ocean scientists have just announced that 2015/16 may see the worst global bleaching event on record.

There are other even more worrying effects. Oxygen is the magic ingredient that fuels the Ocean's metabolism, but warm water holds less dissolved oxygen than cold, so as the Ocean warms many creatures will find it increasingly difficult to breathe. But the problem's not just limited to the surface layers. As we learned in Chapter 4, the deep Ocean relies to a large extent on the thermohaline to deliver oxygen from surface waters, so as surface oxygen declines, the deep Ocean will suffer in turn.

For various reasons, some mid-depth areas of the Ocean naturally contain less oxygen than others. Known as *oxygen minimum zones*, they are increasing in size as the Ocean warms, and new areas covering millions of square kilometres, are forming at an alarming rate. In these zones oxygen levels are so low that virtually no oxygen-dependent life can survive.[15] Most worrying is that they have appeared in three out of the four major eastern boundary current upwellings, traditionally some of the most productive areas in the entire Ocean. Changing wind and current patterns caused by warming are partly to blame for these zones, but as we'll see, both pollution and overfishing are also contributing to this growing catastrophe. The Ocean may be heading for a period of low oxygen, where those with high oxygen needs (pelagic fish, sharks and so on) will struggle, but those with low oxygen needs, such as jellyfish, will thrive.

Perhaps the most frightening impact on the Ocean's metabolism, as well as her respiration, is the sharp decline in global phytoplankton. A review of phytoplankton records taken since 1899 shows that the Ocean has lost as much as 40 percent of her phytoplankton biomass, with most of this loss occurring since the mid 20th century.[16] Scientists believe this dramatic decline is due to warmer surface waters, which are increasing the thermocline stratification of the water column, preventing essential nutrients being recycled back to the surface.[17] Phytoplankton are at the very core of the Ocean's metabolism. Wherever phytoplankton populations decline, entire food webs will suffer.

Nutrient availability is the primary limiting factor for phytoplankton growth – we've already seen that acidification can affect the availability of iron – and now we can see how warming is limiting other essential nutrients as well. The loss of oxygen-producing phytoplankton will of course exacerbate the Ocean's oxygen depletion, but we should also remember the critical role they play in the global carbon cycle and the positive climate feedback loop their loss will create. The complex relationship between phytoplankton, oxygen levels and carbon cycling may be the single most important factor in the whole climate change story. During the 'great dying' of the Permian extinction, the Ocean suffered from a dramatic loss in both oxygen and phytoplankton, and this may have led to the release of massive quantities of poisonous hydrogen sulphide gas from the Ocean floor, 'snuffing out' the vast majority of Ocean life, as well as 70 percent of terrestrial life.[18]

We're all familiar with tragic images of polar bears swimming in open expanses of water, or clinging precariously to tiny ice floes where once there was solid sea ice, but there are even more disturbing ramifications to the retreating ice fields. As mentioned earlier, polar regions of the Ocean are warming faster than most, partly due to a positive feedback loop caused by melting ice. The white surface of the ice reflects about 80 percent of the sun's warmth back into space, but as it melts the dark surface of the exposed Ocean absorbs 95 percent of that warmth, leading to even higher temperatures and more melting. It's predicted that the Arctic Ocean will have ice-free summers by 2040. But it's not just the sea ice that's melting, it's also Greenland's ice sheet. As it recedes, vast fields of methane gas, locked in permafrost on the Ocean floor for millions of years, are being exposed. As the warmer water melts the permafrost, massive plumes of this powerful greenhouse gas will be released, adding yet another positive feedback loop to the warming equation.[19]

The accumulating meltwater in the Arctic could potentially interfere with the thermohaline circulation. During previous warming events over the last 120,000 years, meltwater has caused the thermohaline to slow down, or even stop, with highly unpredictable repercussions.[20] At the present rate of Arctic warming this could become a reality in a matter of decades. The Ocean has been through this kind of circulatory upheaval many times before and has taken it in her stride, but many of her inhabitants will have to adjust their lifestyles, migrating to warmer or cooler waters as required, or following food supplies as circulation patterns change. But those who are unable to move may not be so lucky.

Rising Tide

Sea-level change is nothing new for the Ocean; in fact it is in a continuous state of flux. The difference, once again, is the speed of change. The rate of sea-level rise has doubled in the past two decades, and predictions are that it is going to speed up even more. Two factors contribute to sea-level rise – expansion of the water as it warms, and the melting of ice shelves. Melting sea ice doesn't contribute to sea-level rise as it's already floating on the Ocean. Both the Greenland ice sheet and the West Antarctic ice shelf are melting much faster than predicted, and may have reached a stage of positive feedback that will lead to a sea-level rise of at least two metres by the end of this century.[21]

There are obvious and disastrous ramifications for coastal dwellers, but our focus here is on how this rapid sea-level rise will affect the Ocean herself. By itself it probably wouldn't be too much of an issue, but with the cumulative effects of other factors it may become a disastrous tipping point for a wide range of shallow water ecosystems. For example, coral reefs would normally be able to grow their calcified skeletons fast enough to keep their living tissue close to the sun-drenched surface, but with the combination of acidification, increased extreme storms and coral bleaching, many reefs will struggle to keep pace with the rising waters.[22] Other coastal ecosystems, such as mangrove forests and seagrass beds, may struggle even more. These areas are critically important nurseries for the juveniles of many species, as well as natural filtration areas for sediment runoff from the land.[23]

Perhaps the most worrying and potentially damaging aspect of rapid sea-level rise is one that the Ocean has never before had to contend with. As her liquid body inundates low-lying land she will be flooding through some of the most industrialized and polluted areas that humanity has yet produced, including some of the largest mega-cities on the planet. This 'mother load' of toxic filth will exacerbate an already deadly problem.

Pollution

From an ecological perspective, pollution is a sign of biological imbalance. If one or more species undergoes a population explosion, the usually beneficial chemical or nutrient waste products of their metabolism, overwhelm the system and become toxic. A classic example is the great oxidation event, some 2.5 billion years ago, when cyanobacteria conquered the primordial Ocean with their newly invented photosynthesis and created an ecological crisis with their metabolic waste product, oxygen (Chapter 2). Our own population explosion since the industrial revolution has also lead to a biological imbalance on a global scale, but the waste stream we have created goes well beyond metabolic waste. We're not only polluting the Ocean with chemicals and nutrients at toxic levels, but we're also choking her with plastic and deafening her with noise pollution.

Too Much of a Good Thing

Most rivers lead to the Ocean. They carry with them much-needed nutri-ents from the land, but now they now also carry the leftovers from our oil-fed industry, agriculture and transport, as well as our treated (and un-treated) sewerage and 'waste' water. The result is a toxic overload of chemicals and nutrients that are creating coastal *dead zones* where nothing but bacteria can survive. Like other oxygen minimum zones, these dead zones are starved of oxygen, but in this case it's an over-supply of nutri-ents like nitrogen and phosphorous that's causing the problem. These nu-trients fuel unnaturally massive plankton blooms that overwhelm the best efforts of filter feeders to keep them in check. When plankton die and sink to the bottom, they trigger an explosion of bacterial decomposition, which uses up all the available oxygen. Any oxygen-breathing organisms not fast enough to escape literally die of asphyxiation.

In the Gulf of Mexico a dead zone the size of Connecticut and Rhode Island States combined is fed by millions of tons of petroleum based, syn-thetic fertilisers used in intensive farming across the Mississippi delta.[24] Every spring when the dead zone forms, the sea floor is littered with dead fish, crabs, shrimp, worms and shellfish. Another massive dead zone fills Northern Europe's Baltic Sea, where agricultural, industrial and urban ef-fluent has overwhelmed this semi-closed sea's limited circulation. Scien-tists have now identified 400 dead zones worldwide, covering a quarter of a million square kilometres, but it's estimated that there could be as many as a thousand or more coastal dead zones in the Ocean.

Nutrient-soaked runoff from the land is also fueling the rapid growth of smothering blankets of algae that literally choke the life out of tropical coral reefs, temperate rocky reefs, seagrass beds and sandy lagoons. These so-called *nutrient indicator algae* (NIA) form dense filamentous mats, block-ing out the sunlight crucial for photosynthesizing corals; clogging the pores of filter feeders such as sponges; strangling the tentacled polyps of anemones and corals; and burying sand-dwellers such as shellfish and other invertebrates under a thick layer of algae. Overfishing of grazers such as parrotfish and sea urchins, often exacerbates the NIA problem. For a reef already stressed by coral bleaching, overfishing and acidification, there's no way back once the algae takes hold. Up to 80 percent of the Car-ibbean's corals reefs are affected, many of them now nothing more than NIA covered skeletons.[25]

Another phenomenon related to excess nutrients is toxic algal blooms, also known as *red tides* – so named for the reddish coloured slick covering the surface during a bloom. These happen when particular plankton species bloom, releasing potent bio-toxins, which can build up in filter feeding organisms such as shellfish, poisoning anything that eats them. Plankton-eating fish are also at high risk of ingesting the bio-toxins, which in turn affects their predators including other fish, sharks, whales and dolphins. Marine mammals are also in grave danger of inhaling the toxins when they come to the surface to breath.

Worldwide, the death of whales, dolphins, seals, dugongs and manatees due to toxic algal blooms numbers in the tens, possibly hundreds, of thousands. Indeed, red tides have now become a yearly event in Florida, killing more endangered manatees than any other cause - 149 in just one year. Red tides occur naturally when wind and currents bring deep-water nutrients to the surface, but the combined influence of excess nutrient run-off from human activity and changing wind and current patterns caused by climate change, has seen their frequency and severity skyrocket in the past few decades.[26]

Persistent Organic Pollutants and Heavy Metal Poisoning

Our toxic lifestyles are producing an even deadlier threat to the health and wellbeing of the Ocean and all her beings, not only threatening her physiology, but her psyche as well. The Ocean is now a poisonous soup of heavy metals, along with a suite of man-made chemical concoctions collectively known as *Persistent Organic Pollutants* (POPs). These include many chemicals now banned in some countries (such as DDT, PCBs and dioxins) but as the name suggests, once in the Ocean they persist for many decades, even centuries. What's worse is that they accumulate in the bodies of Ocean beings, starting with plankton, and working their way in ever increasing concentrations through virtually every Ocean food web. This process of *bio-magnification* reaches its climax in apex predators such as tuna, swordfish, sharks and marine mammals, who can end up with accumulated toxins many thousands of times more concentrated than in the surrounding water.[27]

The effects of these poisons on the immune systems are severe, even life-threatening, but they also play havoc with hormones produced by the endocrine system, which not only affect reproductive health and neurological function, but can also lead to tumors and various cancers. For example, mercury, which makes its way into the Ocean via the burning of coal and other industrial air pollution, has been shown to cause severe neurological dysfunction, fatigue, depression, tremors and heart disease in some marine mammals. Dolphins killed in the yearly slaughter at Japan's Taiji Cove have been measured with more than 100 times the level of mercury considered to be safe.[28] The growing number of marine mammal fatalities associated with POPs is alarming, as are the ramifications for all Ocean life, not least of which is the effect they are having on the mental health of many Ocean dwellers. Some areas of the Ocean are more affected than others, but there is nowhere that Ocean beings can escape the inevitable accumulation of these deadly toxins.

Plastic 'Indigestion'

The spectre of Ocean plastic pollution is now well publicized; most of us have heard of the 'Great Pacific Garbage Patch' in the North Pacific Gyre, and many will be aware of similar accumulations of plastic in the other four sub-tropical gyres (Chapter 4). While the gyres do act as irresistible vortices, plastic is another one of our pollutants that has now reached every part of the Ocean's body, not just on the surface. About half of all plastics are denser than water and will eventually sink, so even the depths of her great body are becoming clogged with plastic fragments of all sizes.

The scale of plastic pollution is staggering: it's conservatively estimated that there are at least 5.25 trillion plastic pieces, ranging in size from less than 1mm to larger than 200mm, floating at the surface.[29] The amount that's below the surface is anyone's guess, but based on the latest models as well as benthic surveys around different parts of the continental shelves, it would appear that the plastic problem may be analogous to an iceberg: with the vast majority hidden below the surface.[30] It's sobering to think that plastic has really only been widely used for around six decades, and yet it is now one of the Ocean's biggest challenges. She has never faced an ecological crisis quite like this, and every year it's getting worse by an estimated eight million tons: that's equivalent to about 15 grocery bags full of plastic for every metre of coastline on the planet.[31]

The Ocean's metabolism is severely impacted by this plastic invasion in two ways. At the surface plastic photo-degrades and breaks up into smaller and smaller pieces. These micro-plastics act as sponges, soaking up POPs, as well as giving off their own toxins. Micro-plastics are ingested by plankton and other small beings, such as the hugely important and prolific lantern fish, who are in turn eaten by larger fish and so on until the entire Ocean food web is permeated with plastic. These toxic time bombs then accumulate in larger beings: tuna, sharks, swordfish, squid, marine mammals etc, releasing their poisonous load into the fatty tissues, muscles, circulatory and nervous systems, adding to their toxic distress.

The other impact of plastic ingestion is equally devastating; indeed some of the individual tragedies involved are truly heartbreaking. In a report just released it's estimated that at least 90 percent of the world's seabirds have ingested plastic from the Ocean, and it's not just adult birds that are suffering. Most species of seabirds forage at the Ocean's surface, returning to land to feed their hungry chicks.[32] Tragically, these doting parents are inadvertently regurgitating plastic instead of food into the waiting mouths of their young. Chicks of all species are dying in their millions, either by intestinal blockages or through slow and agonizing starvation because their guts are so full of plastic that there's no room for food.

Plastic ingestion is having a similarly devastating impact on turtles – 50 to 80 percent of turtles found dead or dying have plastic in their gut.[33] So too are whales, dolphins and seals succumbing, as plastic bags, hard plastic items, synthetic ropes and discarded fishing gear get lodged in their throats and block their digestive tracts. The number of whales and dolphins washing up on beaches with ingested plastic is increasing alarmingly, but this may be another 'iceberg' situation, where these beached whales are just a fraction of the real numbers being killed by our addiction to plastic.

Drowning in a Sea of Sound

In Chapter 7 we got a sense of how critically important sound is in the lives of many Ocean dwellers, not only as a form of communication, but also for navigating, hunting, mating and even finding a suitable home. But in the past half-century or so, the natural sounds of the Ocean have been increasingly drowned out by more and more noise pollution from our industrial activities. This noise pollution comes in two forms: background noise and sudden, explosive sound bursts.

Background noise comes primarily from shipping – although in localized areas offshore installations such as wind farms and oilrigs contribute significantly. In the last six decades the number of large ship propellers thrumming through the water has risen exponentially, as have the size of the ships, and consequently the volume of their noise. A large container ship will emit a constant roar in the range of about 90 decibels, which travels in all directions for long distances. With many thousands of ships plying the Ocean today, it's estimated that on average, background noise is eight times louder than it was in the 1950s.[34] Not surprisingly, all this background noise is having a huge impact on the lives of Ocean dwellers, affecting long range whale communication, dolphin sonar, fish mating, hunting and so on. But it's also causing increased anxiety and stress, with related long-term health risks.[35]

Sudden explosive noises from seismic testing associated with oil and gas exploration, military sonar, sea floor surveying and underwater detonations have a more immediate and lethal impact. Marine mammals are especially vulnerable, as their sensitive internal air spaces can suffer traumatic damage from the intense pressure waves caused by the violent blasts. Ocean-wide the number of whale and dolphin deaths attributed to sudden noise trauma is in the tens of thousands, some washing up dead on beaches with blood seeping from ruptured ear canals, while others are driven ashore in mass strandings, either in overwhelmed confusion or in an attempt to escape the intense pain of the blasts.[36]

Industrial-scale Fishing:
Stealing the Ocean's Life-force

It took humans roughly 50,000 years to deplete the planet's large land animals, 5000 years to exhaust most of the planet's coastal environments, 500 years to fish out the continental shelf, 50 years to impoverish the open ocean and 5 years to run through the creatures of the deep ocean.
– Alanna Mitchell, (2008) Sea Sick

We continue to denude the Ocean of her life-force at a rate many times faster than any of the mass extinctions of the past, and in the process we are causing the total, or near total ecological collapse of the vast majority of commercially targeted fish species. We have already removed 90 percent of the large predator fish and are now working our way down the trophic levels, to ever more fundamental species within Ocean food-webs, often with destructive fishing techniques that destroy their habitat and therefore any chance of recovery.[37]

In the past two centuries, and especially in the last 50 years, species after species have succumbed to our profit-driven greed. A 2006 paper published in the esteemed scientific journal *Nature* predicts the total collapse of all commercial fisheries by 2048 unless there is urgent change in fishing practices. The title of that paper, *Impacts of Biodiversity Loss on Ocean Ecosystem Services*, highlights the wider ramifications of our insatiable appetite, but even here, the reference to 'ecosystem services' reflects our prevailing attitude of 'what's in it for us'.[38] Despite the dire warnings of this and many other scientific reports and papers, the fishing industry as a whole, as well as the majority of fisheries scientists, continue to focus solely on single species and their exploitation for maximum profit.

A stark example of this 'profit before sustainability' mentality is the fact that more than one third of wild-caught fish are ground up and used as feed to grow high-profit farmed species, such as salmon and shrimps. It takes 2.5kg of wild-caught fish to produce just 1kg of farmed salmon. The tragedy for the Ocean's wellbeing is that it's the hugely important foraging species like anchovies, menhaden, sardines and pilchards that are being decimated to supply the highly profitable, but ecologically disastrous aquaculture industry.[39]

While organisations like The Food and Agricultural Organisation of the United Nations (FAO) concentrate on overall tonnages, fish consumption per capita, 'catch per unit effort' and socio-economic development (all within the optimistically titled *Blue Growth* framework that at least in principle, recognizes these wider implications) the prevailing attitude is still one of resource exploitation for 'maximum sustainable profit'.[40] The current estimated commercial tonnage of wild-caught Ocean beings is approximately 79 million tons per year, but this doesn't include the estimated 26 million tons taken illegally and a further 39 million tons discarded as by-catch.[41,42] These yearly tonnages represent a declining catch, which peaked in the mid 1990s. But the numbers only tell part of the story, and in fact mask what is described by some marine scientists, as the …'precipice of a major extinction event.'[43]

Another important, but often ignored, consideration is how much effort is required to catch the same amount of fish today as compared to past ages. Taking into account man-hours and energy used, it takes on average 17 times more effort to catch the equivalent amount of fish today as it did at the beginning of the 20th century.[44] Not only this, but fisherman now have to travel further, with ever more sophisticated equipment to maintain even these dwindling numbers. Every night long-lines bristling with millions upon millions of baited hooks – enough to encircle the planet 500 times – are set across the Ocean.[45] Hundreds of thousands of kilometres of nets are deployed everyday, either towed behind ever more powerful trawlers, anchored to the bottom as set-nets or set adrift on the high seas. Tens of thousands of kilometres of these nets are lost or discarded every year, and the heavily subsidized global fishing industry simply 'writes-off' this loss as part of standard operating costs.

The cost to the Ocean though is incalculable.

Habitat Destruction and Fishing Pollution

Individual species, as well as whole ecosystems, are being annihilated by this wholesale slaughter, with virtually no regard for the suffering of the countless billions of lives, nor the Ocean's overall wellbeing. The price we pay for our shrimp cocktail, smoked salmon or fish sushi doesn't take into account the staggering degradation of Ocean environs through destructive fishing technologies, nor does it encompass the horrific impact that lost or discarded fishing gear has on Ocean life. It pays no heed to the substantial contribution that the world's commercial fishing fleet makes to carbon emissions – 1.2 percent of the total world oil usage – and therefore Ocean acidification, warming, sea-level rise, direct pollution of the Ocean through overboard discharge, and of course, noise pollution.[46]

Besides the sheer volume of life being dragged from the Ocean, it's the shamelessly destructive way in which we are doing it that is also causing unprecedented damage to her living systems. Bottom trawling and dredging for species such as orange roughy, hake, hoki, squid, shrimp, scallops and oysters is the most destructive and wasteful. By-catch in this highly unselective fishing method can be as high as 80 to 90 percent of the overall catch. Whole benthic communities including sponges, corals, starfish, shellfish and crustaceans are uprooted, crushed and torn to pieces as the heavily weighted net or dredge gouges its way across the Ocean floor. Every year industrial-sized trawlers 'bulldoze' an area equal to half the Ocean's continental shelves, destroying entire ecosystems that have been part of her complex living process for millennia.

Habitat destruction is a predominant feature of the aquaculture industry. Mangrove forests in particular bear the brunt of this rapidly expanding alternative to fishing. Nearly 40 percent of mangroves worldwide have been destroyed, the majority have made way for shrimp and fish farms, mainly in areas where mangroves are the best, and sometimes only, defense against rising sea-levels. Of greater concern for the Ocean's wellbeing is that mangroves are the primary nursery areas for the juveniles of count-less Ocean beings.[47]

Entanglement in lost, discarded or carelessly placed fishing gear is the other great destroyer of the Ocean's vibrancy. Every year millions of sharks, turtles, dolphins, whales, mantas, seals and seabirds end their lives in a desperate and terrifying struggle to free themselves from ghost-nets, abandoned long-lines, set-nets, lobster pots and so-called shark-nets (a barbaric and outdated policy of setting nets parallel to popular swimming and surfing beaches to 'protect' human users – still being used in Austra-lia). Researchers estimate that worldwide at least 800 cetaceans die every-day in nets and other fishing gear, making entanglement the biggest dan-ger they face.[48] In New Zealand the world's rarest dolphin – Maui's Dol-phin – is dying at a rate many times faster than their meagre population of around 45 can reproduce, because set-nets are still being used in their breeding area. And it's not just commercial and industrial fishing that are creating this entanglement nightmare. Recreational fishing is one of the most popular pastimes in many parts of the world, but as every angler knows, a day's fishing nearly always includes losing gear to snagged lines on the bottom.

Biodiversity = Resilience: Loss of Biodiversity = Collapse

The Ocean's metabolism has evolved over billions of years into a finely tuned, nutrient-cycling process of mind-boggling complexity, and in the process given birth to a truly awe-inspiring collection of diverse beings. This biodiversity is the cornerstone of Gaia's ability to maintain habitable conditions over geological time, as well as her ability to bounce back from tumultuous upheavals. The wholesale removal of so much life can't help but impact on the Ocean's metabolism and the recycling of nutrients, but equally important, the loss of biodiversity reduces her resilience to all the other calamitous health issues caused by pollution and climate change.

By way of example we need only remind ourselves of the critical link between nutrient-rich whale poo and phytoplankton abundance in places like Antarctica and the Gulf of Maine (Chapter 5). With the wanton slaugh-ter of whales throughout the Ocean, entire food webs were impoverished. Scientists point the finger at Ocean warming as the main culprit for phyto-plankton decline over the past century, but this also corresponds with the worst atrocities committed by the industrialised whaling fleets. How much more resilient to rapid warming would the Ocean be if she still had robust populations of whales, and other large beings like tuna, to help keep her phytoplankton supplied with nutrients!

Another example of how the loss of biodiversity from overfishing threatens her resilience is apparent in the 'rotten egg' stench of hydrogen sulphide bubbling to the surface from a dead zone off the coast of Namibia. This dead zone's growth results from a combination of changing wind patterns caused by climate change and overfishing of sardines. Phytoplankton feast on the extra up-welled nutrients from the stronger offshore winds, causing a population explosion, but these same winds blow zooplankton away before they can eat enough of them to avoid massive phytoplankton die-off and eventual oxygen depletion. In the past the Ocean was able to rely on the seasonal proliferation of sardines to keep the phytoplankton in check, but recent industrial overfishing has decimated the sardine population, meaning they can no longer play their part in this complex ecological dance.

Ethical Considerations

These examples give a taste of the complex ramifications of our unbridled pillaging of the Ocean's life-force; but while scientists, politicians, policy makers, and even most conservation organizations focus on the physical, environmental and economic costs of destructive overfishing, very few consider the devastating impact our actions are having from an animal welfare perspective. In Chapter 8 we touched on the moral and ethical implications of our exploitation of Ocean beings when we looked at the fish-pain controversy, but this is really only the tip of another iceberg if we embrace the Ocean as a living, sentient and minded being, alive to herself through the complex, emotional lives of all her offspring.

Can we begin to imagine the intense fear that must surely pulse through the collective mind of the sardine school, when millions of individuals are encircled and slowly crushed together as the purse seine net closes around them? We only seem to care from an ethical or moral perspective when the same fishing technique is used on species like tuna, and only then because there are often other non-target species – dolphins, sharks, turtles and others – trapped in the enclosing circle of fear. But is this selective, ethical *speciesism* justified when we consider the profound interconnectedness of the Ocean as a whole? From an Ocean perspective, should we not give equal consideration to the potential harm we inflict on any part of her vast body as we cast our nets, whether to feed ourselves, and our families, or to satisfy our desire for profit?

Prognosis: Time for a Change

It's clear from our brief health 'check-up' that the Ocean is suffering from serious and systemic physiological stress, which is affecting her respiration, circulation and metabolism in complex and unpredictable ways. It's also apparent that the cumulative effects of all her physical ailments are causing high levels of emotional stress to many Ocean beings, individually and collectively. There is no doubt that all of her various symptoms have a common root cause: us. In medical terms we would be described as an invasive and parasitic pathogen, sucking the life out of our host; robbing her of nutrients and replacing them with our toxic waste. As a result her immune system is severely compromised and her resilience to infection and disease weakened. For individual biological organisms like us a similar diagnosis would be life-threatening. But what does it mean for the Ocean?

The Ocean, like all living systems, works within a relatively narrow set of physiological parameters. Within those parameters she can maintain a dynamic equilibrium, enabling her to adjust to changes and perturbations while maintaining overall balance. Problems usually only occur when a system gets overloaded by too many perturbations, causing it to reach a tipping point, beyond which it moves from its normal steady state into a new semi-stable state. Because of the enormous complexity of the Ocean as a living system, predicting with any accuracy what a new semi-stable state would look like is virtually impossible. Even predicting the tipping point, or points, is extremely challenging. The best we can do is to look into her past for clues.

The last time the Ocean experienced anything like the rapid changes currently occurring was 55 million years ago, in what scientists call the *Paleocene-Eocene Thermal Maximum* (PETM) named for the geological epochs it divides. The PETM was started by the rapid release of massive amounts of carbon dioxide, doubling the existing atmospheric levels in as little as 1,000 years – a geological instant.

The cause of this sudden carbon 'burp' is still being debated, but the repercussions are clear to see in the fossil records of Ocean life from that period. So sudden was the change that many species were unable to adapt quickly enough to the rapid temperature spikes, sea-level rise and increased acidity. Amongst the most affected were calcifying animals such as single-celled foraminifera, of which half the benthic species perished. The fossil records also show that it took about 150,000 years for the Ocean and atmosphere to get back to normal and for new species – including mammals – to flourish, but for most of that period life for the existing species was a precarious thing.

There are differences between the PETM and now though: most notably that Gaia was already in a 'hot state' compared to the relatively cool period we enjoy now. However, this may have worked in many species' favour, as they were already accustomed to a much hotter home. But it's the parallels between then and now that worry climate scientists the most; chiefly the speed with which change occurred and the non-linear way in which the changes, then and now, can suddenly switch into positive feedback, pushing the whole system past it's tipping point into a new and unpredictable state.

The other major difference between the PETM and now is that the Ocean back then didn't have to contend with all the anthropogenic stresses she has to deal with now. Through our own actions we float precariously upon the surface of a completely unique situation, largely blind to the hidden depths of change that may have already surged beyond tipping points only the Ocean herself may be aware of.

What now seems certain is that change is not only coming, but is in fact, already happening. How far-reaching the changes will be, and whether we can minimise them, depend very much on what we choose to do from now on. The task ahead may seem overwhelming, but now is the time to come to our senses, take stock of our situation and allow our hearts to guide us. For some this may bring up feelings of deep despair, but it is only through fully embracing our despair and grief that we can move beyond them and start the process of re-visioning our relationship to the living Ocean.

11

Coming to our Senses

Whatever situation we face, we can choose our response. When faced with overwhelming challenges, we might feel that our actions don't count for much. Yet the kind of responses we make, and the degree to which we believe they count, are shaped by the way we think and feel about hope.
– Joanna Macy and Chris Johnstone (2012) *Active Hope*[1]

At the end of the last chapter I invited you to embrace any feelings of grief or despair about the damage we have inflicted – and still are inflicting – on the Ocean. It may be that your grief and despair are accompanied by feelings of outrage and anger, possibly directed towards the more obvious perpetrators of the worst atrocities of overfishing and pollution. It's also possible that a sense of guilt accompanies the recognition that we are all complicit – whether willingly or otherwise – through our participation in modern, industrial civilization. The purpose of embracing these feelings isn't to apportion blame, seek retribution or 'guilt trip' anyone, including ourselves, into making changes. Rather, it's because by accepting our own grief, despair, anger and guilt, we are able to acknowledge the reality of the situation. This is the first step towards re-visioning our relationship with the living Ocean.

The problems facing the Ocean are big, complex and alarmingly real. There is no easy fix when we view them in the context of our 'business as usual' paradigm, and it's difficult not to feel completely overwhelmed by the enormity of the situation. It's no wonder so many of us suppress, or even deny our feelings of grief and despair, lest we succumb to a paralyzing sense of hopelessness; that all too common feeling that 'there's nothing I can do to change the situation'. This hopelessness is often exacerbated by a sense of isolation when we see others around us acting as if nothing is amiss.

But the tide is turning. Despite decades of ever-increasing denial, the evidence is mounting that continuing with 'business as usual' is simply unsustainable. To continue our abuse of the Ocean will lead us into a spiraling ecological crisis of unprecedented scale. The reality of the Ocean's plight, and the implications for our own survival, is abundantly clear and we can no longer ignore it. The question is: what do we do about it? How do we move beyond 'business as usual'? There is now widespread acknowledgement at the highest levels that all is not well, but even as governments, industry, NGOs, conservation organizations and scientists debate the various issues and try to find common ground, the degradation continues. Despite international treaties and pledges to cut greenhouse emissions, curb overfishing and protect habitats, progress is frustratingly slow.

And what of our own, individual response to this crisis? Do we give in to that sense of hopelessness, cede our *response-ability* to higher authority, and continue to suppress our own feelings of pain and loss? Or do we choose to engender hope by facing up to the situation, accepting the challenges in front of us and giving ourselves permission to act? A personal call to action is the focus of this chapter, not because the big issues are beyond our control to change or influence, but precisely because each one of us is in a position to lead that change by fully embracing our interbeing with the Ocean and all of Gaia. None of us can change the world on our own, but we can change our way of being in the world, and by doing so we contribute to the collective re-visioning of our relationship to the Ocean.

We can think of this as a process of coming to our senses, both figuratively and literally, because it involves not only a re-evaluation of our individual and collective behaviour, but more importantly, because it takes us into our sensual, bodily experience of interconnectedness. Through our physical senses we experience the Ocean's life-force as our own: our grief is her grief, our salty tears mingle with hers as we mourn the loss of so much of her life-force. And yet her strength gives us the strength to face our own part in the destruction, to take ownership of the consequences of our actions and commit to a more life-enhancing path.

When we give voice to our gratitude and feel her life-force pulsing through our bodies, we touch the true nature of our interconnectedness, which lies not in judgment, punishment or reward for our actions, but in our full participation in the life process. As eco-psychologist and wilderness guide Bill Plotkin describes in his book *Nature and the Human Soul*:

> What makes you the individual you are is not your autonomy, but your interdependent and communal relationship with everything else in Nature.[2]

In essence, this coming to our senses could be viewed as an Ocean pilgrimage – we might even say a *soul journey* – in which we honour our interdependence and seek the guidance of her deep wisdom. It's through our sensual, bodily communion with the natural world that we may truly find ourselves, and it's through this communion that we can experience Ocean Spirit.

You may already have a strong connection with the Ocean: many surfers, divers and sailors talk of the deep spiritual connection, the 'nourishing of their soul' they experience when they spend time in, or on, the Ocean. Whatever your connection with the Ocean is, I invite you to make this pilgrimage, with the hope that by being fully present to her living essence something new and life-enhancing may be revealed.

Ocean Pilgrimage

A pilgrimage is a very personal journey of deep connection to something larger than ourselves, and there are many ways one could experience this Ocean Pilgrimage. My intention here is not to prescribe 'the way', but simply to offer some ideas that I hope will be helpful towards deepening your sense of connection to the Ocean. I have presented these ideas as a series of visualizations, but they could be combined or adapted to suit your personal pilgrimage.

Ideally, try to find a calm, gently sloping beach or shoreline that will allow you to enter the water slowly. You may also want to find somewhere that isn't too crowded so that you can focus on leaving behind the sensations, sounds and distractions of civilization. The intention is to clear your mind, and senses, so they're open to receiving information directly through your sensory channels, unfiltered by any terrestrial baggage. You may even want to find somewhere where you can also shed the filter of your clothing, so that you stand naked, vulnerable and fully open to the Ocean's touch.

* * *

Breathing our Gratitude

Stand a short distance back from water's edge, eyes focused on the distant horizon where Ocean meets Sky. Notice the transition between the two: is it a smooth, uninterrupted line, or is there a jagged edginess to their mood – giving away the swirling, tumultuous nature of their relationship? Let your eyes drift out of focus, allowing distance to evaporate into the blurred shades and timelessness of their eternal marriage, then slowly bring your focus back to the water's edge.

Let your attention dwell on the intimacy between the lapping waves and the shore. Notice how the sand and pebbles respond to the Ocean's caress in an endlessly creative dance, surrendering to the moment while the energy of each wave lasts, then resting in anticipation of the next caress. Let the rhythm of their movement seep into your body.

Now close your eyes and shift your attention to the sounds of that movement. Within the slow beat of her rhythm a symphony of gurgles, slurps, rasps, pops and percussive rumbles creates a soundscape of infinite subtlety. Allow the meditative beauty of this Ocean music to permeate your whole being, until you feel yourself becoming as fluid as the Ocean music flowing through you.

Slowly bring your attention back into your body by feeling the sand beneath your feet. Dig your toes into the sand and feel how it moulds to the creases of your skin. If you're close enough to the water's edge you might feel the dampness of the tide's residue, providing a life-line of moisture to sustain all the burrowing sand-dwellers until the incoming tide brings another bonanza of nutrients for them to feast on.

With those nutrients in mind, breathe in through your nose and smell the distinctive aroma of the Ocean: the tangy seaweed smell of DMS, escaping from the bodies of floating algae, or wafting from drying seaweed exposed by the tide. Breathe deeply, infusing your body with the other by-product of their existence: the life-giving oxygen that makes your own existence possible. As you breathe out, offer your gratitude for this gift of life and acknowledge your own gift of carbon dioxide that contributes to their wellbeing. As you continue to breathe, give thanks also to the intricate and complex web of relationships, stemming from these tiny beings, and perme-

ating every facet of life in a continuous cycle of reciprocity that's been in motion for billions of years.

Open your eyes again and take in the immensity of the Ocean. Take a moment to ponder this beautiful life process that sustains you, and of which you're an integral part.

Honouring our Pain for the Ocean

When you're ready – take a few steps forward until you're standing right at the water's edge. With that strong sense of gratitude still fresh in your mind, allow yourself to recall all the atrocities being perpetrated against the Ocean and all her beings. Imagine the coral cities bleaching a deathly white as they succumb to the heat, or crumbling in the acid waters created by the burning of fossil fuels. Contemplate the catastrophic loss of phytoplankton across the surface of the Ocean and the dire consequences to her entire metabolism. Feel the suffocating loss of oxygen in the expanding dead zones and the paralyzing effects of neurotoxins in the ever more frequent toxic algal blooms.

Imagine the slow excruciating death by starvation of untold millions of seabirds because their stomachs are full of plastic, or the millions of turtles, whales, dolphins, seals, sharks and manta rays dying horrific and needless deaths every year through entanglement in lost or discarded fishing gear. Feel the ripping and tearing as industrial trawlers gouge the Ocean floor. Tune in to the mass terror of school after school of sardines, mackerel, anchovies, salmon, tuna, pilchards and others, surrounded and crushed in the closing 'jaws' of giant purse seine nets. Mourn the loss of so much of the Ocean's life-force and vibrancy, the loss of so much sentient intelligence and the irreversible lessening of Ocean Mind.

Allow your emotions to well up inside you and let them flow in an outpouring of pain and grief for the Ocean's loss and for your own. Whatever your feelings are, they will be added to the wellspring of deep experience that is Ocean Spirit. Offer your prayers and sorrow, your anger or guilt. You will be neither judged nor forgiven, just accepted. And with that acceptance comes an invitation to dip into that wellspring of deep experience and discover your true nature as a child of the Ocean.

Coming Home

It's now time to take your first tentative steps towards re-inhabiting your 'Ocean Self'. Walk slowly into the water so you can feel her fluid caress meeting your bare skin as if for the first time. Pay attention to how your skin reacts to the pressure of her touch, the temperature difference and constant movement exciting every pore; as first your feet, then ankles and calves disappear below her surface. Pause for a moment as the tension of her surface 'skin' tickles the sensitive area behind your knees, then slowly continue, inch by inch, until your thighs are submerged and your fingertips are just touching the surface.

Take a moment to check-in with your other senses: notice how the sound of the water's movement now surrounds you, and how the horizon seems much closer, drawing you forward. Breathe deeply and smell the tangy sharpness of the salt-infused air rising from the Ocean's surface.

Moving slowly into deeper water, keep your hands floating palm down on the surface. If you are naked the intimacy of the water's touch on your genitals will serve to remind you of your primal nature. Notice how the thermal change, as the water inches slowly up towards your naval, is more sensual than shocking.

Pause again as the Ocean encircles your waist and enjoy her ticklish, playful caress as the water laps around your midriff. Focus on your hands as they lightly float at the surface. Feel how the surface tension of the water buoys them up and allows them to follow its every subtle movement. Take a moment to really sense how alive the water feels and notice how alive your skin feels in response. Keep walking forward until you are at chest level. Slowly dip your hands and arms into the water and bend your knees slightly so your shoulders are submerged. Feel the slight pressure against your chest as you breathe in, and feel how the water supports your belly.

Now bring your hands together, cupping some water, and lower your face into your cupped hands. Slowly open your hands, letting the water escape. Do this several times, as if washing the pain and sorrow away; just as we wash the sleep from our eyes at the start of a new day. Lick your lips and taste the Ocean's salty vibrancy, then take a small amount into your mouth and swirl it around with your tongue, dispelling the culturally learned fear of having salt water in your mouth, and as you do, savour her life-giving, nutrient richness.

When you're ready, take a few deep breaths, lift your feet off the bottom and duck-dive below the surface. Swim forward and downward towards the bottom so you can feel the viscous resistance of the water moving against your whole body and enjoy the sensation of being within her liquid body. If you can, open your eyes and take in the blurred outlines of the bottom, enjoying the liberation from yet another commonly held cultural fear of opening your eyes underwater.

Rising back to the surface, spend some time floating on your back. Enjoy the sensation of being completely held by the Ocean's embrace, weightless and free from the gravitational restrictions of terrestrial existence. As you float, imagine energetic 'threads' extending out from your fingertips, connecting you with all other Ocean beings in an intricate web of shared history, interdependence and the reciprocity of your interconnectedness.

Deepening the Connection

Our Ocean pilgrimage has so far focused on our own sensual experience of meeting the Ocean and our emotional response to connecting with her life-force. Now we want to deepen that sense of connection by sending our focus outwards, with the intention of seeing the Ocean with new eyes. One way we can do this is by donning mask and snorkel and spending time getting to know a particular area. It might be a reef community, mangrove forest, sea-grass bed, seaweed garden or kelp forest, but the important point is that we are aiming to experience the *living nature* of that particular place by tuning in to its unique, expressive qualities. This is both a sensual, as well as an intuitive process, in which we are fully present to our own direct sense experience, while at the same time opening a space for our intuitive, perceptual awareness of the other.[3]

By tuning-in to the expressive qualities of a particular place we are also moving beyond the generalised idea of *a* reef, or *a* mangrove forest, to the specific expression of *this* reef or *this* mangrove forest. Rather than asking *what are you?* We are instead asking *who are you?* As we move deeper into our connection, the question becomes *what is it like to be you?* We are seeking to connect to the very essence of 'reef-ness' or 'mangrove-ness', as expressed by the particular reef or mangrove forest we are interacting with.

To illustrate this different way of seeing, let's imagine swimming through a swaying kelp forest.

The Ocean Is Alive

* * *

As you snorkel towards the kelp forest you might recognize a particular species of kelp, but as soon as you name it your mind immediately starts to categorize and compartmentalise what you're seeing into what you already know about this particular species: the general shape, colour and height, how it fastens itself to the rocks and so on. If you're not careful you'll lose sight of the actual kelp forest you're swimming through, and only see a generalized idea in your mind's eye.

As soon as you notice yourself doing this you bring your attention back to your direct sense experience by focusing on an individual kelp, undulating lazily in the gentle current. The first thing you notice is the way each frond tip expresses a unique arc through the water, and how this movement translates into a unifying fluidity as it reaches the central stalk. You also notice how the shape of each frond is slightly different, self-similar rather than exactly the same. Gently squeezing one between your fingertips, you're surprised by the feeling of strength and firmness, despite its slightly soft and slimy appearance.

Following the curving trunk-like central stem down to the intricate holdfast, which anchors the kelp to the rock, you can see its root-like structure and sense its enormous strength, capable of resisting the pull of storm surges and powerful Ocean swells. You can also see how the diverse community of encrusting sponges, ascidians and tubeworms weave an entire ecosystem in miniature around the holdfast. As you're watching, a tiny blue-eyed triplefin comes to rest on an orange sponge growing amongst the holdfast. Perched on his translucent pectoral fins, he contemplates you with an obvious curiosity and you sense his complete lack of concern about being so close to a stranger in his territory, despite the fact that you are many hundreds of times his size.

As you widen your gaze, your awareness opens to the wider kelp community, allowing your direct sensual experience to soften into a more intuitive feeling for the essential nature of the kelp forest as a whole. As your whole being connects with the kelp forest you notice your own emotional response; perhaps a deep sense of serenity and wellbeing; but you also become aware of what the kelp forest is expressing of itself. You can feel its vibrancy and strength, and you can also sense its fundamental fluidity; how its life-force ebbs and flows in harmony with the rhythms of the seasons, but also how dependent this life-force is on the diversity of all the beings that call the kelp forest home.

Living Our Response-ability

We ourselves feel that what we are doing is just a drop in the ocean. But the ocean would be less because of that missing drop.
– Mother Teresa

In whatever way it comes about, once we have a deep connection to the Ocean we are faced with a choice: do we carry on with our lives as normal, as if nothing has changed? Or do we acknowledge our complete dependence on her wellbeing, and commit to honouring our deep connection by doing what we can to heal the wounds humanity has inflicted upon her? Or maybe like me, you don't see it as a choice at all, but rather as a natural response to our deep spiritual and physical connection that is as ancient and fundamental as the Ocean herself.

One thing's certain though: on a daily basis we'll be faced with potentially difficult choices that challenge our motivation and make us question our commitment to 'being the change' we'd like to see for the Ocean.[4] However, being the change isn't the same as being perfect, as some of our decisions will very likely involve having to choose between sacrificing our own comfort, pleasure or convenience, for the greater wellbeing of the Ocean. The balance we strike between the two will certainly be influenced by how much we inform ourselves about the issues, as well as how deeply connected we feel to the Ocean. In other words, our choices will involve both an intellectual process – analyzing the pros and cons – as well as our emotional and spiritual connection.

This balance will be different for everyone, but will inevitably involve questioning the sustainability of our decisions, choices and actions. This is important because so often sustainability is seen as a future goal, something to work towards; but in many situations, if our decisions aren't sustainable as we're enacting them they are unlikely to become sustainable in the future! In these cases sustainable is *a way of being*, rather than an end goal to work towards.

A good example of this is our attitude towards plastic. In the middle of last century, the possibility of areas within the Ocean containing more plastic than plankton would have seemed absurd, and yet just six decades later, this nightmare scenario is a reality. Back then plastic packaging seemed like a really good idea; a cheap and convenient alternative to glass, paper and metal. We are now well aware of the ecological disaster our use of plastic is for the Ocean, and yet our use of plastic for packaging and convenience items such as plastic straws, as well as plastic micro-beads in cosmetics and cleaning products, continues to increase. Using plastic in this way is never going to be sustainable or ecologically sound.

Being fully conscious of the impact plastic is having on the Ocean's wellbeing can help us change our fundamental relationship to plastic: honouring its real value in our lives by reserving its use for things that are suited to its special properties of strength and resilience. We are then much more likely to think carefully about the products we purchase and how they are packaged: whenever we can choosing re-useable, fully recyclable, or fully biodegradable alternatives and making simple lifestyle changes, like using a travel mug for our take-out coffee, reusable water bottles and shopping bags. Our deepened Ocean consciousness is likely to lead to us saying 'No' to that plastic straw in our drink when we go to a café or bar. Perhaps it will even lead to us having a conversation with the café owner about phasing out their use altogether, or suggesting alternatives such as paper straws, or re-useable glass straws.

We may have only limited options when it comes to removing the vast majority of the plastic that's already in the Ocean, but we can make a personal contribution by just picking up any plastic we see on the shoreline or along riverbanks.[5] Organised beach cleanups are a great way to experience the positive impact we can have when we act collectively, but every piece you remove from a beach anytime you visit is one less piece that can make it's way back into the Ocean, and you may well be saving the life of a sea bird, turtle or marine mammal.

Making sustainable choices about eating seafood is potentially much more difficult. How do we determine whether the fish on our plate fits into our personal criteria of what we consider to be sustainable? Unfortunately there is little consistency in the use of the term 'sustainably caught', and more often than not it has become little more than a marketing tool. Even industry watchdog organisations, such as the Marine Stewardship Council (MSC), whose logo now adorns more than 12 percent of the world's reported catch, has a narrow range of criteria regarding the ecological and ethical sustainability of the fishery involved in catching it.[6] For example, a number of scallop, prawn and bottom-fish fisheries have been certified, despite the fact that they use highly destructive fishing techniques, resulting in irreparable habitat destruction.[7] Indeed, from the *living Ocean* perspective it's hard to see how any type of industrial-scale fishing could be considered sustainable.

Many other organisations have websites providing 'good choice' guides to eating seafood, but without a consistent and robust definition of what constitutes sustainable we are faced with a real challenge in deciding what, if anything, is currently 'okay' to eat from the Ocean. One option (and my personal choice) is to eat nothing at all from the Ocean. Another is to only eat what you catch yourself, or at least only eat seafood that has been caught locally by small scale, non-destructive fishing methods.

Perhaps it's time to embrace a new vision for a healthy and sustainable relationship with the Ocean, one that acknowledges our indebtedness and provides a framework by which we can find our place – *our ecological role* – while enjoying the gifts of her bounty. From all we've learned, it's painfully obvious that 'business as usual' is leading us towards ecological catastrophe, but how do we address the massive scale of destruction when it seems that we are so entrenched in the current paradigm? Too often we're told that we are naïve, or not being realistic if we suggest large scale changes, but surely it's even more naïve and unrealistic to deny the need for change when the evidence of our destruction is all around us. It's only possible to bring about change if we have a vision of what that change looks like.

12

Finding Our Place

*I seem to have been only like a boy playing on the seashore, and diverting
myself in now and then finding a smoother pebble or a prettier shell than
ordinary, whilst the great ocean of truth lay all undiscovered before me.*

– Isaac Newton

'A little knowledge is a dangerous thing', or so the saying goes, but perhaps the danger's not in how much or how little we think we know, but rather that we believe we know enough to disregard the wisdom of those with greater knowledge. As we explored in Chapter 9, knowledge is a living process in which we participate, and it's through our participation that comprehension arises. We become *knowledged* by increments until some level of understanding arises. Isaac Newton followed this knowledge process in his discovery of gravity, but as the quote above shows, he was well aware that his knowledge was confined to what gravity was prepared to show of itself.

So it is with the Ocean: our knowledge is limited to what she has so far revealed to us. We are like Newton, playing on the seashore, whilst the great Ocean of truth lies undiscovered before us. But perhaps we've learned enough to take stock of our current behaviour and move towards a more life-enhancing relationship. We can start by diving deeply into what we've learned on our living Ocean journey, in search of the core teachings she has revealed and the wisdom they hold.

We Live on an Ocean Planet

Imagine living your entire life on an island, surrounded by the vast Ocean. Whether your island is a high-peaked volcano or a low-lying atoll, you can walk over or around it in a matter of hours, a day or two at most. No matter which way you look you're surrounded by the ever-changing texture of the Ocean's surface. It dominates your world. Even if you choose to live right in the middle of your island, you can't ignore the profound influence she has on every aspect of your existence. If you are to survive and thrive you will at some point have to address your relationship with the Ocean. You'll have to learn her language, understand her moods and meet her inhabitants; you will have to become one of them. This is the condition of being *in* your Ocean world.

When we understand that our Planet Earth is really *Planet Ocean,* it becomes clear that in truth, we are all living on islands surrounded by the Ocean. Some of our islands are indeed large – we call them continents – and over geological time the tectonic plates on which they sit periodically bring them together to form even larger islands. But no matter how large, they are still dominated by the ever more vast Ocean. The deep wisdom for us to embrace is the knowledge that Gaia is primarily an Ocean being, and as such, we are Ocean children.

This in no way diminishes the importance of the land and terrestrial life, just places it in the appropriate context of supporting the *primary* life processes of the Ocean. No matter how large an island we live on, we can never be so far from the Ocean's shores that her life processes no longer affect us, and vice versa. The complete interconnectedness of Gaia as a living system means that even from the middle of her largest islands, the effects of our modern industrialized civilization will reach her shores and beyond.

There's only One Ocean

The Ocean is one vast interconnected whole. Our arbitrary naming of her various parts is simply a geographical convenience that helps us locate ourselves within her vastness. Atlantic, Pacific, Indian, Southern, have no greater meaning than arms, legs, feet or torso: they are the body parts that together constitute a physical description, but don't come close to describing the essence of the whole being. Each part may have its unique attributes, but they only function in relationship with all the other parts and only exist within the context of the whole. We may lose an arm or a leg and still be able to function well enough; we can partially compensate for the loss, but only at the cost of putting more strain on the remaining limb, as well as our system as a whole.

In essence the same principles apply for the Ocean; the difference is in the complexity of her inter-relatedness and the timescales in which her physiology functions. Inevitably her circulation will distribute whatever pollutants we spew forth throughout her entire body; the effects of warming and acidification will permeate every water molecule; the ramifications of habitat-loss and overfishing in one area will eventually be felt everywhere. Such is her enormous resilience though, that until quite recently she has been able to compensate for these losses without unduly stressing her whole system. But this is no longer the case.

The Ocean's resilience is based on two key factors: abundance and diversity. For nearly four billion years she has fostered the evolution of life into ever more diverse beings capable of harnessing and metabolising the raw materials of life – energy and nutrients – then recycling them over and over again. The more diverse life becomes the more ways there are to recycle the nutrients, and the stronger the Ocean's life-force becomes. This naturally amplified nutrient cycling leads to greater abundance as each species benefits from the recycling services of others, until the whole system reaches a dynamic balance and is functioning at optimum levels.[1]

Thus, diversity and abundance are inextricably linked: there can be no abundance without diversity, and yet if we remove too many of even one species, diversity can be irreparably damaged. This dynamic equilibrium between abundance and diversity plays out in different ways and to different degrees in all her various regions: from the intensely productive upwellings to the relatively quiet mid-Ocean 'deserts'; from her deepest trenches to the sun-drenched surface, they all play their part in maintaining her overall wellbeing.

Likewise, abundance and diversity within individual ecosystems is equally important, but here is one of the core teachings we need to embrace. Ecosystems are far more than just an environment inhabited by a collection of species: they are an emergent *living process* that comes into being through complex and non-linear relationships between individuals, groups, whole species and the physical space they inhabit. It's through these relationships that the living nature of each ecosystem is created and maintained, and it's the dynamic reciprocity of the ecosystem's living process that creates its resilience. Every ecosystem is a contextually unique expression of the Ocean's life-force – no two reefs are the same – and they all contribute to her overall resilience and wellbeing.

When we understand ecosystems as *relationships* rather than *real estate* we are tapping into the deep wisdom of the Ocean, which offers us a different perspective on the notions of resource management and ecosystem services. From this perspective, an ecosystem isn't a *thing* to be managed, but rather a *being* to be interacted with in a way that acknowledges, respects and honours its unique contribution to the living process of the Ocean, and indeed to the whole of Gaia. It also invites us to experience ourselves as integral to this living process, rather than outside it, with our own ecological role to fulfill.

By shifting our perception of ourselves as *part of*, rather than *apart from* the ecosystems we inhabit, we not only acknowledge our belonging, but also our responsibility to behave appropriately. Instead of viewing the management process as external – as in resource management – it becomes a process of *self-management*. While we may not physically inhabit Ocean ecosystems, our actions profoundly affect their living processes, and never more so than today. If we can adjust our behaviour to *fit in*, there's potential for us to contribute to, rather than reduce the 'services' they provide.

Understanding our Ecological Role in the Ocean

So, what is our ecological role in the Ocean? Where do we fit in?

Before we explore this question it's important to understand that an organism's ecological role isn't so much a description of its feeding strategy – hunting, grazing, foraging for example – but more how it contributes to the overall functioning of its ecological home. We like to think of ourselves as apex predators, top of the food chain, but is that really an accurate description of our role?

In Chapter 5 we looked at the various trophic levels that make up the Ocean's metabolism: from the primary producers to the primary consumers, all the way up to the apex predators. At each level a huge variety of species create the complex 'living symphony' of interactions that is the Ocean's life-force. Apex predators are the conductors of this 'ecological orchestra', fine-tuning the rhythm and teasing out subtle changes in tempo, creating a seamless harmony: that is their role. But like any good conductor, there's no separation between them and the rest of the orchestra; they are completely embedded within the flow. Their metabolism is an integral part of the nutrient cycle, and when they die their bodies become food for those that were once their prey.

This is clearly not a role we fulfill. In fact, from a nutrient cycling perspective it's hard to see where we fit in at all; our relationship seems one way: we take from the Ocean but appear to give nothing back (except our toxic waste). But we do have a role in the Ocean's nutrient cycle: we are in fact nutrient distributors.

This may not sound as glamorous as being an apex predator, but it is nonetheless an important role, and one that we share with a surprising number of other species. Some are part-time Ocean dwellers, such as seabirds, seals and sea lions, while others are merely Ocean visitors like ourselves. Others include the salmon-loving bears of Alaska, the algae-grazing iguanas of the Galapagos Islands, and a plethora of tidal foragers, such as raccoons, rodents, and even other primates.

What we all have in common is that through our hunting, foraging, grazing and scavenging we are acting as Gaia's biological couriers: transporting essential nutrients from the Ocean and gifting them back to the land through our metabolic waste, where they enrich the soil and contribute to Gaia's terrestrial abundance.[2] Eventually these nutrients make their way back to the Ocean via rivers and estuaries. Most species don't move far from the coast before depositing their 'gifts', but some travel significant distances inland. We happen to be one of those species that are highly mobile, with the potential to 'spread the nutrient love' well inland.[3]

Seabirds are the best example of Ocean nutrient distributors. They forage far and wide across the Ocean's surface, feeding on nutrient-rich zooplankton and small baitfish such as anchovies, pilchards, menhaden and sardines. Some of these nutrients are distributed to different parts of the Ocean as they fly back to their nests, which can sometimes be hundreds, even thousands of kilometres away. When they finally arrive and regurgitate a tasty and nutritious meal for their hungry chicks, they also enrich the area with their nutrient-filled guano. In fact, this sea bird 'nutrient delivery service' is essential for the healthy functioning of offshore island ecosystems.[4]

There are two critically important aspects to being a successful nutrient distributor: 1, feeding low down the trophic levels of the food web – algae, zooplankton, forage fish and so on – and 2, not removing more nutrients than can be replaced by natural processes, such as coastal upwellings, natural runoff via rivers, harbours and estuaries, as well as the biological mixing of nutrients by large animals such as whales. The lower trophic levels of Ocean food webs are where the most abundance is and where nutrient cycling is fastest, and therefore where she can best cope with a limited amount of removal. This limited re-distribution of nutrients contributes to what we might call a dynamic, living balance and is integral to the overall nutrient flow.

The lesson for us here, is that our taste for apex predators like tuna, swordfish and other keystone species is out of step with our role as a nutrient distributor. The other hugely important lesson is that while leaving the apex predators to fulfill their role, we must also be careful not to deplete those lower on the food web, least we inadvertently upset this dynamic living balance.

Unfortunately, our modern lifestyles of industrialized urbanisation, intense chemical agriculture and unbridled pillaging of the Ocean, drastically outweighs any positive contributions we may have had in the past. We are even affecting the ability of other nutrient distributors to perform their ecological role. A study by an international group of ecologists and biologists estimates that the Ocean-to-land transfer of the essential life nutrient, phosphorus, may be as low as four percent of historical levels.[5] A significant contributing factor is the decimation of seabird populations, caused by our industrial exploitation of the Ocean's abundance and diversity. On top of that, our indiscriminant destruction of the living processes, which create ecosystems in the first place, is robbing her of the ability to heal the wounds we inflict with our dredges, bottom-trawlers and discarded or lost fishing gear. The steady stream of plastic and other toxic waste from our industrialized lifestyles adds to her stress and further erodes her ability to recover.

So is there any hope of us 'finding our way back' to a respectful and reciprocal relationship with the Ocean before it's too late?

I believe there is, but it will involve us facing the 'hard truths' of our situation and then collectively acting on them. As a species we are in uncharted waters – not since cyanobacteria caused the great oxidation event 2.5 billion years ago, has a single life form held such influence – and there's no precedent to guide our response except our own deep sense of connection and a desire to re-inhabit our place within the living fabric of our Ocean Planet.

And herein lies our greatest challenge: how do we know how much we can safely take from the Ocean, without further negatively affecting her current state, and at the same time take action that will support her rehabilitation? Figuring this out is even harder now because there are virtually no un-disturbed ecosystems within her vast body that can act as our class-rooms; where we can witness her complex life processes playing out in their full glory, and where we can learn how to be positive contributors to her wellbeing. But perhaps even more importantly, there are precious few ecosystems where she has the chance to re-build her resilience and return to the dynamic living balance that all life forms depend on for their very existence. Remedying this has to be our top priority.

Whether we like it or not, we have no option but to acknowledge our complete dependence on the Ocean's healthy functioning and change our behaviour before we push her beyond the point where she can no longer sustain Gaia as the Ocean Planet. How much time do we have before it's too late? A decade? Five decades? A century? We seem preoccupied with this question, as if we believe we can delay the inevitable and 'eek out' a few more decades of exploitation before we get caught. But all around us the planet is shouting, 'Enough!' It's time to stop playing for time and start living up to our ecological role.

As we explore how we can achieve this it's worth reflecting on this one simple truth: every species – no matter how large or small, no matter how influential or supposedly insignificant they may be – owes an ecological debt to the ecosystems that sustain them.

Honouring our Ecological Debt

When we view our current exploitation of the Ocean from the perspective of our ecological role, it's clear that virtually all of our large-scale fishing practices are far from sustainable and need fixing. But how do we go about changing the nature of the way we fish? One thing's abundantly clear: we can't fix overfishing by using the same principal of *Maximum Sustainable Yield* (MSY) that has created the problem in the first place.

MSY was developed in the 1930's as a theoretical model for determining the largest possible catch that could be taken from a population of fish (or whales) year after year. The basic premise of MSY comes from the antiquated and flawed concept that any given population will produce a surplus over and above what it needs to maximise its ecological niche, and that this surplus will lead to over-population and eventual collapse due to scarce resources. The theory assumes that a population will reach its optimal breeding efficiency when hunted down to approximately half its original numbers, and still produce a yearly surplus. This supposed surplus can then be exploited by fishermen while still maintaining, or even enhancing, a healthy breeding population.[6]

MSY was largely ignored until the 1950's, when an American fisheries scientist who was looking for a model to use for the fledgling tuna industry, resurrected it. Although he used flawed equations and misplaced assumptions, his calculations suited the prevailing political scene and so were adopted. Since then, MSY has been eagerly embraced by virtually every commercial fishery in the world, despite the fact that the theory behind MSY has never been scientifically verified.[7] On the contrary, the untested assumptions that underpin the theory have been stretched, in some cases to the point where the MSY of a fish stock is set at up to 80 to 90 percent of the original population.

Many fisheries scientists have been ringing alarm bells about MSY for decades, but sadly their warnings fall mainly on deaf ears. Instead, fisheries managers often blatantly ignore their warnings and set quotas and total allowable catch limits far above what the scientists recommend. So, not only is MSY a flawed and untested theory, but it is further abused for the sake of short-term – and often heavily subsidised – profit.

Another major problem with MSY is that it focuses solely on the target species and takes virtually no account of the impact on the healthy functioning of the ecosystem as a whole. Even though fisheries scientists have always been interested in population dynamics, much of their research has been, and often still is, primarily focused on target species, and only rarely does the species' role within the ecosystem become part of the research effort. This ecosystem-based approach just doesn't fit into the MSY model. But until industrial fishing is examined from an ecosystem perspective, quotas and catch limits will continue to be profit driven rather than sustainable.

It's time to move away from the idea of maximum yields for maximum profit. Instead we should strive for a dynamic ecosystem balance, embrace the understanding that a healthy and vibrant Ocean in which every ecosystem is important, and has intrinsic value beyond its usefulness to us, would actually provide more sustenance for less effort than a stressed and over-exploited Ocean. We can be guided by what we have already learned about the role biodiversity and abundance play in ecosystem resilience. They provide a natural buffer that enables the ecosystem to cope with change. Working within that buffer and maintaining a dynamic ecosystem balance should be our target.

Creating an Ocean of Hope

The sea, the great unifier, is man's only hope. Now, as never before, the old phrase has a literal meaning: we are all in the same boat.
– Jacques Yves Cousteau

In 2009 world-renowned Ocean scientist and explorer, Sylvia Earle was invited by the 'TED Talk Foundation' to 'make a wish', and this is what she wished for:

I wish you would use all means at your disposal – Films! Expeditions! The Web! New submarines! – to create a campaign to ignite public support for a global network of Marine Protected Areas, "hope spots" large enough to save and restore the Ocean, the blue heart of the planet. How much? Some say 10 percent, some say 30 percent. You decide: How much of your heart do you want to protect? Whatever it is, a fraction of one percent is not enough.[8]

Setting aside areas of the Ocean from exploitation is nothing new. Indigenous Ocean people have been doing it for centuries. Often these *tapu* (taboo) areas were put in place to allow fish and shellfish populations to recover from over exploitation.[9] They were usually enacted for specific time periods and often included a variety of restrictions: from full protection, to limited 'open seasons' for particular species, or restrictions on the type of fishing techniques allowed. The key conservation concept behind their implementation was the 'wise use' of the gifts of the Ocean. They were, and still are, an appropriate response at a local scale, but we now need a global response that recognizes the global scale of the Ocean's plight.

What's needed is a network of large, permanent and fully protected regions, spanning the full diversity of Ocean ecosystems. To offer the hope that Sylvia Earle wished for, these large-scale 'hope spots' not only need to cover a significant percentage of her overall area and volume, but if they are to provide the 'breathing space' for the Ocean to rebuild her resilience and ensure she can carry on her planetary life-support role, they also need to exclude any kind of commercial exploitation, including all forms of industrial-scale fishing.

The United Nations Convention on Biological Diversity has set a target of 10 percent protection by 2020.[10] There is now a coalition of international conservation organizations and research groups – including the

Global Ocean Legacy Project of the Pew Charitable Trusts, and Sylvia Earle's own *Mission Blue* organization – that are working together with the UN and governments throughout the world to turn the rhetoric into reality. Progress is being made. In the past few years several really large marine protected areas have been announced, mostly in the Pacific. They include the islands of Palau, Easter Island, Pitcairn Island, the Kermadec Islands and the Hawaiian Islands, bringing the total area of the Ocean under some form of protection to almost four percent. If this continues we may well reach the 10 percent target by 2020. However, not all of these protected areas are actually full no-take reserves, and even if they were, is 10 percent enough?

When we remember how fundamental the Ocean is to the healthy functioning of the whole planet, it becomes obvious that 10 percent is woefully inadequate. Many marine scientists, researchers and conservation organizations believe it needs to be much higher. Some, like Mission Blue and the Marine Conservation Institute, are aiming for 20 percent protection.[11] Others, including the Marine Reserves Coalition, are aiming for 30 percent.[12] At the University of York in the UK a group of marine and conservation biologists, led by Professor Callum Roberts, have estimated that the area of Ocean with full protection would need to be closer to 35 percent. Their research takes into account factors such as protecting genetic biodiversity, restoring species abundance to at least a reasonable level of health and protecting a variety of ecosystem habitats. And as Callum Roberts points out in his book, *Ocean of Life*, 'not only do we need to protect a third of the Ocean from direct exploitation and harm, but we also need to manage our use of the remaining two thirds much better than we do today'.[13]

From the perspective of our current, materialistic worldview, this may seem unrealistic, but considering that it's this worldview that has led us into the precarious state we're in, perhaps it's time we re-evaluated its worthiness. Here I think we can learn from the wisdom of Indigenous Ocean people and their understanding of the sacredness of our Ocean home. In Pacific cultures, tapu is more than just a resource management tool; it's also a way of acknowledging, honouring and protecting areas of special ecological, cultural or sacred significance. The areas of the Ocean that we collectively agree to put off-limits to exploitation, should surely be considered sacred places of the utmost cultural and ecological importance.

For it's in these special places that we can most honour *Tangaroa*, the great spiritual guardian of the Ocean revered by Polynesian cultures.[14]

For the same reason we also need to create tapu marine reserves that are easily accessible for people. Goat Island Marine Reserve – New Zealand's first fully protected reserve – is just an hour's drive north of Auckland, the country's most populous city. Every year this tiny coastal reserve is visited by close to 400,000 people, more than any of the nation's national parks.[15] Likewise, the world-renowned Poor Knights Marine Reserve further up the coast, is more popular with overseas visitors than the famous Milford Track in Fiordland.[16] Tapu reserves like these provide us with the opportunity to experience the Ocean in her natural state. They are places where we can be awed by her splendour and where we can contemplate our own *Ocean Spirit*.

Creating more easily accessible marine reserves would also serve to protect important coastal fringes, where the Ocean's love affair with the land is played out: the reef lagoons, tidal estuaries, harbours and river mouths. With full protection, the mangrove forests, sea grass beds, marshes, mud flats and tidal pools would become treasured jewels, valued for their critical role as nurseries and safe havens for so much of the Ocean's life-force that we ourselves depend upon.

A New Vision for our Relationship with the Ocean

Katoitu te marae a Tangaroa - katoitu te iwi
(If the realm of Tangaroa endures, so too will humanity)
– Maori proverb

We've travelled far on our Ocean journey and have discovered a living presence that permeates every aspect of our lives: the air we breath, the water we drink, the relatively benign climate we enjoy and virtually every nutrient cycle essential for the food we eat. But more than this, we've connected on a sensual – even soulful – level to the living intelligence of Ocean Mind. Hopefully we've reached the point where we understand that our very survival depends on her continued healthy functioning.

With that understanding it's clear that humanity must change its collective relationship to the Ocean. If we have a clear vision of what we want this relationship to look like, then every one of our individual actions has the potential to create a ripple that will spread and grow into the collective tsunami of change we so desperately need. In re-visioning our relationship with the Ocean we need not be confined by the limitations of our current worldview, but rather, we are free to dream a new reality, one that we can then act upon to bring into existence.

In our new relationship we would re-connect with the deeper ecological wisdom: that all life has intrinsic value, independent of our needs. We would understand that the abundance and diversity of the Ocean's life-force is fundamental to maintaining dynamic ecosystem balance, and we would honour our ecological debt by overhauling the way we fish, so that we become positive contributors to her overall wellbeing. This would include abolishing destructive fishing techniques in favour of ecologically sustainable practices. We would fish only to meet our needs, not satisfy our greed.

We would recognize the inseparable nature of her relationship with the land and atmosphere; what we do to the land, we also do to the Ocean, and what we do to both will be reflected in the atmosphere. We would understand that it's only through the living processes of all the photosynthesising beings, on land and in the Ocean, that the atmosphere can support our existence. But we would also acknowledge that whatever toxic fumes our industrialized lifestyle breathes back into the atmosphere will find their way into the Ocean. This knowledge would inform all our emissions and air quality policies.

Our understanding of this interconnectedness would lead us to take full account of the impact on the Ocean from intensive agriculture and industrial urbanisation. Environmental policies would reflect our commitment to eliminate the runoff of fertilisers, chemicals and other industrial pollutants into the Ocean. We would work hard to restore the wetlands, marshes, mangroves and sea grass beds that provide natural coastal filtration systems. Recognising the fundamental importance of water to all life, and the key role the Ocean plays in the planetary water cycle, we would be completely committed to re-invigorating the water quality of our rivers, lakes and estuaries, so they run clean and pure as they return to the Ocean.

Our new relationship with the Ocean would help us redefine our relationship to plastic. No longer would we see it as a *throw-away* convenience, but rather, we would revere its special qualities of strength and resilience and reserve its use for products built to last and be used again and again. We would also ensure that these products were fully recyclable, so that even at the end of their long lives, they could be transformed into something else of equal use and value, rather than being discarded. Each of us would be committed to doing our part in removing plastic from the Ocean by just-picking-it-up, so that over time we could look with pride at our beaches and coastlines, and know that our efforts had saved countless millions of Ocean lives.

In our new relationship we would honour the Ocean origins of our own sentient consciousness by recognising the sentience of all Ocean beings, acknowledging their complex, social and emotional lives as fundamental to their existence. In this regard, we would hold special reverence for our air-breathing cousins who have returned to an Ocean existence: honouring their right to live unhindered by our activities; not because they are any more, or less, important than any of the Ocean's other children, but precisely to remind us that neither are we. Through our close mammalian bond we would strive to rekindle our deep connection with all life.

Our new relationship with the Ocean would be one of humility, in which we pay homage to her greater wisdom and understand that our true wealth lies not in her exploitation, but in her continued healthy functioning. In our new relationship we would choose to act with gratitude, respect and hope for the future.

The Living Ocean is the cradle of our existence and the heart of our blue home. If we are to survive and thrive we must find our place within her living processes. The choice is ours.

The Ocean awaits our response.

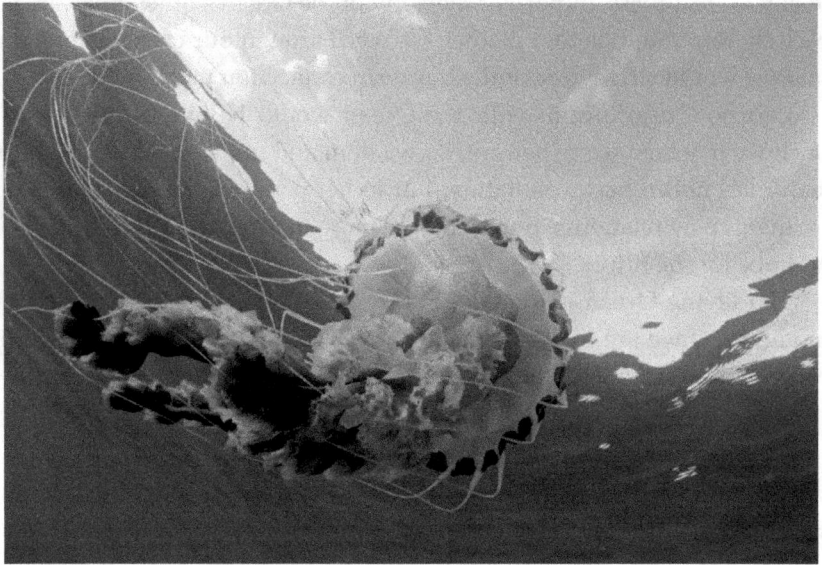

Chapter Notes and References

Chapter 1

1 I have used this theme as developed by Stephan Harding in his outstanding book *Animate Earth*. Stephen Harding (2009) *Animate Earth: Science, Intuition and Gaia – A New Scientific Story* (second edition). Plato quote cited in Animate Earth p.30. Green Books.

2 Cultural ecologist David Abram also postulates in his book *Spell of the Sensuous* that the advent of written language was a major factor in this split. David Abram (1996) *The Spell of the Sensuous*. Vintage Book.

3 The word nature comes from the Latin *Natura*, meaning 'essential qualities' or 'innate disposition'. In ancient times Natura literally meant 'birth'. The use of Nature as a term to encompass the whole natural world has its origins in early Greek philosophy, but became entrenched during the advent of modern scientific method in the last several centuries.

4 Fitjof Capra and Pier Luigi Luisi (2014) *A Systems View of Life*. Cambridge University Press.

5 Ibid.

6 In fact we don't know exactly how many cells make up the human body at any one time. Estimates vary, from approximately 37 trillion up to more than 50 trillion. The figure of 50 trillion used in this book is based on the work of molecular biologist and epi geneticist Bruce Lipton in his books, *Biology of Belief* and *Spontaneous Evolution*.

7 James Lovelock (2000) *Gaia: A New Look at Life on Earth*. Oxford University Press.

8 James Lovelock (1995) *The Ages of Gaia: A biography of our living Earth*. p.20. Oxford University Press .

9 Mark Denny (1995) *Air and Water: The Biology and Physics of Life's Media*. Princeton University Press. Also, Silvia Earle (2009) *The World is Blue: How our Fate and the Ocean's are One*. National Geographic Society

10 James Lovelock (1995) *The Ages of Gaia*. And further developed by Stephan Harding and Lynn Margulis.

11 Stephen Harding's story telling expertise is at its best with his elemental descriptions in *Animate Earth*.

12 This description of an EZ molecule is overly simplistic and doesn't accurately describe the complexity of this molecular alchemy. In fact the molecules form an intricate, hexagonal lattice structure that has some similarity to ice crystals. See *The Fourth Phase of Water* (2013) for a detailed description.

13 Gerald H. Pollack (2013) *The Fourth Phase of Water: Beyond Solid, Liquid, and Vapor*. Ebner & Sons Publishers. This book provides a fascinating overview of his laboratory's in depth research into water.

14 Viktor Schauberger (1885-1958) was a 19th century naturalist who had a deep, intuitive understanding of the living nature of water. He developed many practical theories in how to live in harmony with water's natural movement, including vortices and, what he called 'the half and full water cycles'. (see for example: Alick Bartholomew (2004) *Hidden nature: The startling insights of Viktor Schauberger*).

15 James Lovelock (1995) *The Ages of Gaia: A biography of our living Earth*. p.82. Oxford University Press.

16 Stephan Harding and Lynn Margulis (2000) *Water Gaia: 3.5 Thousand Million years of Wetness on Planet Earth*.

17 James Lovelock (1995) *The Ages of Gaia: A biography of our living Earth*. p.82. Oxford University Press.

18 Stephan Harding and Lynn Margulis (2000) *Water Gaia: 3.5 Thousand Million years of Wetness on Planet Earth*.

19 James Lovelock (1995) *The Ages of Gaia: A biography of our living Earth*. Oxford University Press.

20 Stephan Harding and Lynn Margulis (2000) *Water Gaia: 3.5 Thousand Million years of Wetness on Planet Earth*.

21 Stephen Harding (2009) *Animate Earth: Science, Intuition and Gaia – A New Scientific Story*. (second edition). Green Books.

22 Don Anderson even postulates that the immense weight of the limestone laid down by coccolithophores and other calcifiers, may be one of the drivers of plate tectonics, by softening the underlying basalt at the edges of the subduction zones, thereby making it pliable enough to sink below the Ocean crust. In Lovelock (1995)

23 Stephan Harding and Lynn Margulis (2000) *Water Gaia: 3.5 Thousand Million years of Wetness on Planet Earth*. p.43.

Chapter 2

1 Brian Thomas Swimme and Mary Evelyn Tucker (2011) *Journey of the Universe*. Yale University Press. For a profoundly moving story of this unfolding.

2 Callum Roberts (2012) *Ocean of Life: How our seas are changing*. Allen Lane, an imprint of Penguin Books.

3 Drake, Michael J. and Campins, Humberto (2006) *Origin of water on the terrestrial planets*. Asteroid, Comets, Meteors Proceedings IAU Symposium No. 229, 2005 D. Lazzaro, S. Ferraz-Mello & J.A. Fernandez, eds. c_2006 International Astronomical Union doi:10.1017/S1743921305006861.

4 Valley, John W. et al. *A cool early Earth* Geology; April 2002; v. 30; no. 4; pp 351–4.

5 Callum Roberts (2012) *Ocean of Life: How our seas are changing*. Allen Lane, an imprint of Penguin Books.

6 Stephen Harding (2009) *Animate Earth: Science, Intuition and Gaia – A New Scientific Story*. (second edition). Green Books.

7 The potential life-starting role of EZ water is explored in more detail in Gerald Pollack's book *The Fourth Phase of Water* as well as on his laboratory's website: http://faculty.washington.edu/ghp/research-themes/origin-of-life/

8 Lynn Margulis and Dorion Sagan (1995) *What is Life?* University of California Press.

9 Fitjof Capra and Pier Luigi Luisi (2014) *A Systems View of Life: A unifying vision.* Cambridge University Press.

10 James Lovelock (2000) *Gaia: A New Look at Life on Earth.* Oxford University Press.

11 Lynn Margulis and Dorion Sagan (1995) *What is Life?* University of California Press.

12 Mark Denny (2008) *How the Ocean Works: An introduction to oceanography.* Princeton University Press.

13 Lynn Margulis and Dorion Sagan (1995) *What is Life?* University of California Press.

14 James Lovelock (1995) *The Ages of* Gaia: *A Biography of Our Living Earth.* (second edition). Oxford University Press.

15 Holland, Heinrich D (2006) *The oxygenation of the atmosphere and oceans.* The Philosophical Transactions of The Royal Society, B: Biological Sciences. Phil. Trans. R. Soc. B 2006 361, doi: 10.1098/rstb.2006.1838.

16 James Lovelock (1995) *The Ages of Gaia: A Biography of Our Living Earth.* (second edition). Oxford University Press.

17 Lynn Margulis and Dorion Sagan (1995) *What is Life?* p.114. University of California Press.

18 Ibid p.135.

19 Ibid p.162.

20 Ryan, Joseph et al. *The Genome of the Ctenophore Mnemiopsis leidyi and Its Implications for Cell Type Evolution.* Science 13 December 2013: Vol. 342 no. 6164 doi: 10.1126/science.1242592.

21 Love, Gordon D. et al. (2009) *Fossil steroids record the appearance of Demospongiae during the Cryogenian period.* Nature pp 457, 718-721 (5 February 2009).

22 Lenton, Timothy et al. (2014) *Co-evolution of eukaryotes and ocean oxygenation in the Neoproterozoic era.* Nature, Geoscience.

23 *Timeline: the evolution of life.* New Scientist (14 July 2009) http://www.newscientist.com/article/dn17453-timeline-the-evolution-of-life.html?full=true#.VkIdXIfLRS8.

24 The drop in oxygen may have been due to oxygen-poor deep water welling up to the continental shelves. Paradoxically this may have led to increasing atmospheric O_2 levels that paved the way for land plants to evolve.

25 *Timeline: the evolution of life.* New Scientist (14 July 2009),

26 Lee R. Kump et al. (2005) *Massive release of hydrogen sulfide to the surface ocean and atmosphere during intervals of oceanic anoxia*. Geological Society of America. *Geology;* May 2005; v. 33; no. 5; pp 397–400.

27 Callum Roberts (2012) *Ocean of Life: How our seas are changing*. Allen Lane, an imprint of Penguin Books.

28 Recent archeological research indicates that modern humans migrated out of Africa in several waves. The earliest was probably around 130,000 years ago via a coastal route through the Arabian peninsula to south east Asia and Australia. http://www.livescience.com/44988-humans-dispersed-earlier-than-thought.html

29 Encyclopedia Britannica (2013).

Chapter 3

1   This is a much simplified explanation of photosynthesis. For a more detailed account, see for example: Tyler Volk (1998) *Gaia's Body: Towards a Physiology of Earth*. Springer-Verlag, New York Inc.

2   In fact there is a very small net gain of O_2 over the whole photosynthesis process, which makes up for the small amount of oxygen sequestered during oxidizing reactions with ferrous rocks and volcanic gases.

3   There are three interconnected processes involved in the Ocean's overall carbon *accounting system*: the biological organic pump, the biological carbonate pump and the physical carbon pump. Combined they remove approximately half a billion tons of carbon, equal to the annual input from volcanoes and rock weathering.

4   A small amount of water vapour reaches the stratosphere and dissociates into hydrogen and oxygen, allowing the hydrogen to escape into space (D. Catling and K. Zahnle May 2009, *The Planetary Air Leak*. Scientific American). The influence of life on atmospheric conditions has, however, slowed this to a trickle.

5   Peter Liss and Andrew Watson, environmental scientists from the University of East Anglia, have suggested that algal DMS production cools the planet by 4 °C. *Send in the Clouds*. New Scientist 30 May 1998.

6   James Lovelock was the first to make the link between ocean algae production of DMS, cloud seeding and the sulphur cycle. (*Oceanic phytoplankton, atmospheric sulphur, cloud albedo & climate*. Nature, Vol 326, No 6114, pp 655-661, 16 April 1987).

7   Lynn Hunt *Send in the Clouds*. New Scientist 30 May 1998.

8   The theory of algae intentionally seeding clouds to enhance dispersal was first developed by evolutionary biologist Bill Hamilton and Gaian scientist Tim Lenton. (*Spora and Gaia: How microbes fly with their clouds*. Ethology, Ecology and Evolution Vol 10, pp 1-16. 1998)

9   Lynn Hunt *Send in the Clouds*. New Scientist 30 May 1998.

10 William Marshall, an aerobiologist working for the British Antarctic Survey, cultured organisms, including algae, arriving at the Antarctic, in an air mass that had travelled 1500 kilometres from South America. (Lynn Hunt *Send in the Clouds*. New Scientist 30 May 1998)

Chapter 4

1 Callum Roberts (2012) *Ocean of Life: How our seas are changing*. Allen Lane, an imprint of Penguin Books.

2 Estimates of the circulation time vary between 1,000 to 1,500 years.

3 Stephen Harding (2009) *Animate Earth: Science, Intuition and Gaia – A New Scientific Story*. pp 136-7. Green Books.

4 Ibid. pp 136-7.

5 Stefan Rahmstorf (2002) *Ocean circulation and climate during the past 120,000 years*. Nature, Vol 419, 12 September 2002.

6 This is a very simplified description of a highly complex system. For a more detailed description, see for example, Mark Denny (2008) *How the Ocean Works: An introduction to Oceanography*.

7 Mark Denny (2008) *How the Ocean Works*, provides a good overview of the Coriolis effect as it relates to Ocean currents.

8 See www.oceanservice.noaa.gov/education/kits/currents/03coastal3.html for a useful description of the Ekman transport.

9 Tim Lenton et al. (2008) *Tipping elements in the Earth's climate system*. Proceedings of the National Academy of Sciences, 105: 1786-93.

10 Callum Roberts (2012) *Ocean of Life: How our seas are changing*. Allen Lane, an imprint of Penguin Books.

11 Mark Denny (2008) *How the Ocean Works*. For a detailed (although reductionist) overview of the physical properties of the thermocline.

12 Quoted from Mark Denny (2008) *How the Ocean Works*, but this represents a commonly held view within oceanography. When the thermocline is viewed from the perspective of the whole global climate balance, we can see that rather than being a hindrance, it is in fact a critical factor in the overall balance.

Chapter 5

1 Estimates of the total amount of carbon fixed by the Ocean vary from 40 to 50 billion tons per year. S. Volk (2003) P. Falkowski, Nature (2012), volume 483.

2 For an excellent explanation of nutrient cycling ratios see, Tyler Volk (2003) *Gaia's Body: Toward a Physiology of Earth*. Corpernicus, Springer-Verlag New York Inc.

3 Again, estimates vary as to how much carbon actually leaves the surface layer. The variance is understandable given the vastness of the ocean. 10% is at the lower end of the estimates; the upper range is around 15%.

4 See for example Mark Denny (2008) *How the Ocean Works*.

5   It is also possible that there is a certain amount of leakage from living phyto-
    plankton. One theory (unproven) suggests that this leakage may be an inten-
    tional mechanism to enhance photosynthesis by smoothing the surface, thereby
    enhancing light penetration.

6   There are several species of foraminifera that house symbiotic photosynthesis-
    ing dinoflagellates. The dinoflagellates may be moved out to the pseudopods
    during the day to capture sunlight, and retracted back into the shell at night.

7   I have made an arbitrary distinction here between larger organisms and the
    filter feeders amongst the primary consumers. In reality, filter feeding is an im-
    portant feeding strategy amongst primary and secondary consumers alike.

8   Within an ecosystem a top predator has no predators. Top predators within a
    particular ecosystem are referred to as apex predators, but they may still be sus-
    ceptible to predation outside of their niche ecosystem. On an Ocean-wide scale,
    adult orca and sperm whales are without peer, although juveniles could con-
    ceivably fall prey to large sharks if they become isolated from their pod. Certain
    apex sharks such as great whites would also be top predators once they reach
    full adult size.

9   A study conducted at the Poor Knights Marine reserve in New Zealand showed
    that recycling of nutrients by birds in a marine ecosystem could happen as a
    daily cycle.

10 There are approximately 250 species of lanternfish in 30 generas. Most are
    small, less than 100mm in length. Their total biomass is unknown, but esti-
    mates range from 550 to 660 million metric tonnes, which is several times the
    total annual global fisheries catch. In oceanic plankton tows, lanternfish on av-
    erage make up half of all fish larvae in the plankton layer (Ahlstrom et al, 1976).

11 In fact lanternfish may be the main food source at certain times for many pe-
    lagic predators including giant squid, who predate them below the thermocline,
    but also for animals such as king penguins in the Southern Ocean, marine
    mammals globally and migrating schooling fish such as salmon and tuna. Cur-
    rently there are three main fisheries for lanternfish: the Gulf of Oman, Sub-
    Antarctic and Southern Africa. In all these areas lanternfish are fundamental to
    the whole food web and their depletion could have disastrous results.

12 Dr Steve Nicol, Australian Antarctic Magazine - Issue 21: 2011.

13 Although it is called The Whale Pump, named by marine scientist Joe Roman,
    this phenomenon also refers to other marine mammals such as seals and sea li-
    ons that traverse the thermocline during feeding cycles.

14 Roman and McCarthy (2010) *The Whale Pump: Marine Mammals enhance
    primary productivity in a coastal basin.* PLoS ONE | www.plosone.org October
    2010 | Volume 5 | Issue 10 | e13255.

15 The idea that whales were seeding Antarctic waters with iron was first suggested
    by marine biologist Victor Smetacek. His original hypothesis has since been
    confirmed by several studies showing that the whales are literally acting as
    Ocean gardeners.

16 There may be multiple factors affecting krill populations, including sea ice decline and sea surface temperature changes, but these alone are not enough to
account for the decline in overall productivity in Antarctic waters: Victor Smeta-
cek (2008) *Are Declining Antarctic Krill stocks a result of global warming or
the decimation of the whales.* Alfred Wegener Institute for Polar and Marine
Research Bremerhaven, Germany. Off-print of chapter from: *Impacts of Global
Warming on Polar Ecosystems,* Carlos M. Duarte (ed.) Fundació n BBVA,
2008 http://www.fbbva.es

17 Calculations suggest this biological turbulent mixing could be as significant as
mixing caused tidal and wind turbulence. (Dr Steve Nicol, 2011, Australian Antarctic Magazine - Issue 21).

18 This is an ongoing scientific debate, with estimates of the rate of mixing ranging
from negligible to significant.

19 This trickle of 'new' nutrients arrives primarily via rivers as well as airborne
sources. The severe overloading of nutrients in rivers, caused by human activity,
is creating a metabolic crisis in many areas of the Ocean, as the overload of nutrients overwhelms the natural nutrient cycle.

Chapter 6

1 The so called 'half second rule' is based on the work of consciousness researcher, Benjamin Libet, who described this delay as 'subjective backward re-
ferral of sensory experience'.

2 This is a concept developed by the great French phenomenologist, Maurice Mer-
leu-Ponty, and described with articulate clarity by Tim Ingold in his book *Being
Alive* (2012).

3 For a thought provoking exploration of interoception see: Stephen Harrod
Buhner (2014) *Plant Intelligence and the Imaginal Realm: Beyond the doors of
perception into the dreaming of the earth.* Bear and Company Books.

4 Quoted from: Fitjof Capra and Pier Luigi Luisi (2014) *A Systems View of Life.*
Chapter 12, Mind and Consciousness, provides a wonderful exploration of the
role of cognition in the life process.

5 Fitjof Capra and Pier Luigi Luisi (2014) *A Systems View of Life.* p.256.

6 Stephen Harding (2009) *Animate Earth* Chapter 7. From microbes to cell giants.

7 Ottesen E.A. et al. (2013) *Pattern and synchrony of gene expression among
sympatric marine microbial populations. PNAS*, vol. 110, no. 6, E488-E497;
doi: 10.1073/pnas.1222099110.

8 Stephen Harding (2009) *Animate* Earth. p.159.

9 Gorby, Yuri A. (2006) *Electrically conductive bacterial nanowires produced by
Shewanella oneidensis strain MR-1 and other microorganisms. PNAS* July 25,
2006, vol. 103 no. 30.

10 From the documentary: *Does the Ocean Think,* in the series *Through the
Wormhole.* www.sciencechannel.com

11 Quoted from Alick Bartholomew's excellent book *The Story of Water; Source of Life*. (2010) p.174.

Chapter 7

1   Mollo, E. et al. (2014) *Sensing marine biomolecules: smell, taste, and the evolutionary transition from aquatic to terrestrial life*. Front. Chem. 2:92. doi:10.3389/fchem.2014.00092.

2   Boehm, T. and Zufall, F. (February 2006). *"MHC peptides and the sensory evaluation of genotype"*. Trends in neurosciences 29 100–7. https://www.ncbi.nlm.nih.gov/pubmed/16337283

3   Hasler, A.D. and Wisby, W. J. (1951) *Discrimination of Stream odours by fishes and relation to parent stream behaviour*. Am. Nat. 85: 223-238.

4   *Vision in a Shell: The story of Crustacean Vision*. http://archives.evergreen.edu/webpages/curricular/2011-2012/m201112/web/crustaceans.html

5   Dr James Wood and Kelsie Jackson *An Introduction to Cephalopod Vision*. www.cephbase.utmb.edu

6   My years of interacting with humpback whales showed me just how important vision above and below the surface is to them. They would often 'spy-hop' vertically with their entire heads above the water, so they could watch our activities on the boat. Sometimes individuals would do this for minutes on end, completely stationary.

7   Fields, R.D. (August 2007) *"The Shark's Electric Sense"* Scientific American. Retrieved 2 December 2013.

8   http://en.wikipedia.org/wiki/Electric_ray

9   There is also a second theory that suggests light sensitive chemical reactions may play a role for some species, but it's unclear as to whether this might be a viable theory for Ocean dwellers.

10 http://www.livescience.com/49468-turtles-migration-magnetic-field.html

11 http://www.bbc.co.uk/iplayer/episode/b05vj8hq/shark-episode-2

12 http://www.sharksavers.org/en/education/biology/

13 Map of Life - *"Lateral line system in fish and other animals"* http://www.mapoflife.org/topics/topic_443_lateral-line-system-in-fish-and-other-animals/ October 22, 2014

14 Convergent Evolution is very apparent amongst widely varying Ocean dwellers. Cambridge University's 'Map of Life' website provides an outstanding overview of Convergent Evolution. www.mapoflife.org

15 Narwhals, *Monodon monoceros* ~ MarineBio.org, Inc MarineBio Conservation Society. http://marinebio.org/species.asp?id=336

16 Jenni A. Stanley, Craig A. Radford, Andrew G. Jeffs *Location, location, location: finding a suitable home among the noise*. Proceedings of the Royal Society, doi: 10.1098/rspb.2012.0697. Published 26 July 2012.

17 Lillis A., Eggleston D.B., Bohnenstiehl D.R. (2013) *Oyster Larvae Settle in Response to Habitat-Associated Underwater Sounds*. PLoS ONE 8(10): e79337. doi:10.1371/journal.pone.0079337.

18 An interview with Steve Simpson (July 21, 2010). *Amazing reefs: how corals 'hear'*. http://news.mongabay.com/2010/0721-neme_corals_simpson.html

19 Ongoing research in the area of larval settlement using habitat soundscapes is raising many questions about the effects of anthropogenic noise pollution in the Ocean. But equally important is the loss of *biological* sounds through over fishing and habitat destruction. I believe the evidence is already pointing towards species specific sound recognition, and further research will confirm that some species, crayfish for example, are more likely to settle on a reef that already has adult crayfish in residence.

20 David Rothenberg (2008) *Thousand Mile Song*. Basic Books.

21 The deep sound channel is also called the SOFAR channel, which stands for Sound Fixing And Ranging, and was coined by the US Navy.

22 This was confirmed when the US navy decided to declassify and share decades of sonar surveillance records with whale researchers. It turned out that the Navy Sonar officer who was 'eves dropping' on the unsuspecting fin was able to pick the faint responses from fin whales off the Spanish coast. (David Rothenberg, 2008, *Thousand Mile Song* p.199).

23 David Rothenberg (2008) *Thousand Mile Song*. p.200.

24 James T. Fulton (2015) *Dolphin Biosonar Echolocation: A Case Study*. http://neuronresearch.net/hearing/files/dolphinbiosonar.htm

25 John Stewart Reid and Jack Kassewitz (2013) *Conversations with Dolphins*. Story Merchants Books.

26 Herzing, D.L. (2004) *Social and Non-Social uses of Echolocation in Free-Ranging Stenella frontalis and Tursiops truncatus*. In: *Advances in the Study of Echolocation in Bats and Dolphins* pp.404 410. Springer-Verlag Press.

Chapter 8

1 Riko Riko Cave was measured using laser beams in 2001 and at that point was the largest sea cave by volume that had been measured anywhere in the world. It is quite likely that there are other, larger caves that have yet to be measured.

2 Researchers have found that octopus have 60% of their neurons in their arms and only 40% in their brains. Sy Montgomery (2011) *Deep Intellect: Inside the mind of the octopus*. https://orionmagazine.org/article/deep-intellect/

3 Marc Bekoff (2007) *The Emotional Lives of Animals*. p.31. New World Library.

4 'Think like a fish lives', is inspired by phenomenologist and director of The Nature Institute, Craig Holdredge, who reminds his students that when studying plants they need to 'think like a plant lives'. www.natureinstitute.org

5   Phenomenology has its roots in the 18th century work of people like Johann Wolfgang von Goethe, but was formalized as a scientific method by the German philosopher Edmund Husserl (1859-1938). For a brilliant journey into phenomenology read *The Spell of the Sensuous* by David Abram.

6   Sneddon L.U., Braithwaite V.A., and Gentle M.J. (2003) *Do Fish have Nociceptors? Evidence for the evolution of a vertebrate sensory system.* Proceedings of the Royal Society, London Series B 270 (2003) pp.1115-21.

7   Victoria Braithwaite (2010) *Do Fish Feel Pain?* Oxford University Press.

8   Ibid p.153.

9   Brown, Culum (2015) *Fish Intelligence, sentience and ethics.* Animal Cognition. January 2015, Volume 18, Issue 1, pp 1-17. http://link.springer.com/article/10.1007/s10071-014-0761-0

10 Pascal Fossat et al (2014) *Anxiety-like behavior in crayfish is controlled by serotonin.* Science 13 June 2014: Vol. 344 no. 6189 pp 1293-1297, doi: 10.1126/science.1248811.

11 Bshary, R. Hohner, A. Ait-el-Djoudi, K. and Fricke, H (2006) *Interspecific communicative and coordinated hunting between groupers and giant moray eels in the Red Sea.* PloS Biology 4, 23932398.

12 Vail, A.L, Manica, A. and Bshary, R. (2014) *Fish choose appropriately when and with whom to collaborate.* Current Biology 24: R791-R793.

13 This fascinating account of grouper/eel friendship was recounted on the website www.mongabay.com in refutation of the claim that there is no altruistic behaviour associated with the grouper/eel relationship, as stated in the paper by Bshary et al (2006).

14 Bshary, R. and Schäffer, D. (2002) *Choosy reef fish select cleaner fish that provide high-quality service.* Animal Behaviour 63, 557-564; and Bshary, R, and Wurth, M. (2001) *Cleaner fish Labroides dimidiatus manipulate client reef fish by providing tactile stimulation.* Proceedings of the Royal Society of London B 268, 1495-1501.

15 Raihani, N.J., Grutter, A.S., and Bshary, R. (2010) *Punishers benefit from third-party punishment in fish.* Science 327, 171.

16 Ila France Porcher (2014) *The Shark Sessions.* Tate Publishing & Enterprises (17 Jun. 2014) ISBN-13: 978-1629022635.

17 Ila France Porcher (2014) *Cognition in Sharks.* X-Ray Magazine. Issue 60 May 2014 (pp 68-73).

18 An example of the research focus relating to mother, calf and escort groups. Spitz, S.S., Herman, L.M., Pack, A.A., & Deakos, M.H. (2002) *The relation of body size of male humpback whales to their social roles on the Hawaiian winter grounds.* Canadian Journal of Zoology 80, 1938-1947, 2002.

19 Underwater photographer and naturalist, Tony Wu, has spent many years interacting with humpback whales, and has also noted the more relaxed demeanor of mothers and calves when an escort is present. Tony has also documented a single escort staying with a mother and calf for 16 days, traveling long distances with them and defending them against other males. www.tonywublog.com/journal/swimming-with-humpback-whales-in-tonga-2011-part-6

Chapter 9

1 Rupert Sheldrake (2009) *A New Science of Life*. Icon Books Ltd, London.

2 Ibid.

3 Rupert Sheldrake (2011) *Dogs That Know When Their Owners Are Coming Home: The unexplained Powers of Animals*. p.261. Arrow Books.

4 Ibid. p.259.

5 Despite intense research, no physical mechanism has been found to explain the near instantaneous response of the school as a whole. See for example: Sheldrake (2011) *The Presence of the Past: Morphic Resonance and the Habits of Nature*. pp 357-359. Icon Books Ltd. London.

6 Ibid. pp 252-259.

7 In mainstream evolutionary biology, the mechanism by which cultural transmission occurs is now a hotly debated topic amongst biologists. The neo-Darwinist view, articulated in the 'selfish gene' theory espoused by Richard Dawkins, has been the default story, but this is challenged by the eminent Harvard biologist, E.O. Wilson, who has proposed a multi-level 'group selection' process, which takes into account the very real aspects of altruism and empathy in the natural selection of beneficial behavioural traits. See: Martin A. Nowak, Corina E. Tarnita & Edward O. Wilson *The evolution of eusociality*. Nature 466, 1057–1062 (26 August 2010) doi:10.1038/nature09205.

8 Rupert Sheldrake provides several examples of how new patterns of behaviour evolve and spread through cultural transmission. See: *The Presence of the Past*. pp.259-267.

9 See for example: Brain, J. Williams, (2011) *Revisiting the Ganzfeld ESP Debate: A Basic Review and Assessment*. Journal of Scientific Exploration, Vol. 25, No. 4, pp.639–661, 2011 0892-3310/11.

10 From a documentary interview with Animal Communicator, Anna Breytenbach.

11 William J Long (2009) *How Animals Talk*. p.55. Dover Publications Inc.

12 For an excellent overview of the experimental research, including an in-depth look at why telepathy and other 'paranormal' phenomena continue to attract so much scientific skepticism, See: Dean Radkin (2009) *The Noetic Universe*. Corgi Books, Transworld Publishers, London.

13 See for example: Radkin (2009) *The Noetic Universe;* Sheldrake (2011) *The Presence of the Past*. See also: http://noetic.org

14 Frank Robson (1988) *Pictures in the Dolphin Mind*. Sheridan House Inc, NY.

15 Wade Doak (2012) *Gaia Calls*. Divine Arts, California.

16 Bernard Moitessier (1974) *The Long Way*. Granada Publishing Ltd, London.

17 Jim Nollman (1985) *Dolphin Dreamtime: Talking to the Animals*. London: Anthony Blond, Quoted in: Heathcote Williams (1988) *Whale Nation*. pp 123-124. Jonathon Cape Ltd, 32 Bedford Square, London;

Chapter 10

1   *The Death of the Oceans* by Alex Renton, Newsweek, 11/07/2014.

2   http://www.rollingstone.com/politics/news/the-point-of-no-return-climate-change-nightmares-are-already-here-20150805?page=7

3   http://www.skepticalscience.com/pollution-part-1.html

4   Silvia A. Earle (2009) *The World is Blue: How our fate and the Ocean's are One*. National Geographic Society.

5   http://www.skepticalscience.com/pollution-part-2.html

6   *Past constraints on the vulnerability of marine calcifiers to massive carbon dioxide release* by Andy Ridgwell and Daniela N. Schmidt. Nature Geoscience, published online: 14 February 2010 | doi: 10.1038/ngeo755. See also: http://thinkprogress.org/climate/2010/02/18/205525/ocean-acidification-study-mass-extinction-of-marine-life-nature-geoscience/

7   De'ath, G. et al. (2009) *Declining coral calcification on the Great Barrier Reef*. Science, 323: pp.116-119.

8   Guttuso, J. P. et al. (2015) *Contrasting futures for ocean and society from different anthropogenic CO2 emissions scenarios*. Science, 349 no. 6243.

9   Callum Roberts (2012) *Ocean of Life: How our seas are changing*. Allen Lane, an imprint of Penguin Books.

10 Kawaguchi, S. et al. (2011) *Will Krill fare well under Southern Ocean acidification?* Biol Lett. 2011 Apr 23; 7(2): 288–291. Published online 2010 Oct 13. doi: 10.1098/rsbl.2010.0777.

11 Beaufort, L. et al (2011) *Sensitivity of coccolithophores to carbonate chemistry and ocean acidification*. Nature, Vol 476, 4 August 2011.

12 *The Ocean's Surface Layer Has Been Warming Much Faster Than Previously Thought*. http://thinkprogress.org/climate/2014/10/06/3576234/ocean-surface-warming-faster/

13 https://www.ncdc.noaa.gov/sotc/global/201507

14 Ove Hoegh-Guldberg et al. *Bleaching and Related Ecological Factors*. CRTR Working Group Findings 2004-2009.

15 http://www.oceanscientists.org/index.php/topics/ocean-deoxygenation

16 Daniel G. Boyce, et al. (2010) *Global phytoplankton decline over the past century*. Nature 466, 591–596 (29 July 2010)

17 http://thinkprogress.org/climate/2010/07/29/206497/nature-decline-ocean-phytoplankton-global-warming-boris-worm/

18 Lee R. Kump, et al. (2005) *Massive release of hydrogen sulfide to the surface ocean and atmosphere during intervals of oceanic anoxia*. Geology; May 2005; v. 33; no. 5; pp.397–400.

19 Steve Conner (2011) *Vast methane 'plumes' seen in Arctic ocean as sea ice retreats.* http://www.independent.co.uk/news/science/vast-methane-plumes-seen-in-arctic-ocean-as-sea-ice-retreats-6276278.html

20 Stefan Rahmstorf (2002) *Ocean circulation and climate during the past 120,000 years.* Nature, VOL 419, 12 September 2002 www.nature.com/nature

21 Hansen, J. et al (2015) *Ice melt, sea level rise and superstorms: evidence from paleoclimate data, climate modeling, and modern observations that 2° C global warming is highly dangerous.* Atmos. Chem. Phys. Discuss, 15, 20059–20179, 2015. www.atmos-chem-phys-discuss.net/15/20059/2015/ doi:10.5194/acpd-15-20059-2015.

22 http://www.reefresilience.org/coral-reefs/stressors/climate-and-ocean-change/sea-level-rise/

23 McLeod, Elizabeth and Salm, Rodney V. (2006) *Managing Mangroves for Resilience to Climate Change.* IUCN, Gland, Switzerland.

24 Brian Palmer (2015) *Devil and the Deep Blue Sea.* http://www.onearth.org/earthwire/devil-deep-blue-sea

25 Jackson, J. et al. (2012) *Status and Trends of Caribbean Coral Reefs:* 1970-2012. Global Coral Reef Monitoring Network.

26 Callum Roberts (2012) *Ocean of Life: How our seas are changing.*

27 http://panexplore.com/our-work/ocean-toxins/

28 http://www.bluevoice.org/news_sharedfate.php

29 Marcus Eriksen et al. (2014) *Plastic Pollution in the World's Oceans: More than 5 Trillion Plastic Pieces Weighing over 250,000 Tons Afloat at Sea.* PLoS ONE | doi:10.1371/journal.pone.0111913 December 10, 2014.

30 Lucy C. Woodall et al. (2014) *The deep sea is a major sink for microplastic debris.* The Royal Society doi: 10.1098/rsos.140317. Published 17 December 2014.

31 Jonathan Amos (2015) *Plastic waste heading for oceans quantified.* http://www.bbc.co.uk/news/science-environment-31432515

32 Jonathan Amos (2015) *Seabirds 'blighted by plastic waste'.* http://www.bbc.co.uk/news/science-environment-34108017

33 Allsopp, M. et al. *Plastic Debris in the World's Oceans.* Greenpeace.

34 Callum Roberts (2012) *Ocean of Life: How our seas are changing.*

35 Ibid.

36 http://www.theguardian.com/environment/2015/jun/14/stranded-whales-ocean-navy-sonars

37 Myres, Ransom A. and Worm, Boris (2003) *Rapid worldwide depletion of predatory fish communities.* Nature, 423: pp.280-283.

38 Worm, B. et al. (2006) *Impacts of biodiversity loss on ocean ecosystem services.* Science 314: pp.787-790.

39 http://fishcount.org.uk/farmed-fish-welfare/numbers-of-fish-used-for-feed-in-aquaculture

40 A play on words and the seemingly determined adherence by the FAO (and almost the entire global fishing industry) to persist with 'Maximum Sustainable Yield' as a model for fisheries management. *The State of World Fisheries and Aquaculture: Opportunities and challenges*. Food and Agriculture Organisation of the United Nations (FAO), (2014).

41 http://worldoceanreview.com/en/wor-2/fisheries/illegal-fishing/

42 Davies RWD, et al. (2009) *Defining and estimating global marine fisheries bycatch*. Marine Policy doi:10.1016/j.marpol.2009.01.003.

43 Douglas J. McCauley et al. (2015) *Marine defaunation: Animal loss in the global ocean*. Science, vol. 347, no. 6219; doi: 10.1126/science.1255641.

44 This average increase in fishing effort is even more disturbing when individual species are considered. Callum Roberts and his colleagues have estimated that some species require up to 500 times the effort to catch today as they did 100 years ago. Callum Roberts (2012) *Ocean of Life: How our seas are changing*. Allen Lane, an imprint of Penguin Books.

45 Ibid.

46 Alanna Mitchell (2008) *SeaSick: The hidden ecological crisis of the global ocean*. Pier 9, an imprint of Murdoch Books Pty Ltd.

47 Ivan Valiela, et al. (2015) *Mangrove Forests: One of the World's Threatened Major Tropical Environments*.
    http://bioscience.oxfordjournals.org/content/51/10/807.full

48 http://news.bbc.co.uk/1/hi/sci/tech/2985630.stm

Chapter 11

1 Joanna Macy and Chris Johnstone (2012) *Active Hope: How to face the mess we're in without going crazy*. New World Library.

2 Bill Plotkin (2008) *Nature and the Human Soul: Cultivating Wholeness and Community in a Fragmented World*. New World Library.

3 For a beautifully written and insightful introduction to this 'way of seeing', see: Emma Kidd (2015) *First Steps to Seeing: A Path towards living attentively*. Floris Books.

4 I am of course paraphrasing the saying, 'Be the change you want to see in the world', widely attributed to Gandhi.

5 We run a Facebook page called, 'Just-Pick-It-Up', which encourages people to share their plastic picking-up exploits.

6 Callum Roberts (2012) *Ocean of Life: How our seas are changing*. p.282.

7 Ibid.

Chapter 12

1 For example, recall the story of whale poo and the naturally amplified ecosystem of Antarctica from Chapter 5.

2 Ecologists call this 'mediated nutrient transfer'.

3 Vladimir Vernadsky (1863-1945) was amongst the first to articulate this idea of life forms as primarily nutrient distributors. (see Stephan Harding (2009) *Animate Earth: Science, Intuition and Gaia – A New Scientific Story.* (second edition) p. 62-63. Green Books.

4 Julie C. Ellis (2005) *Marine birds on land: a review of plant biomass, species richness, and community composition in seabird colonies.* Plant Ecology 181: 227–241 doi 10.1007/s11258-005-7147-y.

5 Doughty, Christopher E. et al. (2015) *Global nutrient transport in a world of giants.* Ecology.
http://www.pnas.org/content/early/2015/10/23/1502549112.full.pdf

6 Sylvia Earle (2009) *The World is Blue: How our fate and the Ocean's are one.* p. 56. National Geographic Society.

7 Ibid.

8 Ibid. p.270.

9 Tapu and tabu areas are common throughout Oceania. The English 'taboo' is derived from tabu. In Maori culture a tapu means 'sacred' or 'set apart' and is often used in conjunction with 'rahui' to indicate an area as 'under a ban'. Rahui in its basic meaning is 'to encompass'. Rev. Maori Marsden (1992) *Kaitiaki-Tanga: A Definitive Introduction to the Holistic World View of the Maori.*
http://www.marinenz.org.nz/documents/Marsden_1992_Kaitiakitanga.pdf

10 The goal of 10%, agreed upon in 1997, was originally set for 2012 but has since been extended to 2020.

11 http://mission-blue.org and https://marine-conservation.org

12 http://www.marinereservescoalition.org

13 Callum Roberts (2012) *Ocean of Life: How our seas are changing.* p.276. Allen Lane.

14 Rev. Maori Marsden (1992) *KaitiakiTanga: A Definitive Introduction to the Holistic World View of the Maori.*
http://www.marinenz.org.nz/documents/Marsden_1992_Kaitiakitanga.pdf

15 Established in 1977, the tiny marine reserve at Goat Island receives more than 375,000 visitors per year.
http://www.marinenz.org.nz/documents/leigh_eco_impact.pdf

16 The Poor Knights Marine Reserve gets more than twice the number of visitors than hikers walking the world famous Milford track in Fiordland.
http://www.radionz.co.nz/news/national/267902/search-for-new-marine-arrivals

Selected Bibliography for Further Reading

Ocean Related

Anderson, Ian (2007) *The Surface of the Sea: Encounters with New Zealand's Upper Ocean Life*. Reed Publishing NZ Ltd.

Barnes, R.S.K. & Hughes, R.N. (1999) *An Introduction to Marine Ecology* (third Edition). Blackwell Science Ltd, a Blackwell Publishing Company.

Carson, Rachel (1951) *The Sea Around Us*. Staple Press Limited.

Clover, Charles (2005) *The End of the Line: How overfishing is changing the world and what we eat*. Random House Books.

Cousteau, Jacques-Yves and Dumas, Frederic (2004) *The Silent World*. National Geographic Books, reprint edition.

Denny, Mark (1995) *Air and Water: The Biology and Physics of Life's Media*. Princeton University Press.

Denny, Mark (2008) *How the Ocean Works: an introduction to oceanography*. Princeton University Press.

Doak, Wade (2012) *Gaia Calls: South Sea Voices, Dolphins, Sharks and Rainforests*. Divine Arts.

Dudzinski, Kathleen M., and Frohoff, Toni (2008) *Dolphin Mysteries: Unlocking the secrets of communication*. Yale University Press.

Earle, Sylvia A. (2002) *Sea Change: A message of the Oceans*. Fawcett; 1st Ballantine Books Ed edition

Earle, Sylvia A. (2009) *The World is Blue*. National Geographic Society. 1145 17th Street, N. W, Washington, D.C. 200036.

France Porcher, Ila (2010) *My Sunset Rendezvous: Crisis in Tahiti*. Strategic Book Group.

Getten, Mary J. (2014) *Communicating with Orcas: The whales perspective*. Smashwords e-book edition.

Grescoe, Taras (2008) *Dead Seas: How the fish on our plates is killing our planet*. Pan Books.

Lovelock, James (2000) *Gaia: A New Look At Life On Earth*. Oxford University Press, Oxford, Great Clarendon Road, OX2 6DP.

Lovelock, James (1995) *The Ages of Gaia: A Biography of Our Living Earth* (second edition). *Oxford University Press*.

Mitchell, Alanna (2008) *Sea Sick: The hidden ecological crisis of the global ocean.* Murdoch Books Pty Ltd.

Moitessier, Bernard (1973) *The Long Way.* Granada Publishing Ltd.

Nichols, Wallace J. (2014) *Blue Mind: How water makes you happier, more connected and better at what you do.* Little, Brown.

Reid, John Stewart and Jack Kassewitz (2013) *Conversations with Dolphins.* Story Merchants Books.

Roberts, Callum (2012) *Ocean of Life. How our seas are changing.* Allen Lane, an imprint of Penguin Books.

Robson, Frank (1988*) Pictures in the Dolphin Mind.* Sheridan House Inc. NY.

Rothenberg, David (2008) *Thousand Mile Song: Whale Music in a Sea of Sound.* Basic Books, a member of the Perseus Books Group, New York.

Sardet, Christian (2015) *Plankton: Wonders of the Drifting World.* University of Chicago Press Ltd.

Thorne-Miller, Boyce (1999) *The Living Ocean: Understanding and Protecting Marine Biodiversity* (second edition). Island Books.

Wharram, James (2001) *Two Girls Two Catamarans.* Crociera Totale Edizioni.

Whitehead, Hal and Rendell, Luke (2015) *The Cultural Lives of Whales and Dolphins.* The University of Chicago Press.

General

Abram, David (1996) *The Spell of the Sensuous: Perception and language in a more than human world.* Vintage Books, a division of Random House, INC, New York.

Berry, Thomas (1999) *The Great Work: Our way into the future.* Bell Tower, New York.

Capra, Fritjof (1996) *The Web of Life: A new scientific understanding of living systems.* First Anchor Books.

Capra, Fritjof and Luisi, Pier Luigi (2014) *The Systems View of Life: A unifying vision.* Cambridge University Press.

Coats, C. (1996) *Living Energies: An exposition of concepts related to the theories of Viktor Schauberger.* Gateway, an imprint of Gill & Macmillan Ltd.

Evernden, Neil (1992) *The Social Creation of Nature.* The John Hopkins University Press.

Harding, Stephan (2009) *Animate Earth: Science, Intuition and Gaia – A New Scientific Story.* (second edition). Green Books.

Kidd, Emma (2015*) First Steps to Seeing: A Path towards living attentively.* Floris Books.

Long, William J. (2009) *How Animals Talk.* Dover Publications Inc.

Lovelock, James (2000) *Gaia: The Practical Science of Planetary Medicine*. Gaia Books Ltd.

Lovelock, James (2009) *The Vanishing Face of Gaia: A final warning*. Allen Lane, an imprint of Penguin Books.

Macy, Joanna and Johnstone, Chris (2012) *Active hope: How to face the mess we're in without going crazy*. New World Library.

Margulis, Lynn and Sagan, Dorion (1995) *What is Life? University of California Press*.

Naess, Arne (2008) *Life's Philosophy: reason and feeling in a deeper world*. University of Georgia Press, Athens, Georgia.

Plotkin, Bill (2008) *Nature and the Human Soul: Cultivating wholeness and community in a fragmented world*. New World Library.

Pollack, Gerald H. (2013) *The Fourth Phase of Water: Beyond Solid, Liquid and Vapor*. Ebner and Sons Publishers.

Radin, Dean (2009) *The Noetic Universe: The Scientific Evidence for Psychic Phenomena*. Corgi Books.

Sheldrake, Rupert (2011) *Dogs that Know when their Owners are Coming Home: The unexplained powers of animals*. Arrow Books.

Sheldrake, Rupert (2011) *The Presence of the Past: Morphic Resonance and the habits of Nature* (second edition). Icon Books.

Swimme, Brian and Tucker, Mary Evelyn (2011) *Journey of the Universe*. Yale University Press.

Vernadsky, Vladimir (1986) *The Biosphere: An abridged version based on the French edition of 1929*. Synergetic Press, Inc.

Volk, Tyler (2003) *Gaia's Body: Toward a Physiology of Earth*. Corpernicus, Springer-Verlag New York Inc.

Westbroek, P. (1992) *Life as a Geological Force: Dynamics of the Earth*. The Commonwealth Book Fund Book Program.

Recommended Organisations and Websites

There are literally thousands of organisations involved in Ocean education and conservation. The list of organisations presented here are ones that I find useful, but is by no means a definitive list.

Ocean Education

http://www.howfishbehave.ca
http://marinebio.org Marine Bio Conservation Society.
http://oceanservice.noaa.gov/welcome.html National Oceanic and Atmospheric Administration (National Ocean Service)
http://phys.org/journals/marine-ecology-progress-series/ Peer reviewed research articles.
http://www.whoi.edu/oceanus/ Woods Hole Oceanographic Institution.
http://www.worldoceanobservatory.org/index.php?q=content/one-big-ocean World Ocean Observatory.

Ocean Advocacy and Conservation

www.oceanspirit.org Our own organization, devoted to raising awareness about the Ocean as a living system and advocating for Ocean protection. We also have a Facebook page https://www.facebook.com/Ocean-Spirit-387861044708999/?ref=bookmarks

http://missionblue.org Dr. Sylvia Earle's organization, devoted to protecting 20% of the Ocean by 2020.

http://www.marinereservescoalition.org

http://www.pewtrusts.org/en/projects/global-ocean-legacy

https://marine-conservation.org

http://oceana.org

www.oceanswatch.org a grassroots Ocean conservation organization, working with island communities to protect marine ecosystems, while providing sustainable livelihoods for communities.

Specific Issues

http://www.globalcoralbleaching.org
http://www.sharksavers.org

http://www.planetwhale.com/org-565_WDCS_The_Whale_and_Dolphin_Conservation_Society Whale and Dolphin Conservation Society.

http://uk.whales.org Whale and Dolphin Conservation(worldwide).

Plastic Pollution

http://www.plasticfreeocean.org

http://www.5gyres.org 5 Gyres Institute, carrying out research in the Ocean gyres.

http://www.plasticpollutioncoalition.org The Plastic Pollution Coalition

http://www.plasticoceans.net Plastic Oceans

https://www.facebook.com/Just-Pick-It-Up-412517525469577/ Facebook page devoted to Just-Picking-Up plastic and making a difference every day.

Sustainable Seafood

http://www.goodfishguide.org Marine Conservation Society

https://www.msc.org Marine Stewardship Council

http://wwf.panda.org/how_you_can_help/live_green/out_shopping/seafood_guides/ WWF seafood guides

http://www.greenpeace.org/international/en/campaigns/oceans/which-fish-can-I-eat/ Greenpeace's seafood guides

General Interest

www.natureinstitute.org The Nature Institute (phenomenology).

http://noetic.org Institute of Noetic Sciences (research into telepathy and other paranormal phenomena).

http://faculty.washington.edu/ghp/ Professor Gerald Pollark's water research laboratory.

www.schumachercollege.org.uk Schumacher College, Devon, UK (Holistic Science, Gaia Theory, science of qualities).

http://www.animalspirit.org Inter-species communication.

http://www.sheldrake.org Dr Rupert Sheldrake.

Index

Proterozoic, 48

protoctista, 48-9,

protoctists, 48-9, 51, 58

pseudopods, 88

pterapods, 92

Q

quantum coherence, 110

quantum jazz, 110

quorum sensing, 109

R

radiolarians, 49, 89

red tides, 184

remora, 161, 163

rhabdomeres, 116

rhinophores, 113

Robson, Frank, 164

Roberts, Professor Callum, 216

Rolling Stone magazine, 174

Rothenberg, David, 126

S

Sagan, Carl, 138

salinity, 79-80, 111, 122, 148

Schauberger, Victor, 33

seabirds, 94, 186, 190, 199, 211

sentience, 16-7, 24, 27, 100, 103-11, 137, 169, 174, 219

Sheldrake, Rupert, 154, 159

silicate rock weathering, 36

speciesism, 191

spicule, 51

stromatolites, 46-7

sulphur cycle, 63, 178

superorganism, 29, 105, 109

Systems View of Life, 28

T

Tangaroa, 217

tapu, 215-7

Tarlton, Kelly, 23

tectonic plates, 37, 43, 55, 208

telepathy, 162-3, 168

thermal mixing, 78-9, 99

thermocline, 69-70, 77, 79-81, 87, 94-5, 97, 99, 124, 180

thermohaline, 70-3, 79-80, 95, 180-1

Timaeus, 26

trilobites, 52

trophic levels, 87, 93, 187, 210

U

ultraviolet. 34, 112, 115, 117

The United Nations Convention on Biological Diversity, 215

V

Varela, Francisco, 108

Venus, 30, 34-5, 41, 62

vertebrates, 52, 115, 134, 136-7

W

weak hydrogen bond, 32

whale pump, 97-8

whaling, 11, 98-9, 190

Williams, Heathcote, 169

Z

zooplankton, 23, 85, 90, 92, 96, 98, 106, 191, 211